Process Theory

Process Theory

The Principles of Operations Management

Matthias Holweg

Jane Davies

Arnoud De Meyer

Benn Lawson

Roger W. Schmenner

OXFORD
UNIVERSITY PRESS

Great Clarendon Street, Oxford, OX2 6DP,
United Kingdom

Oxford University Press is a department of the University of Oxford.
It furthers the University's objective of excellence in research, scholarship,
and education by publishing worldwide. Oxford is a registered trade mark of
Oxford University Press in the UK and in certain other countries

© Matthias Holweg, Jane Davies, Arnoud De Meyer, Benn Lawson,
and Roger W. Schmenner 2018

The moral rights of the authors have been asserted

First Edition published in 2018

Impression: 6

All rights reserved. No part of this publication may be reproduced, stored in
a retrieval system, or transmitted, in any form or by any means, without the
prior permission in writing of Oxford University Press, or as expressly permitted
by law, by licence or under terms agreed with the appropriate reprographics
rights organization. Enquiries concerning reproduction outside the scope of the
above should be sent to the Rights Department, Oxford University Press, at the
address above

You must not circulate this work in any other form
and you must impose this same condition on any acquirer

Published in the United States of America by Oxford University Press
198 Madison Avenue, New York, NY 10016, United States of America

British Library Cataloguing in Publication Data
Data available

Library of Congress Control Number: 2017955389

ISBN 978-0-19-964105-5 (hbk.)
978-0-19-964106-2 (pbk.)

Printed and bound by
Ashford Colour Press Ltd.

Links to third party websites are provided by Oxford in good faith and
for information only. Oxford disclaims any responsibility for the materials
contained in any third party website referenced in this work.

PREFACE

We started this book project when we were all based at Cambridge, sharing a common observation: what passed as "theory" in our field was all too often inadequate. In one respect, operations management scholars were bending over backwards to make theories from other fields fit our research problems. In another, questionable assumptions were being used to apply mathematics to operations management problems. Neither proved a good match with what we had observed in practice. Successful operations were managed by considerations that were far more straightforward than much of what was being published in our journals.

So we set out to codify these practical considerations into a set of principles that could be linked to key contributions that have been made to our field over the last century. Identifying principles was simple. Defining a parsimonious set of principles was far from it, however. Writing this book was not the "swift, even flow" ideal that we advocate for managers. We hence are immensely grateful for the patience and encouragement of our editorial team at Oxford University Press—Clare Kennedy, David Musson, and Adam Swallow—who stuck with us as the years went past.

As we complete this project, most of us have moved to pastures away from Cambridge. The team of authors now spans three continents. We have benefited, as always, from the numerous insights we have gleaned from operations of all types and from all over the world. All of these experiences have been important in grounding our work in reality. More than anything, these experiences have reaffirmed our original premise: at the heart of operations management stands a set of enduring principles, generic and time-tested.

Matthias Holweg
Jane Davies
Arnoud De Meyer
Benn Lawson
and Roger W. Schmenner

CONTENTS

LIST OF FIGURES

LIST OF TABLES

ABOUT THE AUTHORS

Matthias Holweg is Professor of Operations Management at Saïd Business School, University of Oxford, where he also chairs the Technology and Operations Management group and Organization Studies department. His research focuses on the application and adaptation of process improvement methods across manufacturing, service, and office contexts. Prior to joining Oxford, he was on the faculty of the University of Cambridge, and a Sloan Industry Center Fellow at MIT's Engineering Systems Division.

Jane Davies is Director of the Cambridge MBA and Senior Faculty in Management Practice at the Judge Business School at the University of Cambridge. Her research focuses on the role of operations management in creating organizational value and growth. Before her academic career, Jane spent ten years consulting to companies in the service and public sectors on process improvement initiatives and technology change projects.

Arnoud De Meyer is President of Singapore Management University. He was Director of the Judge Business School at the University of Cambridge, and was the Founding Dean of INSEAD's Asia Campus in Singapore. He has an MSc in Electrical Engineering, an MBA, and a PhD in Management from the University of Ghent. He serves on several boards as an external director both in Europe and in Singapore.

Benn Lawson is a Senior Lecturer (Associate Professor) in Operations Management at the Judge Business School at the University of Cambridge, and Director of the Centre for Process Excellence and Innovation. His research focuses on the management of global supply chains, particularly issues around strategic sourcing, supplier management, and the interface with new product development. Prior to joining Cambridge, Benn held positions at Queen's University Belfast and The University of Melbourne.

Roger W. Schmenner is Professor Emeritus of Operations Management and the former Randall L. Tobias Chair at Indiana University's Kelley School of Business. He has held faculty appointments at Duke, Harvard, and Yale universities, and has been a three-time visiting faculty member at IMD in Lausanne, and a visiting professor at the Judge Business School at the University of Cambridge. He is also a former President and Fellow of the Production and Operations Management Society. His research interests within in the field include manufacturing strategy, productivity, and manufacturing and service operations location.

1 The discipline of operations management

This is a book about operations management and what it stands for. Those of us who claim this field for ourselves are typically very clear about its mission—to make it faster, less costly, and/or more sustainable to produce the products and deliver the services that add value and enrich our lives, with a quality and a timeliness that satisfy the most discriminating customer. Yet how we accomplish this mission, the essence of what we stand for, comes harder.

We often state that operations is a functional discipline of management. We define it as a function like sales, marketing, engineering, finance, or accounting and our business schools teach it that way. We make a point of stating that the operations function typically accounts for the majority of assets, and largely determines the unit cost for the good or service offered. More importantly still, the way operations are run also determines the day-to-day service levels we offer customers in terms of quality, quantity, and time. We draw on an ample inventory of cases that illustrate how important operations are to the firm as a whole—or more specifically, how important it is to get the operational aspects right.

Yet, what does it mean to be a discipline? For us, discipline means more than the fact that operations management is a branch of learning that business schools teach. "Discipline" connotes a coherent set of concepts, the development of skill, and a point of view about the world. It means holding a particular "lens" to business problems, a lens that both colors how we look at things and brings things into sharper focus. With appeal to our discipline, we can comment more deeply about business issues. Each of the disciplines aligned with business looks at business problems in a different way. Marketing approaches problems differently from finance and from organizational behavior. Economists and accountants have their own perspectives. What is the perspective that is uniquely operations management? What is our "Weltanschauung," our very own view of the world of business?

1.1 Process, discipline, and the role of theory

For us, the discipline of operations management is all about *processes*. Every textbook in operations, it seems, starts out with the transformation of inputs into outputs. Usually little is subsequently done with this process model to explain operations concepts. This is a grave omission in our view, as in that simple phrase lies a treasure chest of insights into exactly how those inputs (what they are, what they cost, where they come from, how they got to us) are processed (by which technologies, by whom, with what quality, in what time frame, with what economy) into those outputs (of what variety and quality, at what cost, how they get to the customer). The choices involved are myriad. And they are important, as these very decisions determine the quality, cost, and delivery of the product or service provided. The discipline of Operations Management can tell us how we should think about all of those choices. Some ways of thinking are more fruitful than others. This is where the "lens" we can hold makes a real difference.

We know a lot about processes, as a body of knowledge, even though we hardly ever express it coherently. We can explain a lot about how they work as they do, and why. We can classify them. We have the tools by which to examine them. We know their strengths and weaknesses. We know which ones are most appropriate in all sorts of circumstances, and we can predict how they will fare. We know how they should be measured and how they should not be measured. We know what it takes to improve them.

We know that when they work well, the rewards can be tremendous. And, when they work poorly, companies are at risk of collapse. Moreover, we know that companies are awash in processes and that they often do not realize how dependent on processes, both good and bad, they are. Importantly, they may not know what to do to improve those processes. Appealing to technology is not, in itself, the path to process improvement. Many cases have shown that having the technology to make something or to deliver a service is only part of the story. Mastering technology does not give you much insight into how to make money from it, nor into how society can benefit the most from it. Here is where *management*—and operations management in particular—can help.

To help shine a light on processes and what we know about them, we have entitled this book, *Process Theory*. We have not done this lightly, as "processes" transcend all business disciplines, and all fields of science.[1] However, processes are at the core of what we do in operations management, and we have been lax at claiming processes as our own and as a basis for theory.

In contrast, the hard sciences are much admired by social scientists, including business researchers, because they appear to be clearly defined by their theories. Physicists have quantum theory, the theory of general relativity, string theory, and more. Biologists have the theory of evolution. Geologists have plate tectonics. One could go on. These disciplines are defined, at least in part, by their theories. On the other hand, what do the business disciplines have? Do we have theories that serve to define us? Do we need theories to define us?

Although we have far to go as a discipline, we feel as though we know enough about processes to frame what we do know as *process theory.*[2] We can explain a lot and we understand how processes work as they do. We can make predictions about them. Process theory is, for us, the grounds for our understanding. It gives us perspective that we would not otherwise have. It is the foundation of our discipline.

DO WE NEED THEORY?

Many management scholars will balk and consider it heretical to even ask whether we need theory, for "theory" is the most important instrument through which researchers come to understand *one another's arguments.*[3] The underlying cycle that tests, expands upon, or refutes the aspects and implications of theory is the most fundamental mechanism that social science has at hand to develop knowledge, and to move the field forward. Theories explain facts and provide storylines as to how phenomena work the way that they do. They can, and should, be used to make predictions. In turn, theories can be disproved by findings that run counter to their predictions or explanations, to make way for better theories.[4]

While the role of theory in the social sciences stands undisputed, it is important to recognize that the operations management discipline combines two distinct approaches to research: the engineering view, and the social science view. These have two very different outlooks on research.

The first one stems from industrial engineering and is focused on "problem solving." Here little if any theory is needed "to explain" or predict, as the research is driven by an often practical problem at hand. Success or failure of the research is purely measured by the degree to which the solution solves the problem. Concerns such as generalization and validity are secondary, as the viable solution is considered sufficient "proof." Whether or not this solution also applies to other cases is of secondary concern. Often mathematics is used to present a new algorithm or procedure to address the problem. Advocates of this approach argue that operations management is dealing with "real-life problems" and is "applied in nature," and thus does not need theory or a theoretical "grounding."

On the other side are those trained as social scientists, who try to work out "how and why things work the way they do." This approach often uses empirics to benchmark and distil best practices. The objective is generally to develop sound predictions of which practices lead to superior performance. Here, theory is seen as the vehicle to develop the implications to be tested, in order to refine, and possibly refute, hypotheses of all sorts.

In short, it makes it all the more difficult when we realize that students of operations management come from so many different traditions and fields of study. Engineers are often analytical, mathematical, and eclectic. Theory may not count so much as problem-solving ability. Others may have science or social science backgrounds, and they often focus on explanations for why things work as they do. Their orientation may be more empirical. They may aim for benchmarking and best practice. Still others may have no science or engineering background at all. Forging a discipline from such diversity can be tough.

Process theory aims to bridge this gap. We build on contributions from across the spectrum of operations management research. We argue that there is a unifying theory of processes at the heart of what we do. And this theory can, and should, be used to make predictions about how processes work.

In our everyday language, "theory" is very often used to describe a state of tentativeness or uncertainty with regards to an explanation. We argue that the definition is exactly the opposite in research; theory provides us with an overarching paradigm, a vehicle to predict and identify cause and effect relationships and interactions between variables. This, in turn, increases our understanding of the world around us.

Theories are generally accepted, but they are by no means uncontested. They emerge, evolve, and are continuously refined. The refinement is a natural process of expanding their scope by applying them to new contexts. They can also be proven wrong altogether. No theory is ever *perfect*, and in fact it cannot be. There is always a better theory on the horizon, which in turn anchors the intellectual development of the field. What we do know, though, is what makes for a *good* theory.[5] First and foremost, a theory needs to offer *predictive value* or *explanatory power*. As Whetten (1989, p.491) puts it, "we must make sure that what is passing as good theory includes a plausible, cogent explanation for why we should expect certain relationships in our data." According to Popper, a theory should make falsifiable or *testable* predictions about things not yet observed. The relevance and specificity of those predictions determine how useful the theory is. Its most fundamental role is to provide us with the ability to better understand causal relationships between variables. As such, theories focus on attributes or variables and their interactions.

Some are concerned that a focus on theory will lead to incremental, less creative, and less relevant research. There may be an element of truth in this, as it is certainly perceived to be "safe" to work on incremental research that "extends the existing literature." This is a matter of choice, however. Theories are not built; they are invented. That is to say, theories cannot be systematically constructed or deduced from facts or existing papers. Theories require inspiration and creativity. Facts and the regularities among those facts may exist for generations before an adequate theory is invented to account for them.

We have made our case for the role and importance of theory in operations management. Yet with so many different theories already out there, the question remains: do we need a theory of our own?

DO WE NEED A THEORY *OF OUR OWN*?

It was a passing comment by our colleague Andy Neely that fell on very fertile ground. He had noticed an intriguing dichotomy between two recent books: *Great Minds in Management* by Smith and Hitt[6] and *Giant Steps in Management* by Mol and Birkinshaw.[7] While the latter lists no fewer than nine fundamental innovations to management in its very first chapter that anyone would immediately recognize as "operations" concepts (of a total of fifty across all management disciplines), the former does not feature a single "great mind" with an operations background among its twenty-four management "gurus." Clearly, operations management has a lot to say to practice. Yet the root cause for its apparent underrepresentation in "management theory" is less clear.

Operations management is different from other fields in management in as far as it does not have a single underlying theory, or even a set of commonly used theories. In fact, operations management covers a broad epistemological spectrum, and tends to borrow theories from many disciplines. On the more naturalist or realist side, more prevalent in Europe, manufacturing systems are seen as sociotechnical systems. Theories tend to be derived from the social sciences, including the resource-based view, dynamic capabilities, and transaction cost economics.

At the other end of the spectrum is the quantitative description and analytical modeling of cause–effect relationships that relies on mathematics as a theoretical foundation. Here, no formal theory is used, although implicitly the *laws* of mathematics are used to justify the approach used. This approach is still more prevalent in operations research circles, as well as in North American academe, where the emphasis on quantitative work is measurably stronger. Few are able to bridge these camps, and, we would argue, this unnatural divide has done a lot of harm to our field.

Regardless of one's personal epistemological stance, a large fraction of operations management research sits somewhere on the spectrum between the social sciences and applied mathematics. While analytical and modeling research in operations management will not be grounded in theory, virtually all empirical operations management research will use some kind of theory to ground its findings.

Most commonly used are management theories borrowed from organizational behavior, strategy, and economics: transaction cost economics, the resource-based view and the notion of dynamic capabilities, information processing, adaptive structuration theory; but also others derived from the sciences, such as evolutionary theory, systems theory, and complex adaptive systems. As Morgan Swink, then co-editor of the *Journal of Operations Management* (whose mission is to "publish original, high quality, operations management empirical research that will have a significant impact on OM theory and practice"), commented: "we have few things that we call our own [theory in operations management]." It is astounding that all operations management research requires theory, yet we acknowledge none of our own devising.

One could argue that borrowing theories from other fields is sufficient. Yet there are three specific dangers in this approach. For one, it can lead to circular arguments. Take for example the work on dynamic capability.[8] Here researchers look at high-performing firms, isolate them from the population of other firms, and identify their distinguishing practices, which are labeled "dynamic capabilities." It is then argued that these practices, such as JIT, Lean, Six Sigma, BTO, lead to higher performance. Not only is this a potentially circular argument, but what actual explanatory value does this have for operations management as a field? We have long known, and empirically proven, that Lean practices lead to superior performance. So what exactly is the *incremental* learning (or explanation) that we in operations management derive from re-coding them as "dynamic capabilities"? A cynical outlook might lead one to argue that theories from other fields serve largely to assist publication in certain journals, and/or to be recognized by other management scholars.

A second real danger in adopting theories from other fields is that while they may be valid theories in themselves, when exported into a new context, namely the operational side of the firm, they lose validity. In other words, one cannot assume that a theory that works in one context, works equally well in another. Theories may or may not retain their *context validity*,[9] and this is a particular danger when borrowing theories from other fields. This is one of the key reasons why operations management needs its own theory.

We *can* borrow, but borrowing brings the danger of compromising the explanatory power of a theory. We see this as one of the main reasons why the theory section seems "bolted on" to some operations management papers. It fits, but overall it has little to say about the actual problem. The main reason, one could speculate, is that operations management is different from other fields of management studies. While marketing, strategy, organizational behavior all share a common grounding in the social sciences, operations management has both a social science and an engineering background. As we discussed earlier, the focus is partly on "problem solving," and partly on "explaining the larger patterns at work." In that sense, operations management has a different outlook on business problems. This should also be reflected in the way it uses theory.

The third danger lies in the *contribution* to theory. The underlying purpose of our research is to make a contribution to theory. All too often new theory is proposed, but then never tested or refuted. As a result we have journals full of papers that all claim to make novel contributions to theory—most of which stand uncontested, and sadly often unnoticed. As Linderman and Chandrasekaran show,[10] operations management is one of the disciplines that is more open to a scholarly exchange with other disciplines. Several other disciplines however are not. This in turn means that making a contribution to one of "their" theories in an operations management journal is likely to go unnoticed. The theory building and testing cycle remains a loop that has not been closed.

So, let us look at what *process theory* is all about.

THE CORE ELEMENTS OF *PROCESS THEORY*

For us, the elements of what we can explain with process theory can be divided into three broad categories: design, measurement, and improvement. Virtually everything we do in operations management hangs underneath these three core activities.

Design is about understanding different kinds of processes, with their strengths and weaknesses. It is about understanding some of the universal truths about processes of any type—their variation, their throughput rates, and their throughput times. It is about the capacity of a process and how that capacity is either constrained or enhanced. It is about matching process to needs, designing the process for the purpose.

Measurement is about what to measure in a process so that we can know its performance, and perhaps influence that performance. Measurement is a critical link between strategy and action. Measurement for operations management is distinctly different from the measurement associated with other disciplines. Indeed, it is sometimes a point of contention.

Improvement deals with how a process can deliver more—more productivity, shorter delivery times, higher quality—in short, better performance along specific dimensions. It is critical to the role that operations can play in the company.

Other students of operations management have sought to characterize what we know about processes. Many of these characterizations have focused on the "factory physics"[11] of operations. Certainly, this perspective on operations is an important one, and all of us are in its debt. We seek a broader perspective, however, one that combines factory physics with the more behavioral aspects of management. The broad and sustaining impact that operations can have on the company merits casting a wider net. That net, for us, must include design, measurement, and improvement, as shown in Figure 1.1.

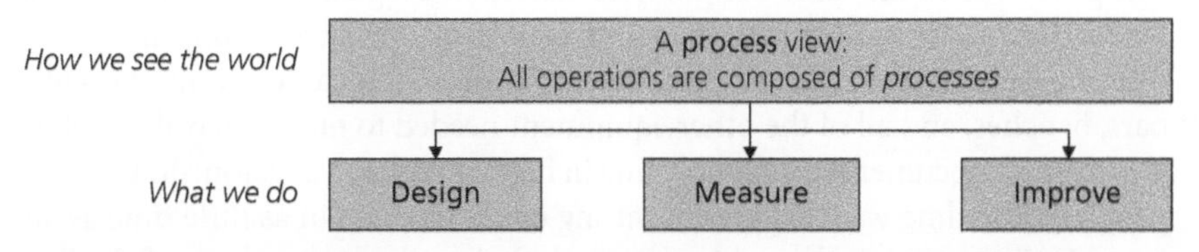

Figure 1.1 The core of operations management: to design, measure, and improve processes.

The principles that define what we term process theory—and that serve as the focal points of this book—are introduced within this framework of *Design–Measure–Improve*. This framework will serve as a touchstone for us. Before we turn to it, however, we first consider some history. Knowing where we come from as a discipline tells us a lot about where we are going.

1.2 **A brief history of operations management**

As with much of business study, operations management routinely neglects its past. Yet its past has much to say about the nature of the discipline and what it stands for. We have argued that processes and their study are at the center of operations management. So it stands to reason that a proper study of operations management begins with a history of processes themselves.[12]

PRE-INDUSTRIAL REVOLUTION

Prior to the Industrial Revolution and the beginnings of the factory system, production was typically done by artisans using the master–apprentice system. The masters often banded together into guilds, and the guilds were the bastions of quality control and the guardians of entry into the field. Production of significant quantities of any product simply could not be accomplished easily, however. The products themselves were unique, in the sense that one product could not be replicated exactly. Products were "fitted"—tweaked—to make them work correctly or assemble properly or look as they should. There were no long runs. Customers typically contracted for what they wanted individually. Production occurred in a series of what we would term "job shops" today.

Still, there are a few noteworthy examples of how early adopters of operations management principles gained an edge. The most spectacular early example of a moving assembly line was the Arsenal in Venice. The Arsenal was charged with building the ships of the Venetian navy. In the 1400s and 1500s, it was the largest industrial enterprise in Europe and famed for producing the galleys that guaranteed Venetian supremacy in the Mediterranean. The galleys, all of the same design, were started in a lagoon within the Arsenal, where their hulls were constructed and their decks planked. From there they were floated past a series of warehouses out of which came the masts, sails, oars, benches, and all of the other equipment needed to outfit a naval vessel. It was the first documented assembly line in history. What was astonishing to the people of the time was that this outfitting could be done in as little time as an hour. Unfortunately, when ship design shifted to the larger ships of the line where the guns were placed along the sides of the ship and not fore and aft as with the galley, the assembly line process could no longer cope, and it fell by the wayside.

Also in other regions of the world there were early experiences with production on an industrial scale and assembly lines. Best known is no doubt the technological and scientific evolution under the Tang and Song dynasties in China, where production of iron, coins, textiles, ships, etc. reached industrial proportions. The discovery in 1998 of a shipwreck from the ninth century in the Java Sea with more than 60,000 ceramics produced during the Tang dynasty provides insights into the industrial production of pottery and the intensive trade between China and what is now Iran and Iraq.[13]

The British Navy's victory in the 1805 Battle of Trafalgar was based on Lord Nelson's superior tactics (using a two-pronged line of attack perpendicular to the Spanish-French Armada), but also on Britain's superior gunnery skills. A 32-pounder cannon required fourteen crew to operate, so "honing" their skills paid off. The British trained their gunnery crews so they could achieve a much higher rate of fire. Although outgunned by thirty-three ships to forty-one, the British Navy greatly benefited from their higher rate of fire. This is certainly one of the most impressive early results of set-up time reduction!

Even before the Industrial Revolution some economic activities had to be done on a larger scale. Shipbuilding, mining, and ironworks, for example, involved significant numbers of people and considerable capital. But none of these operations became early models for higher-volume production. They were simply not productive enough.

THE INDUSTRIAL REVOLUTION

All of this changed with the advent of the Industrial Revolution and the creation of the factory system. The pivotal year was 1776. The seminal place was Cromford in Derbyshire, England. The critical, initial product was cotton thread.

Prior to this period of time, the center for cotton apparel manufacture was India, and the best cotton garments came from there. What cotton garments were made in Great Britain were made according to the "putting-out" system. In the putting-out system, a general contractor, typically a merchant, coordinated the various steps that led to the creation of a shirt or some other garment. It was a cottage industry. Some were responsible for cleaning the raw cotton. Others, elsewhere, carded the cotton into rovings. Still others would take the rovings and spin the thread on a spinning wheel. And then weavers would turn the thread into cloth. From there, a garment could be fabricated. The putting-out system took a great deal of time as materials were shuttled from one person to another. Inventories were substantial. Quality was not always assured, and "shrinkage" was common.

The scale of the operation got a boost with the invention of the flying shuttle in 1733, which doubled the productivity of weavers and moved the bottleneck squarely to the creation of cotton thread. Some of that pressure was relieved by Hargreaves's creation of the spinning jenny in about 1764. The spinning jenny essentially put the spinning wheel on its side and thus permitted work on many spindles at the same time. It was an advance, but nothing like what came shortly after: the waterframe.

The driving force behind the creation of the waterframe was a former barber and wig-maker from the north of England, Richard Arkwright. Together with a clockmaker, John Kay, and through years of experimentation, Arkwright came out with the spinning frame (later dubbed the waterframe because it could use water power) in 1769. The waterframe could produce spun cotton thread of better quality—suitable for the long warp threads needed for weaving—and in much greater quantity than ever before. With this, spinning thread was no longer the bottleneck in the textile process.

The waterframe was the first true production machine, as we would term it now. When coupled with water power, it could produce cotton thread more or less continuously. At its heart was gearing that only clockmakers of the time could design and make. That gearing was able to operate a series of three rollers at progressively increasing speeds so that the cotton rovings could be pulled, stretched, and twisted into cotton thread. Arkwright was able to put rows of them together in what were the first true factories. His first mill in Cromford was a success, employing 200 people twenty-four hours a day, six days a week, but it was his Cromford Mill #2, built in 1776, that became the dominant design. Cromford #2 was immensely successful and was copied throughout Great Britain and elsewhere, including the United States. (Samuel Slater, known as the "Father of the American Industrial Revolution," had worked at Cromford and built his mill in Rhode Island as a copy of Cromford #2.) Cromford #2 combined both the waterframe and the carding machine that Arkwright had perfected in 1775. The mill ran day and night and employed about 450 people. With this mill, the factory system was born. Arkwright went on to build many other mills and, despite not earning much money from his patents, died in 1792 as the richest man of the Industrial Revolution.

When many people think of the Industrial Revolution, they think of a cavalcade of impressive inventions. The steam engine usually heads that list, but an array of textile industry machines, innovations to iron and steel making, the development of canals and railroads and other infrastructure, and the development of a number of other industries can also be cited. Nevertheless, technology did not, by itself, bring on the Industrial Revolution. That took the factory system.

While it was the British who created the factory system, it was the Americans who took it to new heights with standard designs and interchangeable parts. Although the inventor of the cotton gin, Eli Whitney, championed the cause of interchangeable parts, it was John Hall, Simeon North, and their successors who made it happen. Their industry was gunsmithing and the major buyer, the US government, sought a steady supply of better and better performing firearms. John Hall had invented a breech-loading rifle that could be loaded and fired more rapidly than muzzle-loaded ones, and at the Harpers Ferry Arsenal in the 1820s he developed the machine tools, the fixtures, and the gauges that began to make interchangeable parts a reality. Others, such as Simeon North in Connecticut, expanded on his achievement. The Connecticut River Valley—notably the Springfield Armory (Massachusetts)—became the crucible for much of the experimentation with and development of the tools and techniques needed to make parts interchangeable. Veterans of the gunsmithing industry dispersed to other industries and took their knowledge with them. In 1851, at the great Crystal Palace Exhibition in London, the American manufacturer Robbins & Lawrence stunned the British with a display of rifles that could be disassembled, their parts swapped, and the rifles reassembled perfectly. The "fitting" that characterized the final steps in a typical rifle factory in Britain (as elsewhere in industry) was not needed, and its elimination caused such a stir that the British government commenced a study of what they termed "the American system of manufactures." The torch of process-based productivity gain had passed to the Americans.

It still took considerable time to master interchangeable parts. Machine tools needed to become larger and more able to hold tight tolerances. Fixtures, jigs, and gauges needed to improve as well. Only in the twentieth century could one say that interchangeable parts had been mastered. The Ford Motor Company, for example, was acknowledged to have the finest machine tools and was thus the major manufacturer whose output of component parts for the Model T came closest to the goal of interchangeable parts.[14] Timex, in the tight-tolerance watch industry, was the first producer deemed to be able to produce parts that did not need any further processing before they could be put into a watch.[15]

HIGH-VOLUME PROCESSES

Such were the beginnings of batch operations. They were to proliferate in both small-scale and large-scale manufacturing. The archetypal large-scale batch operation was steel. The key invention was British, Henry Bessemer's converter in 1855, but it was a Scot in America, Andrew Carnegie, who oversaw the development of the industry at scale. Carnegie saw the power of designing steel mills with materials handling in mind and of running steel mills flat out—what he termed "hard driving" and "steady and full." The design genius behind the logical and smooth flow of Carnegie's steel mills was Alexander Holley. His Edgar Thompson Works outside Pittsburgh became to steel-making what Cromford #2 had been to cotton textiles.

The late 1800s also saw the creation of the first capital-intensive, continuous flow operations. Here, the grain millers of the Upper Midwest in the United States led the way, using many innovations secured from Europe, especially Hungary. The "automatic all roller, gradual reduction mill," created by C.C. Washburn (a founder of what was later to become General Mills) and perfected by him and his rivals the Pillsbury brothers, revolutionized the way cereal grains were processed. Oats were particularly amenable to milling in this way, and, to exploit this fact, the Quaker Oats Company more or less invented the breakfast cereal industry.

The Bonsack cigarette-rolling machine, whose potential was recognized by James Buchanan ("Buck") Duke, essentially created its industry too. Duke's American Tobacco Company forward integrated towards the marketplace and backward integrated towards tobacco growers in order to exploit the power of the Bonsack machine. It was one of the companies broken up by the US Supreme Court in 1911, in the midst of the trust-busting of the era. The other major casualty of the 1911 trust-busting was another continuous flow process, oil refining. J.D. Rockefeller's Standard Oil Company, the pioneer in fractional distillation, was split into separate companies with brands that we know even today. Indeed, all of the true American trusts of that era—including linseed and cotton seed oils, sugar processing, and lead processing for paint—were continuous flow processes.

The power of the continuous flow process had worldwide reach. Pilkington, in the UK, used the Siemens continuous-tank furnace from about 1880 to seize the leadership in plate glass production in Europe. In Belgium, the Solvay brothers at about the same time developed a continuous, capital-intensive process to produce alkalis, a process that was soon licensed in many countries. In the early 1900s, Courtaulds, a British company, created a high-volume process to produce a synthetic fiber, rayon, and it quickly dominated production worldwide. The German dye makers (e.g. Bayer, BASF, and Hoechst), soon to expand to other organic chemical production, were quick to see how large-scale and concentrated production could lower costs; they dominated world production. Even the making of Scotch whisky benefited from the development of continuous processes. In the 1870s, whisky producers started to blend batch-produced single malt whiskies with grain spirits produced in a "patent still" at higher speeds and volumes and at lower costs. (See Alfred Chandler's *Scale and Scope* for more stories of the international reach and power of continuous flow processes.)

The last major process type to be developed is the process that most people think of first when thinking about factories: the assembly line. The modern moving assembly line is generally attributed to Henry Ford and his lieutenants in a burst of innovation during 1913–14.[16] The popular Model T Ford had been in production since 1908, but with the creation of the assembly line at the Highland Park facility the labor content in the assembly of the Model T dropped from 12.5 hours to 1.5 hours in the space of just a few months. The Model T then truly became a car for the masses. Soon, Ford was producing more than half of all the cars sold in the US.

The creation of the moving assembly line at Ford depended on a number of developments at the company. Critical was Henry Ford's decision to focus exclusively on the Model T, a light but robust car. Other, prior models were abandoned. Producing truly interchangeable parts was another critical goal if the company was to manufacture in high volumes. Ford's engineers became proficient at the design of fixtures, jigs, gauges, and many sorts of machine tools. They also broke from the classic job shop layout of grouping together like machinery, and instead began to place machines in sequence according to the requirements of the parts or subassemblies needed. Gravity slides and conveyors were added to aid materials handling.

The assembly line did not emerge full-blown at Ford's Highland Park facility. It started first in the magneto department and moved on to engine assembly and then axle assembly. The iconic assembly line for the chassis came last, in fact. The idea in all that was done was to move "the work to the men," where before teams of workers would travel from stand to stand assembling cars in place. The chassis assembly line began in sections and used ropes at first, but then over some months became fully connected and run by chains. Workstations, materials handling, and speeds were experimented with until everything was synchronized. Ford's accomplishments were widely reported and the moving assembly line spread quickly to other industries.

The assembly line did have some antecedents. Most immediately before Ford came the "disassembly" lines of the major meat packers, such as Swift and Armour, and these served as inspiration to Ford's engineers. Using railroad cars specially designed to be refrigerated with ice, the meat packers of Chicago could ship "disassembled," dressed meat east and save on the waste and cost of shipping live animals over such a distance. The scale of their operations in Chicago also induced the invention of many by-products from the slaughtering that occurred there.

INTO THE TWENTIETH CENTURY

The moving assembly line that Ford created was both spectacularly productive and massively inflexible. That is understandable for such a pioneering effort. Ford's fortunes were given a shock, however, when General Motors re-engineered the assembly line and the machine tools that fed it, giving it more flexibility to create a succession of different models. The choice that General Motors offered the marketplace and the success that ensued forced Ford to terminate the Model T and to close its operations in Detroit for a turbulent six months so they could retool to match the flexibility that General Motors provided. Ford's sales fell permanently behind those of General Motors.

Still, the power of the moving assembly line continued to reach into other industries. During World War II, for example, as an act of patriotic devotion, the Ford lieutenants that created the Highland Park factory re-engineered the way airplanes were produced. Prior to their re-engineering of the Willow Run facility, where the B-24 bomber was assembled, the best that had been done was the production of a bomber a day. Their re-engineering led to the production of a bomber an hour.

The goal of producing perfectly interchangeable parts was pursued diligently throughout the first half of the twentieth century. Machine tools were constantly being improved, and later in the century they were automated and more precisely controlled, with the innovations of numerical control (NC) and computer numerical control (CNC). With the mastery of interchangeable parts came the need to create statistical process control so that variation that was simply an artifact of statistical randomness could be differentiated from variation that had a specific cause and thus needed to be acted on.

The auto industry was again the source of ground-breaking innovation, with the development of just-in-time (now termed Lean) manufacturing thinking, this time from Japan, and especially Toyota. The creation of manufacturing cells and the development of many techniques to enhance quality and to reduce inventories revolutionized the industry nearly as much as the creation of the moving assembly line itself. The "philosophy" that was developed spread as well to a variety of other industries.

Towards the end of the twentieth century, the computer descended full force on manufacturing. Not only could the computer be used to improve machine tools, but it also served as the driving force behind the invention of robots and other related machines (e.g. vision systems, barcode reading systems) that made production both safer and better quality and the process more flexible. The computer also revolutionized how production planning and control were accomplished, and how supply networks can be coordinated. Its impact will continue long into the current century. All types of operations have benefited greatly from the introduction of information technology (IT) and the Internet. Information flows can be at once faster and more detailed. Materials handling is quicker and more precise. Visibility is greatly enhanced.

The late twentieth century also marked a considerable shift in the operations management field, from the focal firm towards the study of the entire "supply chain" a firm is embedded in. Following Martin Christopher's famous quote,[17] "Value chains compete, not individual firms," it was noticed that the scope for increasing a firm's competitiveness is limited by the partners it is linked with upstream and downstream in the value chain. The initial mention of a "supply chain" dates back to a consulting report of 1982,[18] which commented on the need to manage "total supply chain inventories," but since then the field has developed to include the study of supplier relationships, global supply networks, and the like.

AT THE DAWN OF THE TWENTY-FIRST CENTURY

As we entered into the twenty-first century, a key theme that emerged for operations management research was the globalization of trade, and the global shifts in manufacturing and supply footprints. Enabled by further trade deregulation, low and efficient transportation cost, and a stark difference in labor costs, manufacturing footprints shifted from the West to China. Equally, global supply chains emerged across all sectors and regions, as companies were able to harness the "lowest global cost" options in their supply chain decision making. At the same time, uncontrolled growth in financial markets and the high interdependencies between global markets created by these global supply chains led to a global financial crisis in 2008, followed by a lengthy period of weak recovery. For operations management research, this experience catapulted topics such as uncertainty, risk, and resilience to the front page. For public services, now embattled by strong austerity measures needed to deal with the fallout of the global financial crisis, the mantra became cost-efficiency. Many operations management concepts saw applications in the public sector, with mixed success, at least so far.

Another development—that long predates the turn of the millennium—is the increasing digitalization of all business processes, not just in the office, but also in manufacturing where direct digital manufacturing methods (also known as 3D printing and additive manufacturing) have gained prevalence. Many products have now a high information content and we see all around us "smart" products, from running shoes designed and printed based on the data about how the consumer utilizes them to autonomous vehicles. Many products now also have data as part of their unique selling proposition, such as the origin of meat and vegetables in our supermarkets.

And last but not least, persistent concerns over the sustainability of our world have had a significant impact on how we think about design and improvement of processes. Two major themes have emerged. First, that processes should have less and less impact or even interaction with the environment in which they operate: no immediate interaction while they operate, but also less impact on the stock of natural resources of this world. And second, how we can design closed loop processes, i.e. where we recover and rework the products after their useful life.

1.3 The study of operations management

The interest in studying a firm's operation coincided with the great changes that repetitive large-scale processes instigated. From the advent of the Industrial Revolution through the tremendous growth of the latter half of the 1800s, managers were pursuing these new, primarily technical, innovations in operations. However, they were not writing about them. The study of management and the accounting of what was happening on the shop floor lagged.[19] The first real study of operations began with the creation of the American Society of Mechanical Engineers (ASME) in 1880, whose inaugural meeting was chaired by the steel industry's Alexander Holley. The first mechanical engineering departments in major universities and the first business schools date from this time too. Initially, ASME was as interested in cost accounting as it was in shop floor management. People were just learning how to control these big integrated processes.

The best known of these early students of processes and their management needs was Frederick Taylor. Taylor worked for Midvale Steel, one of the companies not controlled by Carnegie, and even held some patents there for machines and materials. In 1895 he began to argue that costs should be based, not on past experience, but on standard times and outputs that could be determined "scientifically" via time study and more detailed analysis of the jobs involved. In his book, *Shop Management*, Taylor advocated for the creation of a planning department that would run the entire operation, wrenching control from the line managers. Although aspects of Taylor's thinking were adopted widely, no company fully adopted his thinking. Rather, roles such as those that Taylor argued should be housed in an all-powerful planning department (e.g. purchasing, engineering, inspection, time and cost accounting, scheduling, shipping) became instead staff roles reporting to the plant's line management.

Taylor himself was not a particularly able manager. He was too dogmatic and hard-headed. His ideas about how work should be done caught hold, though, and Taylor developed some disciples, including Henry Gantt, and Frank and Lillian Gilbreth (known for motion study and industrial psychology, respectively).

PRODUCTION PLANNING AND CONTROL

Taylor's cause was taken up by his disciples, most notably Henry Gantt, with whom he had worked at Midvale Steel. Before his death in 1919, Gantt developed a host of charts of different types that helped to plan and schedule operations: daily balance of work chart, man's record chart, machine record chart, layout chart, load chart, and progress chart among them. These charts and the follow-on advances made by others were the main tools used to track production prior to the development of the computer. Planning production was done with various static lot-sizing techniques such as the reorder point and periodic review. (The well-known EOQ formula dates from 1913.) In these early systems, all kinds of parts were managed as if they were finished goods. Such simple systems for planning and controlling production were staples of the industry until the advent of the computer.

With the development of the computer, and particularly the IBM 360 computer in the 1960s, one could begin to think how the tasks of forecasting, planning, and tracking production could be made easier and at the same time more detailed. An IBM employee and former J.I. Case manager, Joseph Orlicky, along with two others who had worked together at the Stanley Works, Oliver Wight and George Plossl, took up the cause and championed what became known as material requirements planning (MRP). With the computer, a forecast of production, combined with bills of materials and other information, could be used to coordinate the procurement of materials and the accumulation of inventory to match production needs in close anticipation of their use by the process. IBM created some of the first software to do this work (e.g. COPICS, MAPICS). As part of what came to be known as the MRP Crusade, Wight and Plossl expanded on this notion and advocated an even broader role for the computer, to encompass not only materials but accounting. This became known as manufacturing resource planning or MRP II. An even broader view of the role of the computer in managing the business is evident today in enterprise resource planning (ERP) systems, which have been around since the late 1990s. A number of software firms have contributed greatly to the advance of these tools, including SAP, Oracle, PeopleSoft, and JD Edwards.

While the various lot-sizing techniques and the charts of Henry Gantt were widely used, they could not guarantee that the resources they planned and tracked were used in the optimal way to maximize output or lower cost. Some stunning gains in mathematics, many with roots in World War II, ushered in optimization, and more, with what would become operations research. Mathematical tools, such as George Dantzig's simplex method for solving linear programs (1947), began to be applied to allocation decisions, forecasting, planning, scheduling, inventory, and logistics issues, sometimes with dramatic results. Algorithms were developed in the 1950s for production scheduling (e.g. Johnson's rule, earliest due date, shortest processing time) and the management of inventories. Further gains in mathematical sophistication (e.g. integer and other types of mathematical programming, optimization, search techniques) have only added to the list in the years since. This realm of operations research and the modeling of operations issues have grown to include a wealth of contributions of different types (e.g. scheduling, procurement, logistics, resource allocation) and in different industries (e.g. manufacturing, transportation, healthcare).

Although the "scientific management" movement coincided with the creation of the moving assembly line at Ford Motor Company, historians are convinced that "scientific management" played no formal role in the development of Clarence Avery's thinking or that of the others involved at Ford. The assembly line did usher in the need for line balance, however. Despite being a problem of immense potential, it has proved to be a very difficult problem to solve, even with great computer power. Managers still resort to trial and error, using past history as a guide.

THE MANAGEMENT OF QUALITY

The study of quality in operations began with a concern for conformance to specifications. As the earlier discussion of the American system of manufactures reveals, achieving consistent quality was simply not possible prior to solving the problem of interchangeable parts. Doing that meant creating machine tools of sufficient size and precision, and creating the jigs and fixtures needed by those machines and the gauging required to check the completed parts. As noted earlier, it took until the early decades of the twentieth century for that to happen.

Advances in quality since then have involved coping with the variation of processes. The first great contribution to statistical quality control was the creation of the control chart by Walter Shewhart of Bell Laboratories in the 1920s. For the first time, people could differentiate statistical variation (randomness) from assignable causes (non-randomness). Two disciples of Shewhart went on to make significant contributions: W. Edwards Deming and Joseph Juran. Deming was famed for his work on describing variation and the mechanism for quality improvement (the PDCA or Deming cycle of "Plan-Do-Check-Act" and his program of "14 Points for Management"). Juran was noted for his use of the Pareto principle and his advocacy of the customer in defining quality. Both were early influences on the post-World War II Japanese. Japan's Deming Prize was begun in 1950 as a way to honor Deming and to recognize companies and individuals for their contributions to quality management. The Japanese themselves have also contributed a number of important thinkers about quality, such as Kaoru Ishikawa (the fishbone diagram), Genichi Taguchi (the Taguchi loss function and the importance of meeting the specification exactly), and Shigeo Shingo (mistake-proofing and quick changeovers that keep quality high [e.g. SMED or single minute exchange of dies]).

The tools of quality control (e.g. control chart, Pareto chart, fishbone diagram) are increasingly well known and have repeatedly demonstrated their worth. What has been more problematic is the management of quality. That is, there has been no best way yet devised to organize people so that quality is pursued both well and relentlessly. There have been a number of movements in quality, with varying success. In the 1950s there was work simplification. In the 1960s came the Zero Defects programs, largely associated with the missile programs at Martin Marietta. After the publication of Philip Crosby's *Quality is Free* book in 1979, the reawakening of the US economy to quality, and the re-emergence of Deming and Juran, came quality circles and the total quality management (TQM) movement. TQM sought to get everyone involved in managing for quality and for everyone to think in terms of customers and suppliers, both internal and external to the company. During this movement, the Malcolm Baldrige National Quality Award started in the US (1987) and the European Foundation for Quality Management Award (1988) in Europe. The ISO9000 program also began at this time.

TQM has since faded as a movement, and for the time being has been largely replaced by Six Sigma, a means of improving quality through the actions of specialized actors (e.g. black belts and green belts) employing the statistical tools of quality control to reduce variation and achieve what has become known as the six-sigma level of quality (3.4 defects per million opportunities).[20] Six Sigma, although started by Motorola (an early winner of the Baldrige Award), took on added significance with its adoption by General Electric (GE). TQM and Six Sigma use the same statistical tools for attaining quality, but TQM advocates more decentralized control while Six Sigma advocates more centralized control over the management of quality.

THE JAPANESE CONTRIBUTION

Intimately involved with quality is the way of thinking about operations epitomized by the Toyota Production System. Although initially termed "just-in-time" during the late 1970s and early 1980s, today this thinking is more often termed "Lean production," following the 1990 success of the book, *The Machine that Changed the World*. The Toyota Production System was fathered by Taiichi Ohno, who developed it when Toyota was scrambling to improve its quality and productivity in early post-World War II Japan. Ohno's thinking has roots in what Ford did, in how the company's prior product, the Toyoda automatic loom, worked, and in how shelves were replenished in American supermarkets of the 1950s. It is a multifaceted system that seeks to uncover and remedy deficiencies in production and to avoid waste. However, it should be seen more as a people development system than as a toolkit of techniques. It begins with careful study of each workstation in the facility and what people have to do to produce a quality product. It recognizes inventory as a means by which mistakes can be hidden from view, and thus seeks to reduce inventory so that the process can be better studied and improved. To this end, quick set-ups and "pulling" work through the factory rather than "pushing" it into the factory, even in coordinated fashion, are viewed as the most effective actions. "Pulling" materials through the process acts to replenish what has recently been used up. Better, it is thought, to have a process that makes today what was sold yesterday. The goal for Lean production is continual study of and improvement to the process.

As this description suggests, Lean production is wide-ranging and has much to contribute to a variety of the facets of operations management. It is rooted in quality management, but it influences inventory management, production scheduling, line balance, equipment choice and deployment, supplier management, and the management of the workforce.

SUPPLY CHAIN MANAGEMENT

The first companies to create supply chains that they managed themselves were Singer and McCormick in the mid-1800s (more on these companies in Section 1.4). The Chicago meat packers also created their own supply chains with their ownership of refrigerated railroad cars and the creation of warehouses in the East. American Tobacco, Standard Oil, and others began integrating backward as well as forward. By 1900, many large companies grew to control their own supply chains, both downstream and upstream.

The latter half of the nineteenth century witnessed tremendous advances to transportation and communications. Railroads were a huge industry and leaders in developing key elements of management, such as accounting and purchasing. As transportation and communications matured, logistics became more regular and easier to manage. People could trust logistics like never before and thus maintain their ownership of goods throughout multiple levels of the supply chain. It became easier to manage sourcing, procurement, and distribution channels. There was an explosion of choice that affected upstream and downstream, involving the design of the network, warehouses, modes of transportation, inventory policies, choice of suppliers and policies towards them, and the nature of supply contracts. Elements of logistics were among the first topics to be studied in business schools. At first people studied purchasing, warehousing, and transportation as separate topics. As IT advances became widespread, these elements were often integrated into materials management, and then later into what we now term supply chain management.

The first solid evidence of a bullwhip effect occurs in 1919 with Procter & Gamble. Richard Deupree, then sales manager and later CEO, wanted to end the feast or famine that was affecting the company's manufacturing. Procter & Gamble sold through wholesalers at the time and those wholesalers typically bunched their orders seasonally. Even though Ivory soap sold steadily through the year, its manufacture was highly cyclical, forcing the company into chronic layoffs and factory shutdowns. Deupree convinced the company to sell directly to retailers. It meant that the sales force had to be expanded from 150 to 600; 125 more warehouses had to be acquired; 2,000 contracts had to be written for deliveries by trucks; and the accounting department had to be reorganized to handle 450,000 accounts. But Procter & Gamble's investment in its own distribution channel paid off; the bullwhip was thwarted.

The first academic work on the bullwhip effect was in the 1950s by MIT engineering professor Jay Forrester and his study of what came to be known as system dynamics.[21] That research stemmed from a cyclicality problem that GE's Appliance Park complex in Louisville, Kentucky could not figure out. As it turned out, GE's own policies contributed to the cyclicality. The formal definition of a "supply chain," however, was not to come until 1982, when consultants started to wonder whether it would not make sense to manage "total supply chain inventories," as opposed to each firm managing their own stock levels. From there on a wealth of research into supply chain inventory management, logistics, and supplier relationships started—that to date remains one of the most active streams in operations management.

THE EMERGENCE OF MASS-CUSTOMIZATION AND FLEXIBILITY IN PROCESSES

Until the early 1980s most manufacturing processes aimed at producing standardized products at the lowest cost and of the highest quality. Customization was left to artisanal workshops. With the emergence of more powerful computers, companies were able to produce customized components on flexible manufacturing systems (FMS). In the 1980s companies began to combine powerful CNC machines with automated materials handling and centralized computerized production planning. In the beginning these FMS were limited to relatively simple mechanical components. But these experiences and the early "robotization," in particular in the automotive industry, made people dream of the totally automated factory where management "could turn off the lights" (because robots don't need light), and where one would be able to produce standardized products in a batch size of one.

Flexibility became a new objective in manufacturing.[22] For many consumer durables like cars, PCs, and laptops, companies started offering customized end products by combining in the assembly stage a large series of optional components. In other industries they developed the concept of delayed differentiation. The idea was to redesign the product so that the ultimate customization could be applied in the last step of the production or assembly process. This could be applied to detergents, perfumes, food, beverages, etc. Consultants came up with the term mass-customization.

Soon management discovered that some of these completely automated flexible processes required heavy investments and maintenance, and that in many cases a clever combination of people and robots was more effective. This led to the current trend towards "co-botization."

The use of analytics and big data in combination with 3D printing had a further impact on customization. Based on the data from multiple sensors, one can now design products such as running gear that is perfectly adapted to the needs of an individual and produce it with relatively simple 3D printers.

There is still a big question about the effectiveness of such customization. Does the final customer really want it, and what are the economics of total customization?

PEOPLE

The impact of process change on people's lives has often been dramatic and it cannot be overstated. The building of Arkwright's mills, the first factories, pulled people off the land and into a regulated work environment for the first time. It signaled a momentous shift to the way people led their lives. One has only to read Dickens to recognize how tumultuous this was as the Industrial Revolution spread to other industries and how profound a set of societal questions have been raised by it.

The moving assembly line at Ford led quickly to the "$5 day," a significant jump in pay for the company's unskilled workers that brought many into the middle class. However, this innovation was implemented primarily to stem the tide of worker attrition that escalated because of the upheaval that came with the establishment of moving assembly lines everywhere in Ford.

The assembly line also brought with it acceleration in the influence of unions. Unions predated the assembly line; the American Federation of Labor was founded in 1886, although individual craft unions had existed well before then. Indeed, one could look on the guilds that sprang up in the Middle Ages in Europe as the origins of the labor movement. Union strength has varied over time and across countries. Unions tend to be in decline now, but their historical influence has been substantial and something that line management in a number of industries and countries have had to deal with.

The most appropriate way to pay people has been debated for years. Hourly pay is a standard mechanism, but Frederick Taylor and others were advocates for incentive pay such as piecework. Indeed, piecework itself dates from the time of the putting-out system. Others have supported gain-sharing plans of various types (e.g. the Scanlon Plan dates from the 1930s).

What determines a worker's willingness to put in effort has been a management issue for years. Pay has always been a factor, since the time when factory jobs started luring people from off of the land. An important experiment at Western Electric's Hawthorne Works outside Chicago from 1924–32, however, concluded that change and interest in the workforce can lead, in themselves, to short-run productivity gains. Since then, there has been research into what has been termed "quality of work life," trying to assess what aspects of the job and the environment surrounding the job are most effective.

STRATEGY

The production/operations function at so many early companies was inextricably tied to the founder and to the company's initial product and its development. Simply getting the product made or the service delivered was a big part of the strategy. As companies and economies matured, the production/operations function became more standardized. Observers began to speculate that the production "problem" had been solved (e.g. John Kenneth Galbraith's 1958 book, *The Affluent Society*, and his 1967 book, *The New Industrial State*). Strategy drifted away from the production/operations function at the same time as discerning customers were beginning to demand more options and choice, which increased the variety and variation that the operations function faced.

Enter Wickham Skinner, of the Harvard Business School, who is generally regarded as the father of manufacturing strategy. Skinner, beginning in 1969, wrote a number of articles that reasserted the production/operations role in corporate strategy. He noted that manufacturing could not be all things to all people, and he introduced trade-offs into operations thinking and the need for consistency of choice in operations design. Thus began a stream of research on strategy that debated the extent and character of those trade-offs, and, once the power of the Japanese just-in-time contribution was recognized, whether indeed those trade-offs were real or whether they could be mastered as "cumulative capabilities."[23]

The introduction of strategy issues to operations has triggered an explosion of empirical work in operations as researchers have strived to uncover the effect of various policies and actions on the performance of company operations.

SMALL-N PROCESSES

Although most of operations management research is focused on repetitive processes ("large-n" processes), the truth is that much of what we do in operations management practice are "projects," or "small-n" processes. Even when we aim to improve a repetitive process using Lean or Six Sigma, the actual process is an improvement "project." While Lean and Six Sigma are standard methodologies, each improvement project will be different depending on the context.

The key distinction for "small-n" operations is that we are deprived of one of our key tools: the learning curve. More specifically, as projects are different from each other (although quite possibly similar in nature, scope, and objective), it is not possible to directly transfer the learning from one project to another. Replication is a core principle for how process improvement works. With replication, any learning from running a process can be transferred and the operation can do better each time around.

The 1950s saw the creation of algorithms to improve the scheduling of projects. The critical path method (CPM) originated with DuPont in 1956 as that company pondered what could be done effectively with one of the first computers, the Univac. The program evaluation and review technique (PERT) came two years later, in 1958, as a means of coordinating better the US Navy's Polaris missile program.

This sets out the main challenge: how does one capture and codify cross-project learning? In their seminal book, *Product Development Performance*, Clark and Fujimoto provide a parallel view to the *Machine that Changed the World*, and demonstrate how Lean principles can equally be applied to small-n processes.

More generally, as the limitations of the early normative view of project management became apparent, the study of projects, and especially major projects, programs, and portfolios, recognized the need not just to manage the conversion process, but also to manage stakeholders and their perceptions of the project output and wider outcome.

1.4 Service vs. manufacturing: the artificial divide

Much of the initial attention in operations management research was devoted to manufacturing, largely because that is where the great changes took place. Yet the history of services parallels that of manufacturing. The early services were family operations and branches were largely a function of the family and its coordination. For example, bank branches such as those created by the Rothschilds and others were family affairs. Although merchants often acted as agents and coordinated some production activities (such as many did with the putting-out system), they did not stray much from their chief activity of selling. As the putting-out system declined, more specialization came to the commercial supply chain (paced by the cotton supply chain). That specialization affected both the goods moved and the paperwork and money transfer that permitted that movement. Jobbers and others surfaced. Nevertheless, services stayed highly fragmented.

It was only with the Singer Company and with the McCormick Harvesting Machine Company, two companies not known for their manufacturing prowess, that we first see the creation of a distribution channel that was owned and operated by a single company. Singer, for example, starting in the late 1850s, owned and operated its own retail stores where sales and repairs were made, where inventories were kept, and where a cadre of women demonstrated the sewing machine for customers. Singer also instituted a "hire-purchase system" whereby customers could buy in installments. In the late 1870s, McCormick took over its entire distribution channel. The formerly independent agents that represented McCormick became salaried managers within the McCormick Harvesting Machine Company and the lower-level sales organization became franchised dealers. Service and repair people operating in the field also became salaried workers of the company. Supply chains as we know them took shape, and, interestingly, they did so in part to compensate for weaknesses in their manufacturing abilities.

The development and geographic spread of the railroads and of communication lines and the speed and regularity that they provided were integral to this growth and innovation. Services such as retailing were subject to the same forces. New kinds of services, such as department stores, and then catalogue operations, began to flourish in the United States after the Civil War. From then on, branches and franchises became more widespread, and distribution channels became more coordinated. Chain stores developed whose high inventory turns and low costs began to dominate sectors that had previously been the province of smaller wholesalers and retailers. Mass distribution joined mass production.

In terms of contribution to the national economy, the service sector has long outgrown the contribution of the manufacturing sector in all developed countries. The nature of Western economies has changed considerably over the past century, which has seen a formal study of operations management: from an agricultural and cottage industry, to an industrial society, and more recently towards a service economy. We do not wish to start the debate as to what level of "balance" is right between manufacturing and service; however, it is undisputed that services now account for the majority of economic activity (75–80 percent) in developed countries, while manufacturing has declined (16–20 percent). The interest in service operations research reflects this trend.

Old hands in our discipline remember when many operations management courses were simply termed "production." Around 1970, calling our field production became more uncomfortable to many because it seemed to neglect what was fast becoming the dominant source of jobs, namely services. In recognition of the increasing importance of services, the field took on names such as production and operations management, or simply operations management.

A good deal of the early research in services dealt with determining which aspects of manufacturing management had easy parallels in the service realm and with categorizing just what services were and how they differed from manufacturing. Many definitions of service include characteristics such as intangibility, the visibility of the service process to the customer, the short time between the production and consumption of the service, and the ease of entry into many services. None of these is fully satisfying. More modern characterizations point to the interaction of the customer with the process as the best distinguishing feature of the service operation. The fact remains, however, that services are not readily defined.

Service research has been particularly sensitive to perceptions and expectations. Research on quality, waiting lines, service recovery, and loyalty all reflect this. Yield management, where service firms that gather reservations can exploit customers' willingness to pay, has been another fruitful topic.

More and more, however, the walls that we have tried to erect between manufacturing and services are seen to be porous or fragile, or just plain artificial. Labeling a company as one or the other is often pointless. An electricity utility is classed as a service, but for many it is a "factory" for producing electricity and lies far away conceptually from what most people have in mind when they think of services. Is IBM a manufacturing company or a service company? It is clearly both. And with what is now termed "servitization," more and more companies are not selling their products so much as the services that can flow from their products (e.g. Rolls-Royce's famed move to sell "power by the hour" instead of selling jet engines per se). However, as we saw with Singer and McCormick, even servitization is not a new concept.

We can lead this argument *ad absurdum*, by stating that all firms are service providers: the car factory provides the service of assembling a car from pressed steel parts, the component supplier provides the service of pressing steel into components, the steel company provides the service of melting ore and coke into steel, and the mining firm provides the service of digging the ore out of the ground. All firms provide services, while Mother Nature provides all the goods—without ever having "manufactured" anything.[24] Similarly, grocery retailers could be defined as selling the good of "convenience" that saves us from growing our own vegetables, while restaurants "assemble" and "manufacture" foods from a range of ingredients in a very similar way to how manufacturers build their products from components. Clearly this distinction makes no sense.

Not all operations are the same, yet a classification into a binary "service" vs. "manufacturing" is simply wrong. The common denominator for all operations is their processes, which generally contain both manufacturing and service elements. The discipline of operations management has always been tied to processes. As processes matured, the study of them began in earnest. The topics of operations management—quality, production planning and control, capacity, new product and process development, supply chain management, strategy, services, and so on—are all linked to process needs. As processes have changed, so too has operations management. Be they the efforts of Taylor and his disciples with the shop floors of the late 1800s, or the line balance needs of the Ford Motor Company in the early 1900s, or the innovations in quality management from the 1920s on, or the development of Lean manufacturing principles after World War II, or the importance of supply chain management in a world that is more open and connected than ever before, the subject matter of our discipline of operations management has always taken its lead from processes and the innovations swirling around them.

1.5 In essence...

For us, the discipline of operations management has everything to do with processes. In this book we present a case to make a lot of implicit theory explicit, by bringing it together into a formal "process theory" that is our own. The core of this process theory is not new, and all of its "components" have been widely discussed as integral parts of the operations management field as concepts, and even as "laws." However, it has never been formally documented and thus is not being used to explain operations management phenomena. This book is an attempt to formalize this "process theory," as a skeleton that allows our operations management concepts to fit into a larger whole.

"Process theory" combines what we know about the three core activities in operations management: to design, measure, and improve the conversion of inputs into outputs. Not only will this help to "ground" our research in theory. It can also help in framing our teaching. In a recent discussion, Kate Blackmon of Oxford described operations management textbooks as "cook-books that feature lists of ingredients, but without any recipes." Another colleague described his approach to writing his textbook as "selling dog food"—that is sold to the owner, not the dog. In other words, textbooks are written to suit what lecturers are comfortable teaching. The unwillingness to deviate from well-honed curricula stifles innovation in how we present our field.

Yet innovation is as critical for us as a field, as it is for firms. There remain many "puzzles" for which we think explanations are needed. This is not meant to be an exhaustive list, by any means. Rather, it is simply meant as an illustration of what we in our discipline can wonder about and ponder over. Why, for example, is one operation more productive than another, and why does it often stay that way for a considerable length of time? What are the ways by which a company's operation can "lose it"? Why does such backsliding occur? To which things should we pay most attention? Does it matter what performance measures an operation uses? Is there a proper set? Under what conditions could a quality initiative (or some other operations initiative) sustain itself, or are all such initiatives doomed to morph into some other initiative, as seems to be the history? How prevalent and disruptive is entropy—increasing disorder—within operations? How does the proliferation of products/models put pressure on the operations function, and what is the best way to cope? The list seems endless.

We, as a discipline, need to share our ignorance more than we do. And we need to be more critical of what it is we think we know. Only then might we capture some of the cachet of the hard sciences. This book is an effort to put forward "what it is we think we know," and at the same time to recognize our ignorance. It is our attempt at defining the "habit of mind" that students of operations management can adopt and the "lens" through which the world of manufacturing and service operations can be seen clearly.

The remainder of this book takes this perspective. First, we spend some time describing processes in more detail. We then move on to outline the ten principles that we think anchor our discipline of operations management. And we apply these principles to important topics such as process design, process improvement, the supply chain, new product development, project management, environmental sustainability, and the interfaces between operations management and other business school disciplines.

NOTES

1. We are aware that many management scholars distinguish between "process" and "variance" theories. See for example: B.T. Pentland, 1999. Building process theory with narrative: From description to explanation. *Academy of Management Review*, 24(4), pp.711–24, and T. Hernes, 2014. *A Process Theory of Organization*. Oxford University Press. Process theory is a commonly used form of scientific research study in which events or occurrences are said to be the result of certain input states leading to a certain outcome (output) state, following a set process. In simple terms, process theory provides an explanation for "how" something happens, and a variance theory explains "why." In the context of operations management we use the term "process theory" to denote the theoretical foundations of our discipline that build on the notion of an input-conversion-output process model that underpins all operations.
2. The notion of a "process" is a well-established concept, and dates back to Leontief's input–output analysis of national economies. See W. Leontief, 1951. *Input Output Economics*. Oxford University Press, and O. Bjerkholt, 2016. *Wassily Leontief and the discovery of the input–output approach*. SSRN working paper.
3. R.W. Schmenner, L. Van Wassenhove, M. Ketokivi, J. Heyl, and R.F. Lusch, 2009. Too much theory, not enough understanding. *Journal of Operations Management*, 27(5), pp.339–43.
4. C.G. Hempel, 1965. Typological methods in the natural and social sciences. In *Aspects of Scientific Explanation and Other Essays in the Philosophy of Science* (pp.155–71), University of Pennsylvania Press.

5. R. Dubin, 1969. *Theory Building*. The Free Press, and J.G. Wacker, 1998. A definition of theory: research guidelines for different theory-building research methods in operations management. *Journal of Operations Management*, 16(4), pp.361–85.
6. K.G. Smith and M.A. Hitt, 2005. *Great Minds in Management: The Process of Theory Development*. Oxford University Press.
7. M.J. Mol, J. Birkinshaw, and J.M. Birkinshaw, 2008. *Giant Steps in Management: Creating Innovations that Change the Way We Work*. Pearson Education.
8. K.M. Eisenhardt and J.A. Martin, 2000. Dynamic capabilities: What are they? *Strategic Management Journal*, 21(10–11), pp.1105–21.
9. D.A. Whetten, T. Felin, and B.G. King, 2009. The practice of theory borrowing in organizational studies: Current issues and future directions. *Journal of Management*, 35(3), pp.537–63.
10. Kevin Linderman and Aravind Chandrasekaran, 2010. The scholarly exchange of knowledge in Operations Management. *Journal of Operations Management*, 28(4), pp.357–66.
11. W.J. Hopp and M.L. Spearman, 2011. *Factory Physics*. Waveland Press.
12. Much of this history is taken from several outstanding books. Of particular importance are Alfred D. Chandler, Jr, *The Visible Hand*, Belknap Press, 1977, and David A. Hounshell, *From the American System to Mass Production, 1800–1932*, Johns Hopkins University Press, 1984. Chandler's *Scale and Scope*, Belknap Press, 1990, is also an important source. On the Industrial Revolution, see Robert C. Allen, *The British Industrial Revolution in Global Perspective*, Cambridge University Press, 2009. The source for the Arsenal is Frederic C. Lane, *Venetian Ships and Shipbuilders of the Renaissance*, Johns Hopkins University Press, 1934, pp.129–75; and Lane, *Venice: A Maritime Republic*, Johns Hopkins University Press, 1973, pp.361–4.
13. Medieval China had developed real large-scale factories. The exhibition of the ceramics of this shipwreck is impressive and can be seen on: http://acm.org.sg/collections/galleries/tang-shipwreck
14. D. Hounshell, 1985. *From the American System to Mass Production, 1800–1932: The Development of Manufacturing Technology in the United States*. John Hopkins University Press, p.230.
15. D.S. Landes, 1983. *Revolution in Time*. Belknap Press.
16. For an outstanding description of what occurred at Ford, see Hounshell, *From the American System to Mass Production*.
17. Martin claims these are not his own words, yet he is still widely credited with saying this.
18. The first mentions of "supply chain management" date back to the early 1980s, when Booz Allen's consultant Keith Oliver was interviewed by Arnold Kransdorff of the *Financial Times*, during which Oliver proposed that firms should manage their "total supply chain inventories." See Arnold Kransdorff, Booz Allen's rather grandly titled supply chain management concept. *The Financial Times*, June 4, 1982. Oliver proceeded to publish a full report that same year: R.K. Oliver and M.D. Webber, 1982. Supply-chain management: Logistics catches up with strategy. In M. Christopher (ed.), *Logistics: The Strategic Issue* (pp.63–75), Chapman & Hall.

19. The references for this section are many, including Chandler and a series of articles in a special issue of the *Journal of Operations Management*, Vol. 25, No. 2 (March 2007) edited by Linda G. Sprague. This brief history of operations management has especially benefited from the articles by Sprague, Chase, and Apte; Holweg, Jacobs, and Wewton; Lewis, Mabert, Schonberger, and Skinner. Also used was "A History of Production Scheduling," by Jeffrey W. Herrmann, Chapter 1 of *Handbook of Production Scheduling*, International Series in Operations Research & Management Science, 2006, Volume 89.
20. In reality, 3.4 defects per million opportunities corresponds to a 4.5-sigma level of quality, but that is intentional. The idea is to aim for a 6-sigma level of quality but permit the mean of the distribution to drift up to 1.5 standard deviations. Hence the resulting 4.5-sigma level's number of defects per million opportunities.
21. J.W. Forrester, 1961. *Industrial Dynamics*. MIT Press.
22. A. De Meyer et al., 1989. Flexibility: The next competitive battle. *Strategic Management Journal*, 10(2), pp.135–44.
23. K. Ferdows and A. De Meyer, 1990. Lasting improvements in manufacturing performance: In search of a new theory. *Journal of Operations Management*, 9(2), pp.168–84.
24. Arguably this point is subject to theological debate, which is not our forte.

FURTHER READING

De Meyer, A. and Wittenberg-Cox, A., 1992. *Creating Product Value: A Strategic Manufacturing Perspective*. Pitman (London); also published as "The Manufacturer's survival guide" (Irwin) and "Nuevo Emfoque de la Funcion de Produccion" (Biblioteca de Empresa, Folio).

De Meyer, A. et al., 1989. Flexibility: The next competitive battle. *Strategic Management Journal*, 10(2), pp.135–44.

Ferdows, K. and De Meyer, A., 1990. Lasting improvements in manufacturing performance: In search of a new theory. *Journal of Operations Management*, 9(2), pp.168–84.

Pilkington, A. and Meredith, J., 2009. The evolution of the intellectual structure of operations management—1980–2006: A citation/co-citation analysis. *Journal of Operations Management*, 27(3), pp.185–202.

Schmenner, R.W., 2001. History of technology, manufacturing, and the industrial revolution: A rejoinder. *Production and Operations Management*, 10(1), pp.103–6.

Schmenner, R.W., 2001. Looking ahead by looking back: Swift, even flow in the history of manufacturing. *Production and Operations Management*, 10(1), pp.87–96.

Schmenner, R.W., 2009. Manufacturing, service, and their integration: Some history and theory. *International Journal of Operations and Production Management*, 29(5), pp.431–43.

Schmenner, R.W., 2012. *Getting and Staying Productive: Applying Swift, Even Flow to Practice*. Cambridge University Press (Cambridge, UK).

Sprague, L.G., 2007. Evolution of the field of operations management. *Journal of Operations Management*, 25(2), pp.219–38.

2 The process

With this chapter, we begin defining the discipline of operations management using the framework of *Design–Measure–Improve*. We do this by setting forth some principles that define what we think operations management stands for. The first principle states our fundamental world view that processes are the bedrock of operations management. This principle is a prelude to four principles that deal with the "design" of operations.

Principle #1: All operations are composed of processes.

This first principle should come as no surprise. Indeed, Chapter 1 addressed processes and their history. Processes are the focal points of operations management. Repetitive work, of whatever kind, is accomplished through processes that convert inputs into outputs.

When we consider processes, we often think of manufacturing processes and service processes as distinct. In reality, the two are not as different as we suppose, but there are some features that we associate more with one than the other. With that proviso, let us turn first to manufacturing, then to services, and finally to overhead functions in the company.[1]

2.1 What is a process?

THE PROCESS MODEL AS CONCEPTUAL LENS

At its most basic, a "process" is the sequence of activities that turns inputs (or resources) into outputs (products or services)—see Figure 2.1. It is the sequence of operations and involved events, taking up time, space, expertise, or other resources that lead, or should lead, to the production of some outcome. The basic process model thus consists of inputs, conversion, and outputs. A process also has a *purpose*, which is to provide a particular desired output. In converting the inputs into outputs, it may also produce undesired outputs, such as emissions and waste in the form of defects, rework, and the like. The basic process model is shown in Figure 2.1.

This model is the most generic representation of what happens in any business process. Various aspects of this model warrant a closer look.

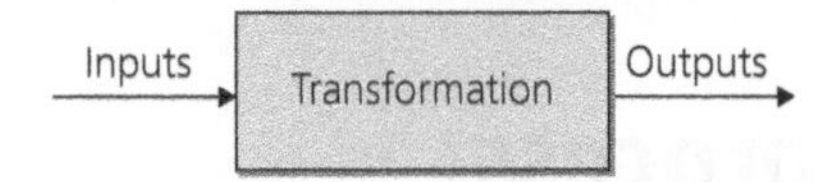

Figure 2.1 The process model.

PURPOSE

It may seem obvious, but processes have a purpose, namely to produce the desired output. The reason this is not as straightforward as one might think is because there are an infinite number of process (or asset) configurations that can convert inputs into a desired output, outsourcing portions of the entire process to third parties aside. Thus there are many possible variations of process design, but only one (or a few) that provides the best fit between the external requirements (market) and the operational resources. It is at this intersection that our process model interlinks with operations strategy (we will return to this point in Chapters 5 and 6).

INPUTS

Resources of all kinds are needed for a process to operate. These inputs come in many forms and modes of delivery. First and foremost, there are production resources: materials, components, and labor. The former two are sourced, or procured, from external organizations: suppliers. Labor, in turn, is an internally developed resource. Through training, education, and process improvement, so-called "human capital" is built up: a firm's workforce. Although labor is technically also "sourced" from the labor market, it is naïve to assume that one can readily buy and sell labor. The lead times involved in hiring and training make this a near-static resource for many firms, and thus more of a fixed cost as opposed to a variable cost. More recently, information has become a production resource of its own. It is used to inform the design of the process, as well as the conversion of the resources in a high-value product.

Other, more generic resources include energy needed to run the process. And capital is required to procure the resources needed and to finance the inventories of raw materials, components, work in process, and finished goods. We deliberately exclude the capital needed for investing in the "conversion assets" (factory building, production machinery), as the nature of capital flows for the *operation* of a process is very different from that needed to *set up* the process. All resources are of equal importance, simply because they all are necessary but insufficient in their own rights. You need all of them for the process to function.

While this way of thinking about processes—this discipline—seems natural to us as students of operations management, these concepts are not the only way to regard production. Economics and accounting take a significantly different approach. They think of production in terms of "factors of production." Factors of production examine the equipment (capital), labor, and materials that go into the products and services that the company markets. Materials, both consumables and non-consumables, typically constitute the inputs that are transformed by the process into outputs. Capital and labor are required for the transformation process itself.

The factors of production are clearer for manufacturing processes than for service processes. In manufacturing, the materials to be transformed are typically marshaled in plain sight, and both the equipment to which it is destined and the labor associated with that equipment are evident. For services, the materials to be transformed may not be so evident, and may only be information or data. Nevertheless, transformation occurs through the application of capital and labor.

The ratios of capital to labor can differ greatly from process to process. Continuous flow processes and service factories, respectively, have considerably larger ratios of capital to labor than job shops or professional services. The materials (inputs) for some processes are more uniform than others, too.

In more recent years information has come to be often considered a fourth factor of production. In particular in services, but increasingly also in manufacturing, data have a significant influence on the production processes. Sometimes they are needed for the customization of the product. In other cases, particularly when traceability of the origins and transformation of the product is essential, e.g. in pharmaceuticals or food, data "accompanies" the product through the process.

This perspective of "factors of production" is of interest to economics and accounting chiefly because those disciplines are interested in costing inputs and outputs. Economics and accounting do not examine as critically as does operations how one can assemble together the factors of production more effectively. Rather, they take the factors of production as more or less given, and they are, for those disciplines, the elements that account for the costs a company incurs. We, on the other hand, as students of operations management, acknowledge the need for the various factors of production, but they are of less interest to us, perhaps with the exception of information and data. The factors of production are, for us, the givens. They are sunk costs. Our job is to use them effectively—to design and operate the process to create the throughput that the company sells, and as much of it as is needed by the marketplace.

CONVERSION

The conversion that takes place is the actual transformative process within the firm. Here the inventory of materials and components turns to work-in-process (or work-in-progress) inventory as it moves from process step to process step, until it is complete. "Complete" here refers to the state at which it is useful for the customer of this process—which may well be another manufacturer, not necessarily the end consumer. A finished good or product can also both be used as input for another firm's process, and be consumed by end consumers. For example, tires are used both by vehicle manufacturers to build new cars, and by vehicle owners to replace their existing ones. A process can have both "original equipment" and "aftersales" customers.

While the "inputs" are generally seen as the "supply chain," the "conversion" step is where the actual operational improvements are generally focused. The downstream end is generally called "distribution" or "retail."

OUTPUTS

The "outputs" are the actual products or services the process provides. In fact their production represents the aforementioned "purpose." It should not be assumed, however, that all resources are converted into outputs; in fact the quality of a process is, among other things, measured by the degree to which it is able to convert inputs into outputs completely or efficiently. Typical losses occur due to defects during start-up or production that lead to scrap, or inefficient use of raw materials that leads to wastage. As we will discuss in greater detail in Chapter 7, the most fundamental metric of a process is its productivity, which is defined as the ratio of its outputs to its inputs. The fewer inputs a process needs to deliver a desired output, the more productive it is.

CONTEXT

Processes do not happen in a void—they are embedded in a national, an industry, and intra-firm setting. As such it is important to understand how this context influences the process. Most directly this context can be seen through its impact on items such as working hours, break times, and emissions in manufacturing. Also, the national and regional differences in energy provision result in differences in cost and carbon intensity for the energy consumed by the process.

All regulation and taxation issues that affect the process are part of the context. The ones most commonly cited by companies refer to business taxation, labor hours, and safety regulations, as well as emissions and other environmental standards. Tariff and non-tariff trade barriers for international trade are also important. Conjointly these define the context in which the process operates, which has a significant impact on the performance of a process, and at times may restrict the freedom of the operations manager to act in the most efficient way from the business' point of view.

MANAGEMENT SYSTEM

The management system is the "control unit" of the process, which plans and oversees all activities, as shown in Figure 2.2. Effectively, it is what puts the *management* into *operations management*. The management system has the fundamental function of "running" the process, which starts with the basic planning and set-up, but also covers the control of the process while it is running, and improving the process over time based on what has been learned from running the process.

Planning involves the provision and allocation of resources for the process to operate against a given plan or schedule. This includes setting the production schedule, procuring the required materials and components, and scheduling all work centers or machines so that the process can function. This part is the traditional production planning and scheduling function.

Process control involves measuring the process before, during, and after it has operated. Once the process has run, it is important to measure its performance. This, however, is only meaningful if one has a "baseline" to compare against. A common mistake is to omit the "baseline" measurement in process improvement, yet measuring the outcome of a process run is meaningless unless one has a standard or baseline—or a "before"—to measure it against. The fundamental premise of any operational improvement is to measure outcomes on a continuous basis.

The management system also is responsible for improving the process, which is one of the creative parts in operations management, where the main objective is to increase the performance, measured for example through total factor productivity or the ratio of outputs to inputs—either through reducing the inputs for a given output, increasing the outputs for a given set of inputs, or both. The ratio of outputs to inputs is no doubt the most fundamental performance metric of a process. We will return to this when

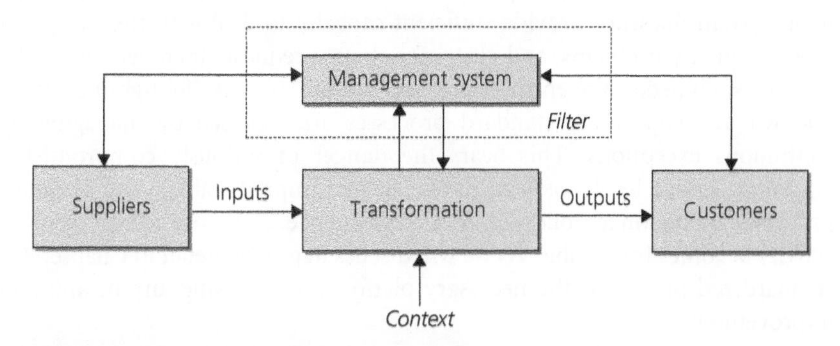

Figure 2.2 Process model with management system.

we discuss productivity and efficiency in Chapters 7 and 8. But improvement can also be about reducing the time to delivery at constant output over input, or increasing the flexibility of the process, thus allowing for more variety coming off the production line.

The actual design of the process is in the first place also part of the management function. But few operations managers will actually have the opportunity to design their processes from scratch. Most processes are already operational, or even if new, have to follow the corporate global standard in terms of layout, machinery, and IT backbone, so there are considerable constraints that need to be adhered to. So, even many "greenfield" processes feature less design freedom than one might imagine.

Lastly, it is important to mention that the information that the management system faces is filtered. It would make little sense to inform the production scheduler about every single product sold from inventory in the marketplace, and neither would it make sense to reorder components and materials in single units. Instead, this information is aggregated through a filter, which reduces the total amount of information that the management system has to deal with.

This has been known in the field of cybernetics for almost half a century, and is known as "Ashby's Law of Requisite Variety." Applied to the process model, it essentially says that the management system's capacity for dealing with requests needs to be equal to or greater than the actual requests that it faces. Requests could be any kind of information needed for the process to run, from supply uncertainties to machine breakdowns, and other issues that need to be rectified for the process to run. In the "rock–boat analogy" (see Section 8.3) these issues would be the "rocks" that are buffered with inventory and capacity in the system.

In a cybernetics context, having insufficient processing capacity at the controller means that the robot simply falls over at the point in time when the sensors in the arms and legs are sending too many signals to the controller at the same time. It is unable to process these in time to devise counterbalance actions. The same principle applies to a management system. If the management system does not provide sufficient capacity to deal with the exception reports, quality problems, and customer change requests then eventually the schedules, and soon the entire processes, will fall over. A "firefighting" scenario will develop where standard processes are replaced by managing by continuous exceptions. This bears the danger of seriously compromising customer service levels (as lead times become unpredictable), and standard processes are no longer followed. As a consequence, any process improvement activity becomes impossible. As we will discuss in greater detail in Chapter 8, a standardized process is the necessary platform for devising any meaningful improvement.

2.2 Understanding a process as a sociotechnical system

It is very easy to describe a process as a mechanistic system, but this misses an important point. Processes are inherently sociotechnical in nature, which means that they rely on a combination of human and machine as their key resources. In order to succeed, both need to be considered—each in isolation, as well as their interaction. Seminal studies in the Hawthorne Works at Bell Labs (incidentally, the same factory where Walter Shewhart was developing his early theories on process quality) in the early twentieth century showed how limited the mechanistic approach to understanding and managing sociotechnical systems was. In fact to this day you hear statements like "Turn the lights up a bit brighter, and they work faster," which stems from Mayo and Roethlisberger's famous study,[2] where they experimented with the effects of lighting on worker productivity. In essence: when they increased the lighting levels, productivity went up, as expected. But when they decreased the lighting levels, productivity went up even further, clearly showing that the effect of being observed was far greater than the effect of lighting.

Since then we have developed a much more sophisticated understanding of what drives the performance of sociotechnical systems, which must include "soft" systems aspects of incentives, rewards, and motivation—as well as aspects of *structuration*, whereby process and technology co-evolve together. In fact virtually no technology is used entirely in the way it was intended—its use generally emerges as the technology is implemented and being used.[3]

In short, when we look at processes, we need to consider the *hard system* (machines, equipment, and materials) as well as the *soft system* (the people), which each have their own rules and dynamics, yet conjointly determine the performance of a process.

2.3 Processes within processes: the level of resolution

Principle #1 states that operations are composed of processes. The operations of a factory or of a service firm are often a combination of different manufacturing, service, and/or overhead processes. For example, different products are often produced with different processes. And a variety of overhead processes are common to any operation. The largest-scale operations are typically supply chains. Supply chains link different operations, often different manufacturing and service operations. For example, a supply chain could begin upstream with suppliers that are manufacturing operations that feed an assembly operation, another sort of manufacturing operation. Between them, transportation companies and perhaps warehousing, both classed as service operations, provide a vital link. The assembly operation would then ship its products to a series of distribution centers, and the product would then be on its way to the market and the end consumer. The distribution channels that the company uses to reach the consumer can themselves be an amalgam of service operations of various types and the overhead processes that help to run them.

Processes span across departments within the firm, and of course across all firms in the value chain: from raw materials to finished product, from customer order to service delivery, and from internal request to completed task (see Figure 2.3). At the micro level, every single machine or process step also conforms to the input-conversion-output logic. So we have processes within processes. Furthermore, processes are essentially embedded in a web of interrelated processes, where the manufacturing process interacts with the purchasing, finance, and human resource processes, and so on. So how does one define what is part of the process and what is not?

The answer is "It depends!"—mostly on the question one is setting: the relevant level of "resolution" one takes to analyze a given process is a function of what problem is being investigated. If the productivity of a given machining center is in question, the relevant level of resolution is at the micro or machine level. If dynamic distortions are experienced in the supply chain system (such as the infamous "bullwhip effect," which we will explain further in Chapter 9) then the resolution level should be at macro or supply chain level. A particular danger, which we will also return to in Chapter 9, is to create local optimization, or "islands of excellence." By considering a process

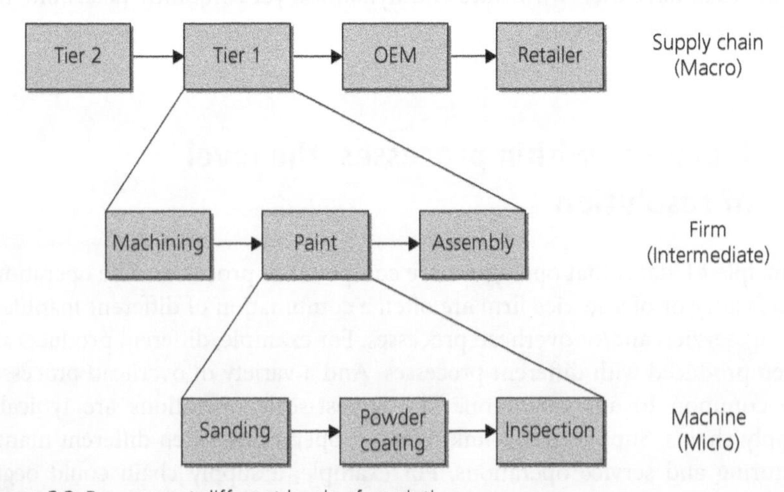

Figure 2.3 Processes at different levels of resolution.

in isolation, and then "optimizing" it by improving its productivity, one can easily fall into the trap of improving a subsystem at the expense of the performance of the overall system, firm, or supply chain. Such islands of excellence form easily where managers lack visibility of the whole system, and thus cannot judge the implications of their behavior for the whole system. They can also happen easily where functional metrics are poorly designed, and not aligned to the objective of the firm (found, for example, by using a Hoshin Kanri or policy deployment process).

There are several ways in which business processes can be classified. A typical list of business processes would group them by their respective outputs, or objectives, such as order fulfillment, or order-to-delivery, which describes the activities from a customer placing an order to that order being fulfilled.[4] Others include sales and operations planning (SOP), which describes all activities related to providing the appropriate capacity and processes within which current and future demand can be fulfilled, or new product development and introduction, which describe all activities from concept to launching a new product, and to the first production run, respectively.

Derivatives of the above processes that are more common in practice include the "order to cash cycle," the "complaint to resolution" process, and the "concept to launch" process. In general, several process classification schemes have been proposed. Douglas Lambert, for example, identifies eight business processes: customer relationship management, customer service management, demand management, order fulfillment, manufacturing flow management, procurement, product development and commercialization, and returns.

The definition of what is and is not a relevant process is entirely dependent on the question one is asking. Nonetheless, we would like to propose the list of selected business processes in Table 2.1, as most relevant to operations management, as a starting point.

Another often-used classification groups processes by thematic flows. These tend to span across several cross-functional business processes that are often mentioned. These are "high-level" processes that connect many business functions:

- **"Order to delivery"**: from order submission, through manufacture, to distribution and delivery of a product.
- **"Order to cash"**: from submission of a customer order, through order fulfillment, to delivery, to payment for that product.
- **"Complaint to resolution"**: from submission of a customer complaint towards resolution of the problem.
- **"Concept to launch"**: from initial product concept, through product development, towards launch of the new product—the traditional NPD (new product development) process.

Table 2.1 Key operations processes

Key business process	Definition
Order fulfillment	The process from a customer order being placed, to that order being fulfilled.
Sales and operations planning (SOP)	The planning process that sets the framework in terms of production capacity, labor, and processes to fulfill current and future (forecast) demand.
Product life-cycle management	The process of managing all aspects from new product introduction, to upgrading the product, to phasing out the product, as well as all aspects of service and maintenance related to the product.
Technology, plant, and equipment management	The process of procuring, operating, and conducting maintenance on production equipment in order to maximize their utilization.
Human resource development	To hire, develop, and retain the right levels of skills needed for the operation and its support functions.
Strategy and policy deployment	To develop and deploy key performance metrics throughout all levels of the organization that support the goal at organization or firm level.
Purchasing and supplier integration	The process of selecting, contracting with, and developing suppliers of direct and indirect goods and services.
Continuous improvement	To continuously improve the various aspects of performance of manufacturing, service, and overhead processes.
New product development (NPD)	To design a new product from a concept up to the point of the new product introduction (NPI) process, where the product enters volume production.
Closed loop logistics	To distribute the product, to monitor its use, and to take it back and remanufacture or recycle it at the end of its useful life.

2.4 Types of processes

Processes come in a wide range of forms, and even for similar purposes a wide range of resource configurations are feasible. While each process is unique, there are common features that determine a process' essential character. In fact there are two main dimensions that determine which types of processes are economically viable, and which ones are not. We capture the two dimensions in Volume and Variety, but others are possible. For example, in Schmenner's terminology for the service process matrix these are *labor intensity* and *degree of customer interaction*, and in his later book *Getting and Staying Productive: Applying Swift, Even Flow to Practice* they are called *speed of flow*, measured as throughput time of materials, and *variability*. Common to all these descriptions are the notions that the volume of the process and its variation determine which types of processes are economically appropriate and feasible.

Plotting these two dimensions in a chart (see Figure 2.4), one can generally observe that economic processes tend to be located along the center line from Low volume/High variety to High volume/Low variety. This is driven by the facts that low-volume, low-variety processes are not economically viable, and

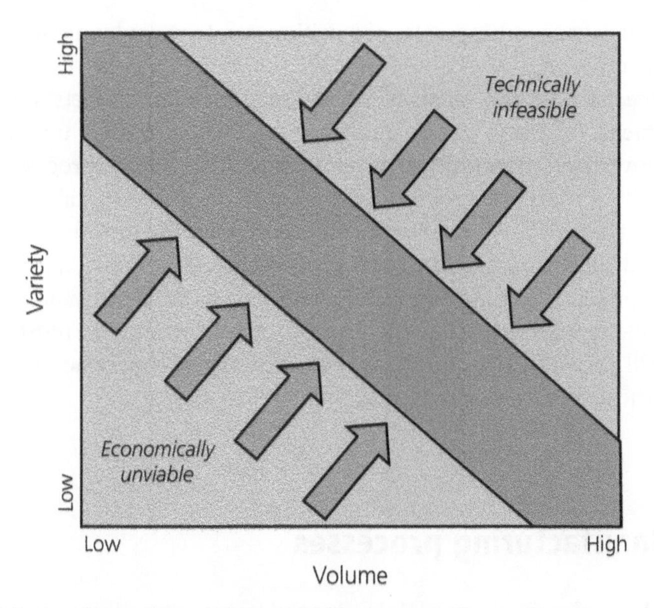

Figure 2.4 Economic pressures pull processes to the center line.

high-volume, high-variety processes are currently difficult to accomplish technically. In a low-volume setting one expects a high degree of customization to warrant the high margins required to make this kind of operation feasible. Equally, for high-volume processes to produce highly variable goods, the technical requirements are currently too stringent.

Please note that while the underlying economic principles, in our view, will always hold, this is not to say that new technologies will not challenge the product–process matrix. 3D printing, for example, is largely agnostic to product variety and does challenge the "top right-hand" corner. So technology certainly can shift the boundaries of what is economical and feasible! We will return to this point in Section 8.7.

These two dimensions have been found to be the main features that determine the process' fundamental character. This relationship was initially discovered by Robert Hayes of Harvard Business School in the spring of 1976. Hayes was trying to summarize the variety of cases that were being taught in the required operations management course for MBAs. He, together with Steven Wheelwright, the course head at the time, called this relationship the "product–process matrix" and shared their thoughts in a pair of *Harvard Business Review* articles that were published in 1979.

We will use these two dimensions to classify the main three base types of processes: (1) manufacturing and (2) service, which are both "order to delivery" processes that deliver a product (good or service, or combination of both) to a customer, and (3) overhead processes, which are internal to the firm (financial accounting, sales acquisition, strategy deployment, budgeting/planning, etc.).

In a special class are "small-n" processes (which are projects, new product development, etc.) that can be customer-oriented (projects), but can also be internal/overhead (new product development). This class of processes exists in all three basic types of process, as "projects" or "professional services" and "artful overhead." The fundamental difference with the three base processes is the limited ability to learn from past process runs. This constrains the amount of cross-project learning, and thus requires a different kind of process improvement strategy to the repetitive processes common in most firms.

We will discuss each of the main process types—manufacturing, service, and overhead—in more detail in Sections 2.5 to 2.9.

2.5 Manufacturing processes

Although students of operations management sometimes differ on the terminology, there is broad agreement on the variety of manufacturing processes that are typically encountered. Besides projects, we identify four "pure" processes, which form a spectrum (see Figure 2.5). Hybrids of these pure processes are also possible.

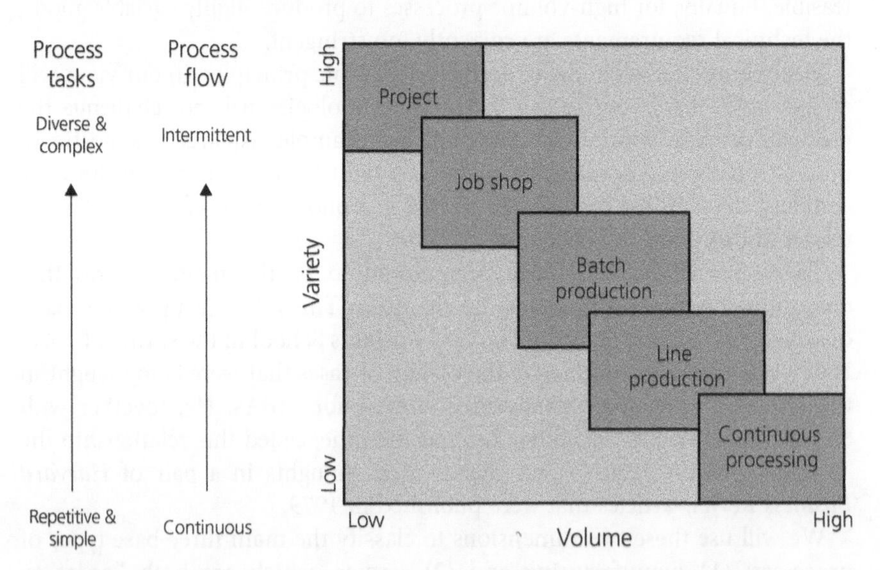

Figure 2.5 The spectrum of manufacturing processes: the product–process matrix.
Adapted from Hayes and Wheelwright (1979).

THE PROJECT

Projects are the epitome of customization, in as far as the entire product design and delivery processes are geared to delivering a single, unique product. Typical features of projects are that resources are very generic in nature, operated by highly specialized workers. Often the materials and production equipment are brought to the location of production, for example in the case of construction. The equipment used for projects tends to be general purpose, so that it can be reused for the next project. The workforce, on the other hand, needs to be highly skilled in their respective tasks, as they need to execute a wide range of diverse tasks.

A key operational challenge with projects is the lower level of repetition: many projects are executed only once. Thus this process form is often deprived of the repetition needed to improve the process by identifying problems and investigating their root causes in order to codify practices that prevent these problems from reoccurring at subsequent executions of that process. The focus shifts towards learning about the *methods* used to carry out certain tasks, codify this learning into best practices, and apply these to the next project.

There are of course many different types of projects. Loch et al. make a distinction between different projects based on the complexity of the project as well as the degree of uncertainty with which the project team is confronted.[5] They refer to "task complexity" and "relationship complexity." Uncertainty can be the normal variance one would expect due to different contextual circumstances in which the project needs to be implemented. But the project can also be confronted with "known unknowns" or "unknown unknowns." They see projects not as a sequence of tasks, but as a sequence of decisions. Depending on the degree of complexity and uncertainty, the project management will need to be adjusted. At low levels of uncertainty and complexity we use the traditional network techniques like PERT or critical path methods. They call this the instructionist approach: i.e. a project can be defined in a certain set of instructions to be implemented. But with higher levels of uncertainty and complexity the project manager will have to shift to high-reliability projects (which we will discuss later in Chapter 5) or a combination of a "Darwinian" selectionist approach (i.e. launching several projects in parallel and weeding out the unsuccessful attempts) and a learning approach. Loch et al. observe that the degree to which learning can be achieved is determined by the type of project management approach that is selected.

A construction project may be unique because of the design of the building, but the methods used can easily be transferred and learned from one to another. Research projects, on the other hand, are confronted with a high level of uncertainty or unintended consequences and therefore learning is more difficult. Still, it is often possible to generate general best practices from project executions, and transfer learning across with regards to organizational structures ("heavyweight project managers"), resource allocation ("front-loading"), and review schemata ("stage gates").

THE JOB SHOP

Beyond projects, where a single product is designed and made, the job shop is the most flexible process for creating a wide variety of products in significant quantities. Machine shops, tool and die shops, kitchens, and many plastic molding operations are job shops that work to fulfill particular customer orders.

The job shop's layout groups similar equipment together ("process centers"), primarily because no single product generates enough sales volume to justify the creation of a product-specific array of equipment. A job shop typically contains a diverse array of equipment with different capabilities. Some of that equipment will be used heavily and some may not be used much at all.

The flow of material in a job shop can be complex and far from straight-line in character. Materials can be routed in many directions and can loop back to the same equipment later in the processing cycle. With each order (job) capable of such complexity, it is absolutely essential that information on how the order is to be routed through the factory, what is to be done to it at each step of the way, and how much time and effort are actually spent on it, follows the job. A well-functioning job shop depends heavily on its information flows. This information is vital, because job shops typically bid for work. Without good information on costs, times (run times, set-up times, labor content times), routings, and process steps, a job shop would not be able to bid intelligently or schedule itself effectively.

THE BATCH FLOW PROCESS

One step towards the continuous flow process from the job shop is the batch flow process. The job shop and the batch flow process have much in common. Their layouts are similar, with equipment grouped by function rather than by product. The product moves from department to department within the factory. Like a job shop, a batch flow operation depends on information such as routings and process steps and it tracks costs and times spent. However, batch flow processes typically have a set menu of products that they produce, frequently in set quantities (lot sizes). The batch flow operation is thus somewhat more standardized than the job shop, particularly as it relates to routings and costs.

While the job shop usually operates to fulfill an outside customer's order by an agreed-upon due date and in whatever quantity is ordered, the batch flow operation usually produces in established lot sizes that move into an inventory from which further production or final customer orders are filled. Batch flow processes are commonplace; much "fabrication" is done this way.

Batch production is not always directly associated with smaller lot sizes. Sometimes batch production is the only way that is technically possible. Production processes that require fermentation or the development of living organisms—e.g. brewing beer, fermenting cheese, or producing vaccines—can only be achieved in a batch process. Other examples of batch flow processes include much of the chemical industry, semiconductor fabrication, apparel, much of the steel industry, and huge chunks of the metal bending, metal forming, and metal machining industries.

THE LINE FLOW PROCESS

Between the batch flow and continuous flow processes, along the process spectrum, lies the line flow process. In reality it lies closer to the continuous flow process because it presents some substantive distinctions from the batch flow. The line flow process is most popularly exemplified by the moving assembly line that one finds in the auto industry. But it is also found in a host of other assembly industries such as consumer electronics, computers, and other consumer goods. In contrast to the batch flow process, the line flow process exhibits the following characteristics:

- A product-specific layout with different pieces of equipment placed in sequence ready to perform operations on the product. There are, of course, mixed-model lines that can produce distinctly different models of the basic product, but the more diverse the products made, the less satisfactory the line becomes at producing them.
- The product moves readily from one operation to another so that there is little work-in-process inventory, nor is there a stockroom in the product's path. This also means that there is a great need to examine the "balance" of the process so that the different tasks to be accomplished take roughly the same amount of time to perform and have the same capacities, not just over weeks of time, but over minutes of time.
- The paperwork needs of the line flow process are less demanding than the batch flow process or the job shop. Routings are not needed and operations sheets can frequently be simplified, if not eliminated altogether. Products have set "recipes" that remove the need for tracking labor and machine inputs to particular products/parts.
- In contrast to the continuous flow operation, the line flow is somewhat more flexible, generally less automated, and more labor-intensive.

As one proceeds across the spectrum from project to continuous flow, one tends to move from a highly individualized, flexible process to one that is much more inflexible in the products it can make, but at the same time much more productive and efficient in how it makes them.

THE CONTINUOUS FLOW PROCESS

At the other extreme of the process spectrum lies the continuous flow process. Many high-volume consumer goods and commodities are made by continuous flow processes, for example oil refining, papermaking, and food processing. In a continuous flow process, materials move without much, or any, stopping. They are typically guided and transformed in their journey by some impressive engineering. Each process step typically involves some equipment that is specially designed for the task, and the equipment for each process stage needed to produce the product is integrated and synchronized with the equipment for the other process stages. Thus the materials progress constantly from one process operation to another. Indeed, one can estimate realistically how long it takes to transform the raw materials into a specific product. Work-in-process inventories exist at well-defined levels and are low relative to the value of output the continuous flow process generates. Capital investments and automation, on the other hand, are often higher than those of other processes, frequently dramatically so, especially when contrasted with the workforce employed. Layouts are almost always product-specific, often with a straight-line character to them.

Continuous flow processes can be very productive and very profitable, assuming normal sales levels. Only when sales levels plunge is the profitability of the continuous flow process in jeopardy.

HYBRID PROCESSES

The four process types introduced in the previous sections—job shop, batch flow, line flow, and continuous flow—are all "pure." Many factories are combinations of two (or sometimes more) of these pure processes. Popular hybrids are the batch flow–line flow hybrid (e.g. auto engines, air conditioning, furniture) and the batch flow–continuous flow hybrid (e.g. drinks and food canning/bottling, many high-volume consumer products whose raw materials are made in batches).

In these processes the first part of the flow of materials looks like a batch flow process (often this part of the process is labeled "fabrication") while the latter part resembles a line or continuous flow process (this part of the process is labeled "assembly" or "finishing"). Importantly, the two portions of the hybrid are separated by an inventory, typically termed a "decoupling" inventory. The batch flow process fills up the inventory with parts or semi-finished product which then is drawn down by the line or continuous flow process for assembly or completion.

The reason the hybrid process is divided into two parts is that the batch flow process is not normally as nimble as the line flow or continuous flow process. It may not be able to switch from product to product as quickly. Significant chunks of time may be needed to set up the existing machines for a different component or version of the finished product. This puts pressure on the batch flow process to produce in longer runs than would be needed to match precisely the product mix and quantities produced by the line or continuous flow process. If the batch flow process tried to match the line or continuous flow process precisely (say, hourly or daily), it would lose a lot of time to set-up and this downtime could rob the process of the capacity it needs to keep up with overall demand. Thus the batch flow process does not attempt a precise, real-time match of the line or continuous flow process' product mix and quantity, but rather a quantity and product mix match over a much longer period of time, say days or weeks. The batch flow process then replenishes the decoupling inventory, while the line or continuous flow process fills particular customer orders. The two types of process are governed by two distinct production plans.

2.6 Comparing manufacturing processes

Arrayed as they have been here, the different processes introduced demonstrate some distinct trends involving the types of products manufactured and how those products compete against others. Specifically, the more one goes from a project towards a continuous flow process, the more it is generally the case that:

- The number of different kinds of products made (variety) declines.
- Product volumes increase to the point where the continuous flow process is essentially producing a commodity for the mass market.
- Product customization declines and product standardization increases.
- New product introductions become less frequent and are more costly to do.
- Competition is more likely to center on price.
- Competition, at least in the middle ranges of the array, is more likely to emphasize aspects like workmanship, product performance, and product reliability; but as the process becomes more and more a continuous flow, any differences between rival products become narrower and narrower.

GENERAL PROCESS FEATURES

One can observe some complementary trends in some general process features as well. For example, as one progresses down the array of processes from job shop to continuous flow, it is generally true that:

- The pattern of the process becomes more rigid, and the routing of products through their various process steps becomes less individual, more prescribed, and better defined.
- Process layouts, with like machines grouped together, give way to line flow, or product-specific layouts.
- Process segments become more tightly linked together and synchronized.
- Equipment becomes more specialized.
- More, and generally larger, equipment is part of the process.
- There are more opportunities for automation.
- Proprietary process knowhow becomes more important.
- The operation becomes bigger, and economies related to that scale are possible.
- Equipment is less likely to be idle; pieces of equipment become better balanced to one another in size and speed.
- Equipment set-ups are fewer and run lengths are longer.
- The pace of the process is determined largely by machine capabilities or regulated by machines or conveyors.
- The pace of production keeps increasing.
- The notion of capacity becomes less ambiguous and more measurable in physical, rather than monetary, units.
- Additions to capacity come in large chunks, and incremental additions to capacity become less viable.
- Bottlenecks become less and less movable, that is, less and less influenced by the mix of product produced at any time, and thus better understood.
- Incremental change to the process itself becomes relatively more frequent and routine, but the impact of radical change to the process is likely to be more sweeping, even daunting.

MATERIALS-ORIENTED FEATURES

Again, keeping the array of different processes ordered from job shop through continuous flow process, some general trends in materials-oriented features can be observed. For example, as the process becomes more and more a continuous flow, it becomes more and more the case that:

- The span of the process (vertical integration) becomes broader. A plant is more and more likely to start with "commodity type" raw materials and to transform them into products that may need little or no finishing before consumers purchase them.

- Raw materials requirements are large, but their purchase and delivery can be made steady.
- Supplier ties are long term, with frequent deliveries.
- Because of large production volumes and steady purchases, control over suppliers for price, delivery, quality, design, and the like is great.
- Control over the delivery time of the finished product becomes greater.
- Because of process design, work-in-process inventories become scant, and queues of work cease to exist.
- Finished goods are sold through formal distribution channels and can sometimes be forced down those channels for the sake of keeping production running smoothly.

INFORMATION-ORIENTED FEATURES

A number of trends are evident for many information-oriented features of the various production processes. As the process changes from job shop to continuous flow, generally it is more and more likely that:

- Production is not instigated by a bidding procedure.
- Longer-term sales forecasts are used, and orders are "frozen" long before production is scheduled to start.
- The corporation outside the plant is an integral part of the plant's scheduling and materials movement tracking (the plant is likely to be one among others owned by the corporation).
- Order scheduling is done on a very sophisticated basis.
- A finished goods inventory is managed.
- The flow of information and paperwork between management and workers is less.
- Quality control measures become increasingly formal.
- Inventory adjustments become important in responding to seasonal or business cycle changes in demand.
- The process is less flexible in making swift adjustments to demand changes, and so production must be carefully planned in advance.

LABOR-ORIENTED FEATURES

Again, trends are evident across the spectrum of production processes explored, this time concerning labor issues. Progressing from job shop to continuous flow process, it is more likely that:

- The labor content of the product is smaller, relative to the product's value.
- As a result of the smaller labor content, less skill is needed to perform the repeating task.

- Labor is paid by the hour or salaried rather than by some incentive system (in fact, the progression of wage payment schemes tends to go from hourly or individual incentive rates for the job shop, through individual and then group incentive schemes, and then on to hourly rates or monthly salaries).
- While the importance of setting standards for labor remains high, the mechanization of the continuous flow process means that such standards are useful, less to define the process and its capacity than to assign the workforce to the equipment.
- As production moves more and more to mechanical or technological pacing, the scramble to complete a lot of production to meet monthly goals or billings becomes less and less prevalent.
- The path of worker advancement becomes better defined and formalized.
- Job content moves from doing (i.e. producing the good) to overseeing and controlling the process.

MANAGEMENT FEATURES

Finally, some trends can be identified for several aspects of the management of these diverse production processes. Progressing from job shop to continuous flow process, it is more and more the case that:

- Staff operations concerning such topics as materials movement, scheduling, capacity planning, new technology planning, and quality control become more important relative to line operations.
- The size of the plant's management (line and staff) is larger relative to the size of the workforce, both because the capital intensity of the operation is greater and because staff operations are more important.
- Given that the plant involved is part of a multi-plant company, the involvement of managers situated at the corporate offices (rather than at the plant itself) becomes greater; the corporation's influence may extend to operations as well as to capital planning and spending.
- The operation is controlled more as a cost center, as opposed to a profit center.
- The major challenges that management faces are significantly altered, largely shifting from day-to-day operational considerations to very long-term, high-expense items.

2.7 Service processes

The realm of services is vast and diverse. A host of different traits can describe them. Some services are "pure" (i.e. intangible) and some involve "facilitating goods." The customers for some services interact repeatedly with those services' providers, while the customers of other services scarcely interact with their providers at all. Some services are delivered quickly and their benefits are enjoyed right away. Other services take a long time to deliver and their benefits might stretch out over longer periods of time. Many services cannot be inventoried (e.g. a night's stay at a hotel). Other services deal with inventories all the time.

One consequence of this diversity of traits is that managers of services are more apt to think of their processes as unique, in comparison with manufacturing managers. After all, the classification of manufacturing processes into job shops, batch operations, assembly lines, and continuous flow operations is of reasonably long standing and is well accepted. Service research, especially in its formative years, spent considerable effort on classifying services in different ways, in part to dispel the notion that each kind of service was unique. The search was on to find categories within which services could share important characteristics.

In line with our focus on processes, we are most comfortable grouping services into process types. Figure 2.6 compares four different types of service operation: service factory, service shop, mass service, and professional service. These service processes can only roughly be equated to the four manufacturing services that have been discussed earlier in the chapter. They contain elements that are unlike the more well-established manufacturing processes.

The four service processes can be described by arraying them according to two dimensions. One dimension is *labor intensity*, which describes the labor input required by the service provider to complete the service offered relative

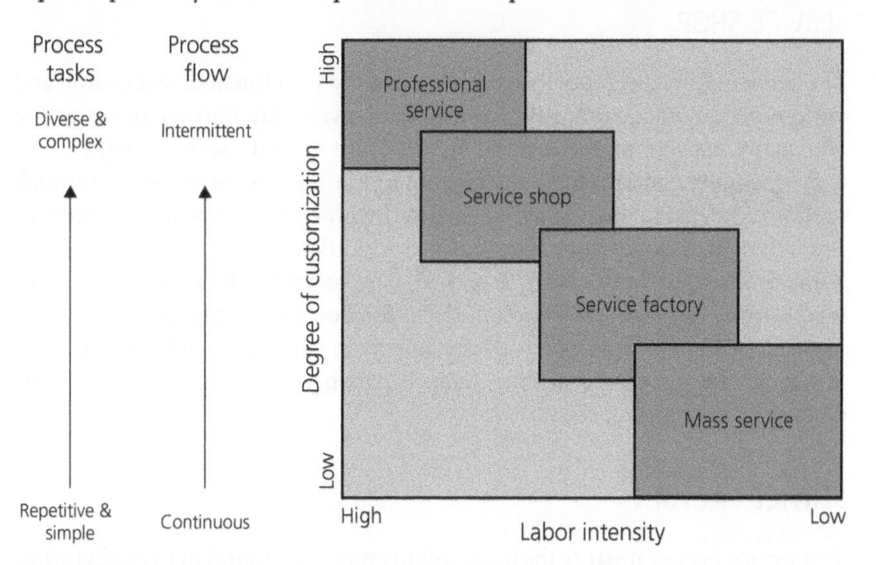

Figure 2.6 A spectrum of service processes: the service process matrix.

Adapted from Schmenner (1986).

to the capital employed. And for the second dimension the *degree of customization* is used—how different each service is from the service offered to another customer. Using these two dimensions, process patterns, layouts, bottlenecks, and a range of other characteristics can be distinguished, much as we did with manufacturing. Other aspects do not match up as well, however, such as capacity, peak vs. off-peak demand, and customer interaction. The challenges that management faces can be very different.

Please note that, just as for manufacturing processes, technologies can challenge and shift the boundaries of what is technically feasible and economically viable. Digital platforms in particular can be customized to a great extent, with little or no labor input required. As such, both the product-process and service process matrices must be seen as dynamic, and bound to change in relation to technological advancement.

PROFESSIONAL SERVICE

The professional service is effectively the "project" or "job shop" of the service world. Here, highly skilled workers ("professionals") provide such services as customized tax advice, legal advice, and personal development services. Very often little equipment is needed beyond general-purpose equipment. As these services are initiated by, and tailored to, a specific customer, the level of customization is effectively infinite.

SERVICE SHOP

The service shop combines lower labor intensity with the high interaction and customization associated with professional service. An auto repair operation and many aspects of the general hospital are typical "service shops." The output is quite specialized to the customer, but the customer moves through specialized departments, often constructed with considerable capital expenditure, that provide distinct operations—e.g. undercarriage work on a car, or X-ray and surgery services for a patient. The patient (either human or auto) travels from "process" to "process," depending on the specific needs. Like in a manufacturing job shop, the pathway any given patient might take will differ; however, the processes within each department will show considerable amounts of repetition.

SERVICE FACTORY

The service factory mirrors the high-volume processes found in manufacturing. They are often the back office operation, the fast-food restaurant, the no-frills airline, and the Internet retailer. They are frequently characterized as having little customization but considerable capital expenditure, and thus only modest labor intensity. They are standard services offered on a large-volume basis.

MASS SERVICE

Mass services are those whose labor intensity is high but for which the customization needed is low. Standard services such as in-store retailing or wholesaling, where the capital needs are modest, are typical examples. Customers are served, but the degree to which customization must be applied in doing so is limited.

HYBRID SERVICE SET-UPS

While factories mostly tend to provide a clear separation of process types (e.g. an assembly line in production, but a separate job shop in the product development area), for service operations this separation is often not apparent. For example, a general hospital will see service factory-type operations for small, standard, elective interventions, a service shop for most patients, offering services that vary according to their needs, and highly complex surgeries or treatments that require a professional service set-up. These all share the same resources, such as wards and operating theatres, which explains to some extent the general difficulties in improving healthcare operations. We call these "hybrid" set-ups, as different process types can occur in parallel.

NEW INFORMATION SERVICES

Over the last ten to fifteen years we have seen the emergence of low-labor intensity mass services like Alibaba's Taobao in online consumer sales, WeChat's portfolio of communication platforms, or Telegram's secured chat platform. In the case of Taobao, customers and suppliers can to a large extent customize their own services and offerings, based on a clever utilization of platforms and data. Some of these services have probably moved off the diagonal and can be found in the top right-hand corner of the matrix in Figure 2.6.

2.8 **Product manufacturer or service provider?**

As we have noted, what constitutes a service is not as easily defined as what constitutes manufacturing. Nevertheless, many of the principles of operations management apply to services as readily as they do to manufacturing. Notions of capacity, bottlenecks, balance, quality, scheduling, and the like are as applicable to services as they are to manufacturing. And, as we have observed, what leads to productivity is the same for both.

Some emphases are different, however. That most services are deemed to be more intangible than manufactured goods means, for example, that perceptions and expectations play important roles in service management. Perceptions get tangled up with service quality. And those perceptions can depend on what was expected. Thus, managing customer expectations so that the service can be seen to "under-promise and over-deliver" can be critical.

As is suggested by the discussion in Section 2.7, services also engage in more customer contact than does manufacturing. Service customers often interact or otherwise become a part of the service process. Some scholars think that this aspect of service, customer contact, is the chief defining characteristic of service.

The fact that many services cannot be inventoried means that service capacity has to be carefully managed, even rationed. Demand management and reservation systems become crucial for many services. Revenue (or yield) management has grown into a major mechanism for rationing capacity by exploiting the demand curve and people's willingness to pay, particularly as time counts down. However, when reservation systems or demand management becomes impractical or insufficient, queues can develop. Managing the queues, and the psychology of waiting, then becomes necessary. Those among us who have waited in endless security check lines at airports will know everything about this. A number of companies, pre-eminently Disney, are recognized masters of this.

Despite the conceptual differences between manufacturing and service firms, it is important to note that virtually all products contain both manufactured and service elements. A manufactured iPad is of little use without iTunes and app-store services, and a restaurant visit without any tangible and manufactured food is equally disappointing. So while it is important to understand the difference in emphasis between manufacturing and service processes, it is equally important to understand their connectedness in the context of the firm.

2.9 **Overhead processes**

Within our discipline of operations management, we conventionally divide repetitive operations into two major categories: manufacturing and service. We have devoted considerable time and effort to characterizing and classifying different manufacturing and service processes and we have developed an arsenal of tools by which to improve one or the other.[6]

Overheads are indirect costs, which are necessary but generally non-value adding activities needed to sustain the business. If you are an accountant, then accounting is your customer-facing service process. The same applies to any professional service. Just because it is accounting or HR, does not mean it is overhead. If accounting firms provide accounting as a service process, then it is value-adding.

Yet there is a third category of repetitive process that is critical to the effectiveness of companies of all sizes and shapes. This category encompasses the processes that are internal to the company and are given the label of overhead or support processes. In the heyday of business process engineering in the 1990s, in the wake of Michael Hammer and James Champy's work on re-engineering,[7] much was made of *core* processes and *support* processes. Core processes typically encompass manufacturing and service while support processes encompass what here is referred to as overhead. Also, one can think of managerial processes that direct strategy and change.[8] However, because of the *sui generis* nature of much of upper management's actions, we leave managerial processes to the side.

Companies are swimming in such processes. Some of the processes are directly tied to the products that a company sells, but others are not. These latter are both overhead and overlooked. Of course, much has been written about the often escalating costs of overheads and alternative ways to allocate them (e.g. activity-based costing, as in the work of Robin Cooper, for example Cooper and Kaplan (1988)).[9] Of concern to this chapter is not how overhead costs should be allocated, but rather what the processes standing behind those overheads look like and whether they can be improved and made more productive.

The internal company overhead processes that are in direct support of the manufacturing or service delivery process have been amply studied and are, in the main, well understood. These are processes such as new product development, purchasing, maintenance, warranty, marketing, and sales lead qualification. Although these processes are often conducted in the background, the scope of their activity is directly related to the sales, either current or projected, that the company enjoys. Change what the company sells in the marketplace and these supporting processes will, of necessity, change as well.

The overhead processes that do not directly support the company's product offerings, what could be termed "pure overhead" processes, are a different matter. They run the gamut of company operations from human resources (e.g. recruiting, executive appraisal, promotions and transfers) to accounting and finance (e.g. monthly close of the books, capital appropriation requests, annual budgeting process) and to a host of others (e.g. regulatory compliance, orders on the IT department). Look into any department of the company and one can find processes that govern how the company operates and processes that company policy firmly dictates must be followed irrespective of what the company is selling.

Although one could presumably argue that processes of this type are simply another form of service process, they are sufficiently different to be flagged here. The customers for and the suppliers of such processes reside within the company. Indeed, it has been fashionable for managers to think of themselves as being a "customer" for someone in the company and in turn being a "supplier" to someone else. Yet there is no external market for these processes, nor are they linked to the market as support processes such as purchasing or new product development are. Thus, although there are customers and suppliers, and these are well known within the company, there are no formal, market-based buyers and sellers. The processes and procedures used are typically those that the company itself has devised or has "borrowed" from other companies; they are not ones that have been honed in competitive battle with other companies. They are only rarely benchmarked and their benefits and costs are seldom explicitly researched.

Companies are typically complex amalgams of various manufacturing and service processes, and of the overhead processes that support them. Indeed, the overhead processes that are found in companies of all types are often more similar to each other than the manufacturing and service processes that are the *raisons d'être* of such companies. In the main, accountants and IT and HR executives, for example, can pass between diverse companies more easily than the operations managers that produce what is sold. Frequently, their allegiance is as much, or more, to their disciplines as it is to the industries they serve. This is another reason to consider such "pure overhead" separately.

Table 2.2 presents a comparison of overhead processes, both pure ones and ones that exist to support the product offered to the marketplace, against both service and manufacturing processes. As can be readily seen in the table, pure overhead processes display some characteristics that are not shared by the others. The fact that overhead processes escape the rigors of the marketplace shows up in these characteristics. Issues surrounding capacity, precise specifications, customer expectations, and customer wait are often ignored.

CLASSIFYING OVERHEAD PROCESSES

As one might expect, not all pure overhead processes are alike. For example, the company's accounting and finance processes (e.g. creation of financial statements, annual budgeting, capture of expense data) are much more standard and less subject to change than some other processes. Figure 2.7 arrays some pure overhead processes according to two traits. One trait relates to the definition of the process, namely whether the process is tightly defined, perhaps enough to be considered a standard operating procedure, or whether it is more loosely defined. The other trait relates to the output of the process, namely whether that output is well understood ("volume") and whether it is subject to change and uncertainty ("variety").

Table 2.2 Comparing manufacturing, service, and overhead processes

Characteristic	Services	Manufacturing	Overhead	
			In direct support of products	Pure overhead, not in direct support of products
Tangibility/ intangibility	The intangible is often what is valued.	Goods are tangible.	The output of such processes is often tangible as it is directly tied to the product on offer.	Process often has a deliverable that is tangible but the value of the process can be intangible.
Quality	Sometimes defined as customer perception–customer expectation. Thus managing perceptions and expectations is critical.	Conformance to well-defined specifications, tied to the customer.	Specifications and customer perceptions and expectations are typically well known.	Specifications, perceptions, and expectations are often not defined at all. Quality is more often seen as speed and definitiveness.
Customer contact and interaction	Lots of customer contact and interaction with the process. This is often a defining characteristic.	Customer does not interact with the process or come into contact with it.	The extent of any customer contact and interaction depends on the circumstances.	People interact with the process all the time, including its customers.
Inventory	Services typically cannot be inventoried.	Inventories of all sorts exist.	Inventories are often relevant to the process.	Inventory is usually not relevant.
Simultaneity of production and consumption	Production and consumption are often nearly simultaneous.	Consumption is divorced from production.	As these processes operate in the background, production and consumption are typically not simultaneous.	Consumption and production can be nearly simultaneous but the lags between production and consumption can also be long.
Managing capacity	Determining the proper extent of capacity and managing the capacity that is available is critical. Reservation systems and revenue management are frequently used to ration capacity.	While capacity is examined regularly, the ability to build up finished goods inventory attenuates the urgency of employing capacity management tools.	The delivery of the product or service is sensitive to the capacity of these processes. Capacity is monitored and managed.	Capacity for overhead processes is often ignored, as the deliverables of the process are not sold to a market.
Managing queues	Given that queuing often involves people and not simply materials, the management of queues and the psychology of queues become important.	The queuing of materials can matter and is handled by production planning and scheduling. The psychology of queues, however, is not relevant.	The queuing of materials can matter a great deal. As the process is often distant from the consumer, the psychology of queues usually has little relevance.	Queuing is often ignored, as there are no buyers in the traditional sense.

Source: R. Schmenner, 2012. Overhead and overlooked. *operations Management Research*, 5(3–4), pp.87–90.

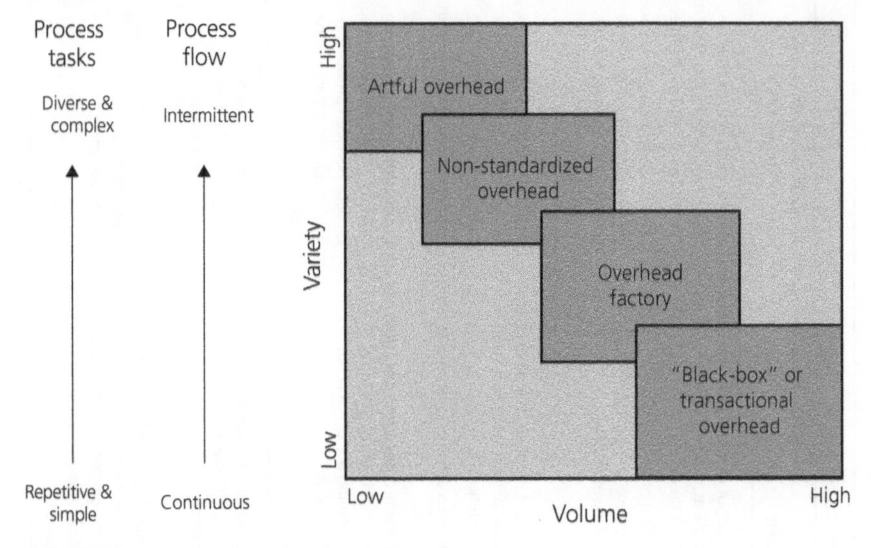

Figure 2.7 Spectrum of overhead processes.

Adapted from Schmenner (2012).

The standard nature of many accounting procedures—characterized as an "overhead factory" in Figure 2.7—is a far cry from the fluidity and uncertainty of dealing with the press. Press relations, in contrast, can be characterized as "artful overhead." Executive appraisals that lead to promotions and advancements and IT projects are in this "artful overhead" category as well. What it is about someone that led to his or her promotion and advancement may not be clear to others in the company, and IT projects are often famous for their opacity and for the uncertainty of their cost and timing.

Some accounting and finance processes are not as tightly defined as expense approvals are. The budget process and the capital appropriations request process are more loosely defined, although both of these processes are typically well understood and not subject to much change over time. They are thus labeled in Figure 2.7 as "non-standardized overhead."

A lot of HR processes like recruiting, layoffs, and salary setting, although more tightly defined than some other HR processes, are not well understood and more subject to change. They fall into the category of "black-box overhead," as they are procedural yet shrouded in some mystery.

THE BURDEN OF OVERHEAD

However these overhead processes are defined, they can be millstones around a company's neck. These processes frequently do not have "owners," or at least "owners" that one can count on to take responsibility for their continual improvement. Prior to the widespread adoption of Lean principles, product changeovers were not routinely studied and worked on to reduce changeover times. Their impact was not appreciated. Overhead processes share much of that same neglect. One characteristic of overhead processes that seems often to be neglected is that they create their own work by imposing new controls and procedures. They can take up valuable time, and if they are done haphazardly they can lead to poor decisions. They are too often the object of employee exasperation or even scorn.

Nevertheless, improving such processes can make a big difference to a company and its employees. Fortunately, the same tools of analysis that apply to manufacturing and service operations can be applied to these internal company processes. They can be flow charted, studied, and improved. The waste within them can be identified and removed. The time it takes to accomplish them can be slashed. The variability they are subject to can be lessened. In this, overhead processes react just like manufacturing or service processes.

NOTES

1. This discussion of process characteristics draws on Roger Schmenner's previous depictions of different processes, as found in his textbook, *Production/Operations Management*, 5th edition. Macmillan, 1993.
2. E. Mayo, F.J. Roethlisberger, and W. Dickson, 1939. *Management and the Worker*. Harvard University Press.
3. S.R. Barley and P.S. Tolbert, 1997. Institutionalization and structuration: Studying the links between action and institution. *Organization Studies*, 18(1), pp.93–117.
4. B.P. Shapiro, V.K. Rangan, and J.J. Sviokla, 1992. Staple yourself to an order. *Harvard Business Review*, 70(4), pp.113–22.
5. C.H. Loch, A. De Meyer, and M.T. Pich, 2006. *Managing the Unknown: A New Approach to Managing High Uncertainty and Risk in Projects*. J. Wiley and Sons.
6. See, for example, R.B. Chase, 1981. The customer contact approach to services: Theoretical bases and practical extensions. *Operations Research*, 29(4), pp.698–706 and R.W. Schmenner, 1986. How can service businesses survive and prosper? *Sloan Management Review* (1986–1998), 27(3), p.21 for early service classifications and see the vast literature on quality, Six Sigma, and process re-engineering for process improvement.
7. M.C. Hammer and J. Champy, 1993. *Reengineering the Corporation: A Manifesto for Business Revolution*. Nicholas Brealey Publishing.
8. U.S. Bititci, P. Suwignjo, and A.S. Carrie, 2001. Strategy management through quantitative modelling of performance measurement systems. *International Journal of Production Economics*, 69(1), pp.15–22.
9. R. Cooper and R.S. Kaplan, 1988. Measure costs right: Make the right decisions. *Harvard Business Review*, Sept–Oct, pp.96–103.

FURTHER READING

Davenport, T.H., 2013. *Process Innovation: Reengineering Work through Information Technology*. Harvard Business Press (Brighton, MA).

Deming, W.E., 2000. *Out of the Crisis*. MIT Press (Cambridge, MA).

Deming, W.E. and Birge, R.T., 1934. On the statistical theory of errors. *Reviews of Modern Physics*, 6(3), p.119.

Hammer, M. and Champy, J. 2009. *Reengineering the Corporation: A Manifesto for Business Revolution*. HarperBusiness (New York).

Hayes, R.H. and Wheelwright, S.C., 1979. Link manufacturing process and product life cycles. *Harvard Business Review*, 57(1), pp.133–40.

Loch, C.H., De Meyer, A., and Pich, M.T., 2006. *Managing the Unknown: A New Approach to Managing High Uncertainty and Risk in Projects*. J. Wiley and Sons (London).

Schmenner, R.W., 1986. How can service businesses survive and prosper? *Sloan Management Review* (1986–1998), 27(3), p.21.

Schmenner, R.W., 1995. *Service Operations Management*. Prentice-Hall (Englewood Cliffs, NJ).

Schmenner, R.W., 2012. Overhead and overlooked. *Operations Management Research*, 5(3–4), pp.87–90.

Schmenner, R.W., 2012. *Getting and Staying Productive: Applying Swift, Even Flow to Practice*. Cambridge University Press (Cambridge).

Shewhart, A., 1931. *Economic Control of the Manufacturing Product*. Van Nostrand (New York).

3 Analyzing processes

As we have stated, the bedrock of operations management is the process. In Chapters 1 and 2 we have described in some detail the distinctions among manufacturing and service and internal company processes of different types. Some processes are clearly more suited to particular business situations than others.

In order to make the best match that one can, managers need to be able to analyze processes on at least two levels: the "as-is" level and the "desired" level. The analysis of the process as it is currently functioning in the business—the "as-is" process—is prosaic, but startlingly useful. Knowing how effective that process is across a variety of dimensions is an essential step in improving operations and the profits they can earn. The bulk of this chapter deals with the analysis of "as-is" processes.

On the other hand, the match of process to business needs—to create the "desired" process—is the domain of operations strategy. The last section of this chapter, Section 3.9, uses economics to discuss the operations role in business strategy.

3.1 Making process mapping work

Process mapping is a fundamental technique in operations management that allows for all parties to develop a common understanding of what the actual process looks like, what the main stages are, and who the main stakeholders are.

For this reason, most process improvement projects will start with a process map, and in our experience it is a very good first step when you are trying to get to know a process you are unfamiliar with. We have found that spending the first day mapping a process is rarely a waste of time and effort.

Methods differ, but the logic of process mapping is universal: you start with the incoming order, and follow it through all the waiting and processing stages until the product or service is complete.[1]

There are three simple rules to obey when thinking about process mapping:

1. **Go to gemba (the real workplace):** It is very important to capture the actual process, and not the process as people think it is supposed to operate. You need to go down to the shop floor or actual workplace to see and map the

process. Often so-called "workarounds" (secondary ad-hoc process steps that develop because the primary process has failed) will occur, that people are not aware of. You need to capture these in order to create an honest overview of the process. In our own experience it may also be helpful to focus on stockpiles of in-process inventories, because they are often the symptom of a difference between the intended and actual process.

2. **Capture the "vital few":** It will not be possible, nor a productive use of your time, to capture the process in every possible detail. So capture the main aspects and stages of the process, and estimate the set-up times and runtimes where needed. Aim for a process map that may not be fully complete, but captures all the vital aspects of the process you are mapping. Make assumptions where needed, and clearly state them. In this context it is important to pick a high-volume product that runs frequently, so that you can confidently argue that the process you are seeing is not an exception, but the norm.
3. **Stick to the mapping methodology:** There is always a temptation to create new icons that may suit the context better than the ones the methodology actually offers. Process maps are a "language" to describe a process to someone not familiar with the process. You need to stick to the standards of mapping for others to be able to read your map. You may wish to add comments to the map where further explanation is needed.

In this chapter, we examine processes using a number of tools that can help us to understand those processes better. There are four different types of diagrams which we have found to be exceedingly useful in visualizing and understanding a process, and which are not used in practice as often as they should be. They are the process flow diagram (sometimes termed the process map or the value stream map), the information flow diagram, the inventory build-up diagram, and the spaghetti diagram, as well as IDEF0 mapping. Let us comment on them in turn.

3.2 **Process flow diagrams**

For beginning a case discussion, or for any other situation when one needs to get acquainted with the as-is process, there is nothing quite as useful as the simple, fundamental process flow diagram. It is the anchor for the discussion, and we and our students, in their own work situations, have seen the process flow diagram become a focal point for managers, engineers, and workers as they wrestle with a process problem. Frequently, higher-level managers have an idealized view of what the process is, and they miss the nitty-gritty detail that the workforce deals with in the process. Discovering exactly what happens

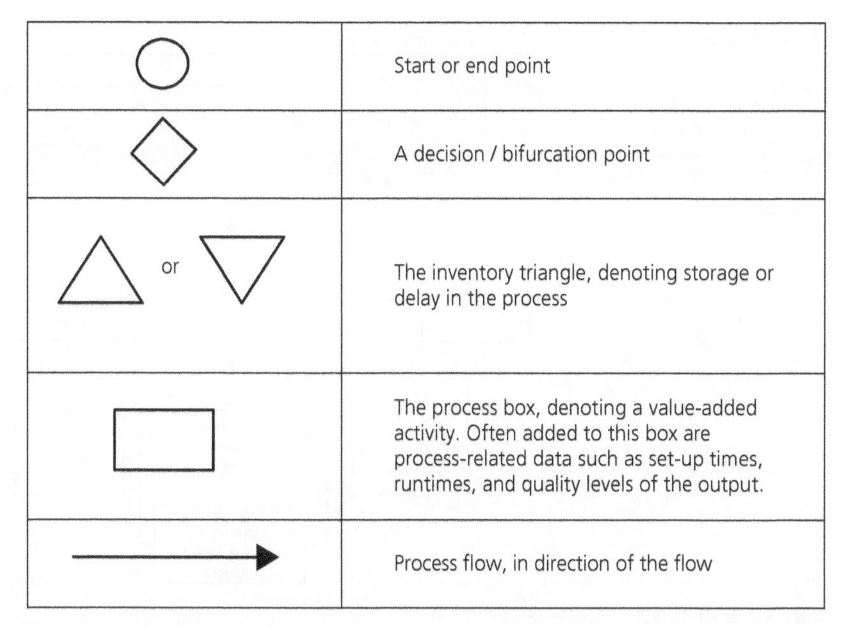

Start or end point
A decision / bifurcation point
or
The inventory triangle, denoting storage or delay in the process
The process box, denoting a value-added activity. Often added to this box are process-related data such as set-up times, runtimes, and quality levels of the output.
Process flow, in direction of the flow

Figure 3.1 Basic process mapping symbols.

under different circumstances is a revelation to some managers, although sometimes a revelation that they do not want to acknowledge right away. It is clearly an effective way for the workforce, who might not otherwise have the opportunity or be able to find the words, to convey what they see as problematic for the process.

It is our convention to use the following symbols, as shown also in Figure 3.1. They may not conform exactly to those used in industrial engineering, but we find them easier to use and write in while diagramming:

- Rectangle—An operation where someone or something is working on the materials or information in the process
- Oval or circle—An inspection or control step
- Triangle—An inventory
- Diamond—A decision point where different decisions (e.g. yes or no) can lead to different subsequent operations.

Figure 3.2 is an example process flow diagram for a back office function.

Figure 3.2 is a simple one. It has only nine activities depicted. Still, it has served well to visualize a case situation and generate considerable discussion. We have found, however, that process flow diagrams of between fifteen and forty symbols are generally the most effective. With such a count of symbols, there can be sufficient detail to spark real understanding about what is going on, without burying any discussion in too much detail.

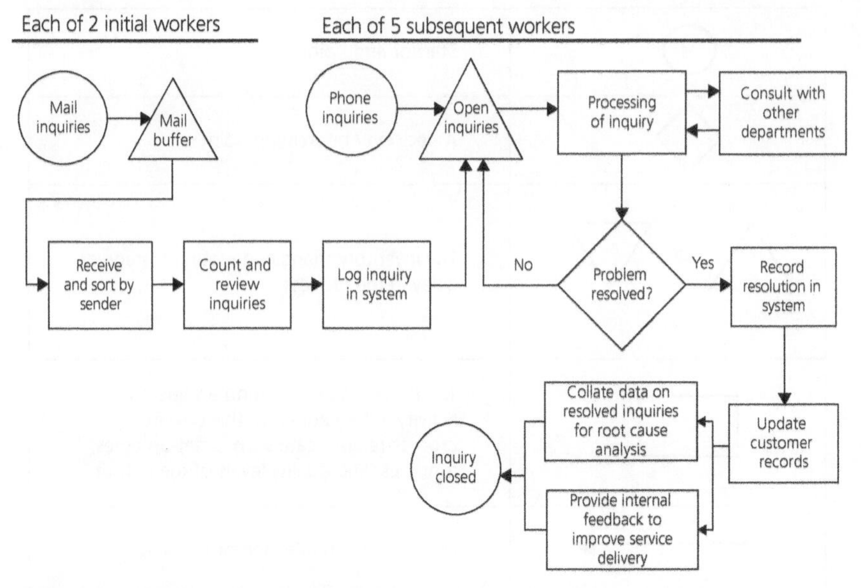

Figure 3.2 Back office process—an example.

Sometimes it is also advantageous to divide the process flow into levels that may correspond to different realms of responsibility. For example, for many service processes, it could make a great deal of sense to divide the process flow into those tasks that are customer-facing (e.g. front counter) and those that are internal or back-of-the-house. Different groups of employees may be responsible for these tasks, and so noting that fact on the process flow diagram can be helpful.

This can naturally complicate the diagram, but segregating the levels of responsibility can be helpful in analyzing what can be done independently and what needs to wait on work done by someone else in the organization. (The information flow diagram in Figure 3.3 divides the information flow into levels.)

3.3 Information flow diagrams

Less used or needed, but still very useful is the information flow diagram. The process flow diagram typically tracks materials as they flow from upstream to downstream. The information flow diagram, on the other hand, is useful precisely because it often tracks information as it flows from downstream back upstream. It can be particularly useful in tracking what happens in a supply chain.

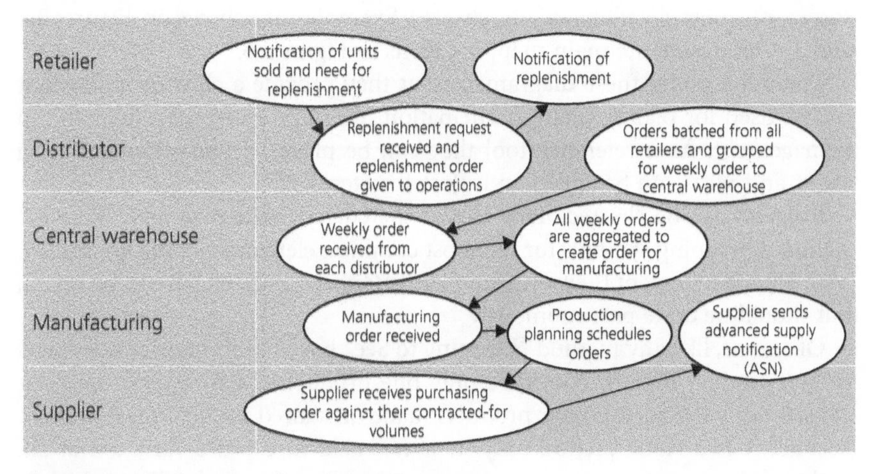

Figure 3.3 An information flow diagram.

Figure 3.3 provides an example of an information flow diagram.

An information flow diagram can quickly become busy. Nevertheless, it is useful to know who is getting informed of what, and, typically, when such information is being passed. It can then be linked to a process flow diagram for a fuller understanding of what is occurring and how it is occurring. In some cases, it is useful to combine the process flow diagram and the information flow diagram into one. The key point is that managing the flow of materials from upstream to downstream in a process often requires that one also first manage the flow of information from downstream back upstream.

Often these information flow diagrams reveal duplication of information flows. While they may be needed for control purposes, often they create non-value adding tasks, which may endanger the measurement and control capacity of the organization.

3.4 **Value stream mapping**

The mapping technique most widely used in the context of process improvement is "Learning to See" or "value stream mapping" (VSM). It has its origins in the Lean Thinking philosophy and was developed originally by Toyota.

The method maps both material and information flows. It is quick to learn because it uses simple boxes to indicate stages, and other obvious symbols such as trucks, factories, and kanban cards. The tool is suitable for repetitive operations, especially where a single product or family of products is made. A powerful feature is that it "closes the loop" from customer order to supply to manufacture, ending with the delivery of the product. (This closed loop is not shown on most detailed activity charts.) Examples are shown in Figures 3.4 and 3.5, alongside the main mapping icons in Figure 3.6.

The point about these diagrams is that they provide a clear overview that can be used for planning and participation meetings, from shop floor to top management. As a reference tool they can be placed on boards in meeting areas, and ideas can be added with Post-it notes.

Progress can be charted. This creates the current state diagram. There are standard mapping symbols for the most common elements—some are shown. Many mappers invent their own supplementary symbols, which can be useful, but should be done parsimoniously.

Of course, like any method "Learning to See" has limitations that one needs to be aware of. First, it considers only one product at a time, and does not consider any linkage to other products made on shared production resources. Second, it is a static picture only. It is not able to capture variation at all. It therefore cannot make any statement about capacity or loading, which is a major shortcoming that the mapper needs to be aware of when analyzing the result!

Value stream mapping, in short, consists of two maps: the *current state* or *as-is* map, and the *future state* or *should-be* map. The former denotes the as-is process, the latter the ideal state one aims to achieve. The gap between these two maps creates the implementation plan.

THE CURRENT STATE MAP

Figure 3.4 is an example of a current state map for a simple, linear manufacturing operation.

Note that the map incorporates both the *information flow* (top right to top left) and the *material flow* (bottom left to bottom right), and thus shows a complete loop from order received to order fulfilled.

Further note the *timeline* at the bottom of the map: here we capture both the *value-added* times (i.e. the actual processing times) as well as the *non-value-added times* (i.e. the waiting times). This allows us to show the degree to which lead time could theoretically be reduced. (In this case the total lead time is 23.5 days, of which 184 seconds are value-added. Typically 95–99% of the total lead time is waste; world-class manufacturers achieve 90% or less.)

THE FUTURE STATE MAP

The creative part of VSM is the development of the future state map, an example of which is shown in Figure 3.5, where an ideal process is depicted. While it is important to design this process in the context of what realistically might be feasible, creativity should not be curtailed by existing boundaries.

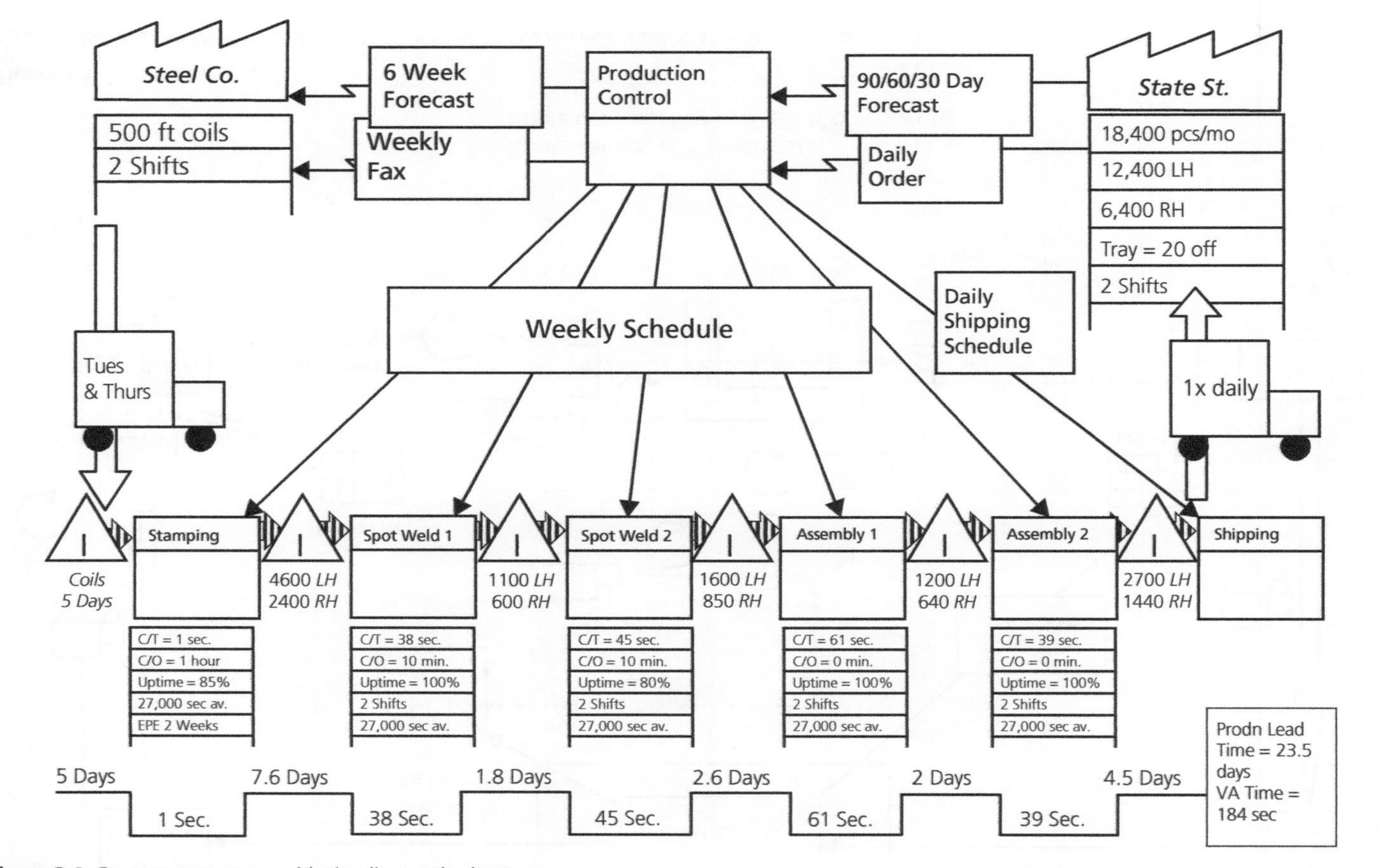

Figure 3.4 Current state map, with timeline at the bottom.

Source: J. Bicheno and M. Holweg, 2016. *The Lean Toolbox: The Essential Guide to Lean Transformation*. Picsie Books.

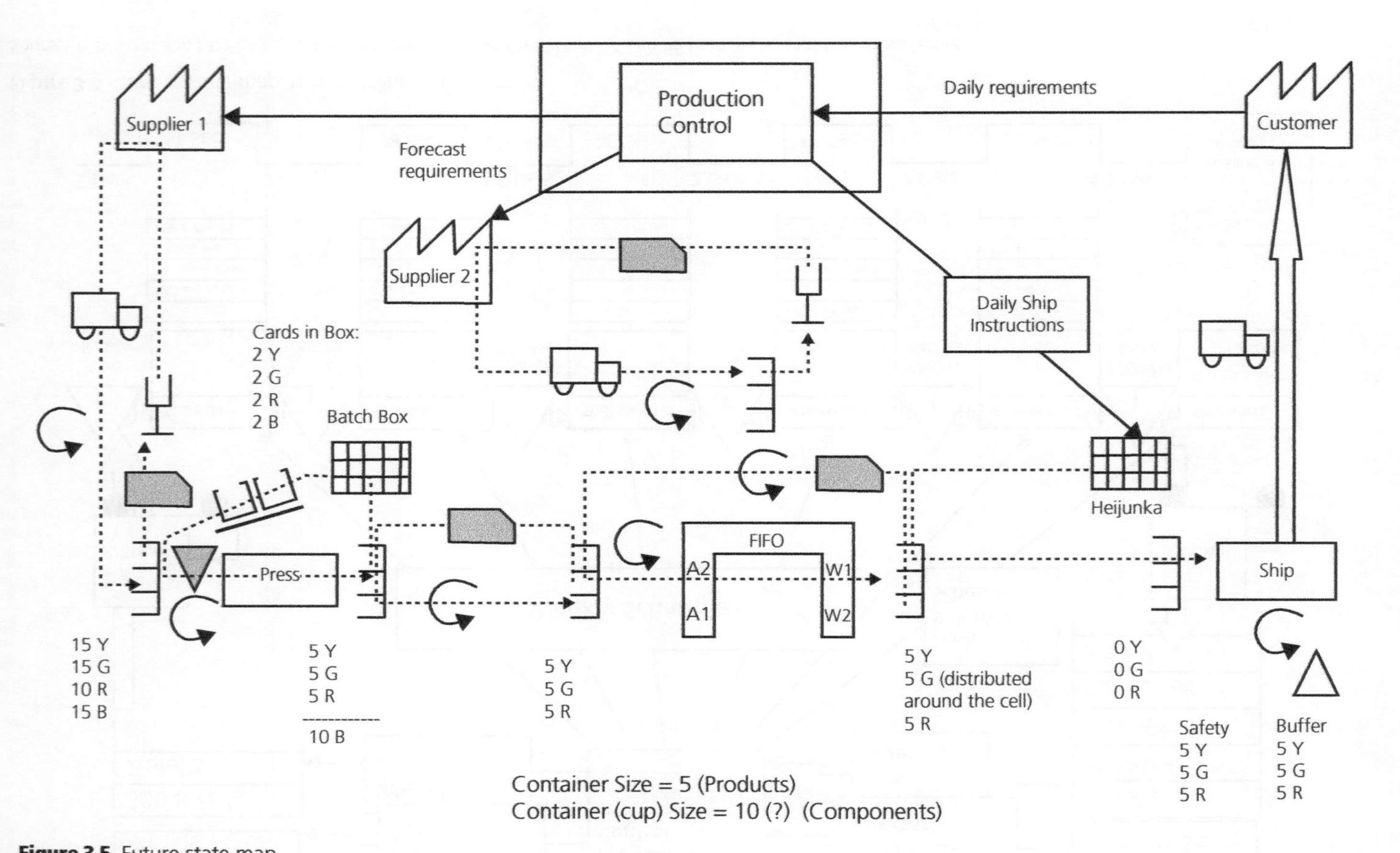

Figure 3.5 Future state map.

Source: J. Bicheno and M. Holweg, 2016. *The Lean Toolbox: The Essential Guide to Lean Transformation*. Picsie Books.

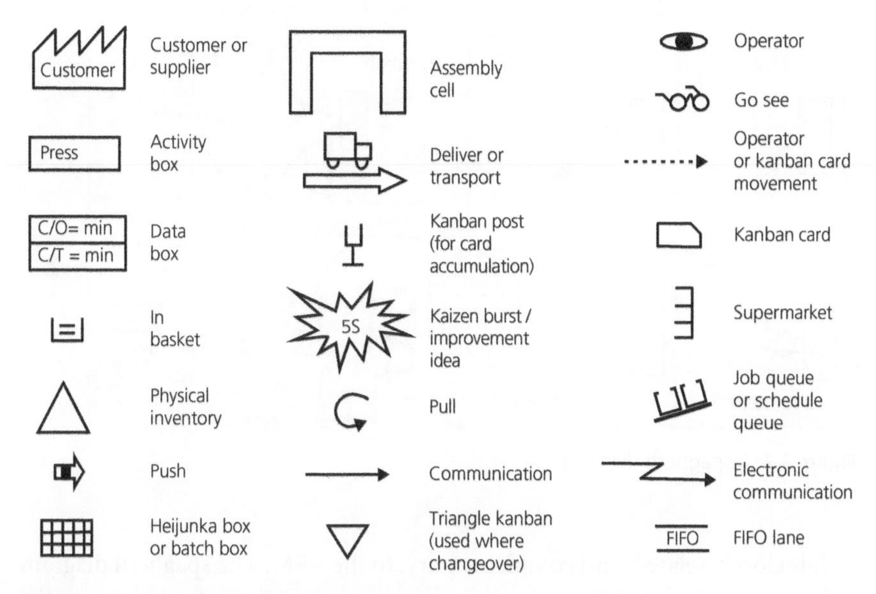

Figure 3.6 Value stream mapping symbols.

Source: Adapted from Rother and Shook (1998).

(For example, changing a global standard is unlikely to be feasible, so the future state process should take this into account.)

One would not expect to ever reach the idealized future state, but instead one would expect to repeat the mapping exercise at regular intervals, and thus move towards an (evolving) future state that incorporates learning from ongoing improvements.

MAPPING SYMBOLS

As stated earlier, it is important to stick to the standard mapping icons so that the maps will be legible by anyone not familiar with the process. Figure 3.6 is an overview of the most common VSM symbols. See Rother and Shook (1998) for more detail.

3.5 Spaghetti diagram (material flow map)

The spaghetti diagram tracks the path of materials through an operation by depicting it on the layout itself. The path that materials take can be tortuous, and thus there can be lines going every which way across the layout. Hence the appellation *spaghetti diagram*.

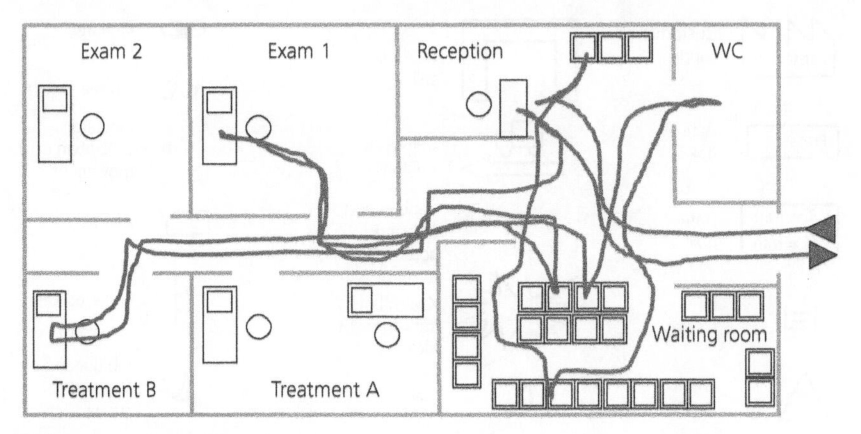

Figure 3.7 A spaghetti diagram.

It is closely related, and complementary, to the VSM. The spaghetti diagram follows a given item (or resource, such as a person) through its way on the shop floor of a factory or service operation.

Figure 3.7 presents a spaghetti diagram example of a patient traveling between different work centers in a hospital (but please note that such maps can also cover multiple buildings or sites). The logistics involved, and likewise the cost of those logistics, can be significant. The spaghetti diagram can help us to come to grips with the logistics and costs.

The purpose of this map is to highlight inefficiencies in the workflow and/or layout of a process. The way to generate a spaghetti diagram is simple: take an A0 printout of the shop floor plan, and map the actual path of a part, material, or resource (i.e. a worker) along the shop floor.

You would capture two aspects:

1. Total *distance traveled*, and
2. *Number of times an item is handled* (picked up and put down).

Your aim is to minimize both.

3.6 **IDEF0 mapping**

IDEF0 mapping is a simple yet powerful technique originally developed by the US Air Force to assess the processes of its suppliers. It's very simple—there is only one symbol to remember (a rectangle = a process), and the key idea is that every process turns a set of inputs into a set of outputs. "Entities" (which could be materials, objects, people, documents—anything really) are shown as arrows that go from one process step to another, and the key idea is that entities remain unchanged as they go from box to box. If they do in fact change, another box is inserted to denote that change.

Optionally, you can add "controls." A control may be a trigger event, or a bit of information used by but not transformed by the process, coming into the top of the box, or "resources" (for example equipment, workers) coming into the bottom. And that's it. It's astonishingly simple, but tricky to do in practice. Why? Because you have to think hard about what actually happens to stuff. And you have to think creatively about how to carve up the activities into processes.

The key word is "transformation": in IDEF0, processes transform inputs into outputs. Perhaps it's easiest to imagine a chunk of metal being transformed in a manufacturing process (e.g. flat metal becomes curved metal), but the approach also works if you think about other sorts of things (e.g. person without loan is transformed to person with loan; unaudited document is turned into audited document).

One of the great advantages of the approach is that you can start with the overall process (a so-called "Level 0" model), and then progressively "zoom in" (Level 1, 2, etc.) to the subprocesses that are interesting. A key part of the process is that you keep on iterating between the levels in your analysis to keep everything consistent; the discipline helps you think hard about the system in question. Once you have a diagram, it is relatively easy to add quantification to the process steps and flows.

Figures 3.8 and 3.9 give a flavor of the technique. Figure 3.8 shows the Level 0 view of a system (a pensions processing operation at a fictional government department here called the DIA).

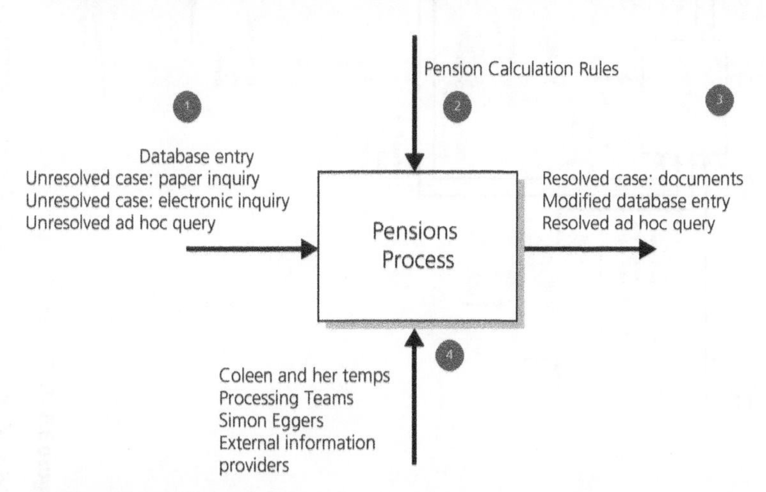

Figure 3.8 IDEFO Level 0 map.

Source: M. Holweg and S. New, 2017. Process Mapping, Saïd Business School, Teaching Note.

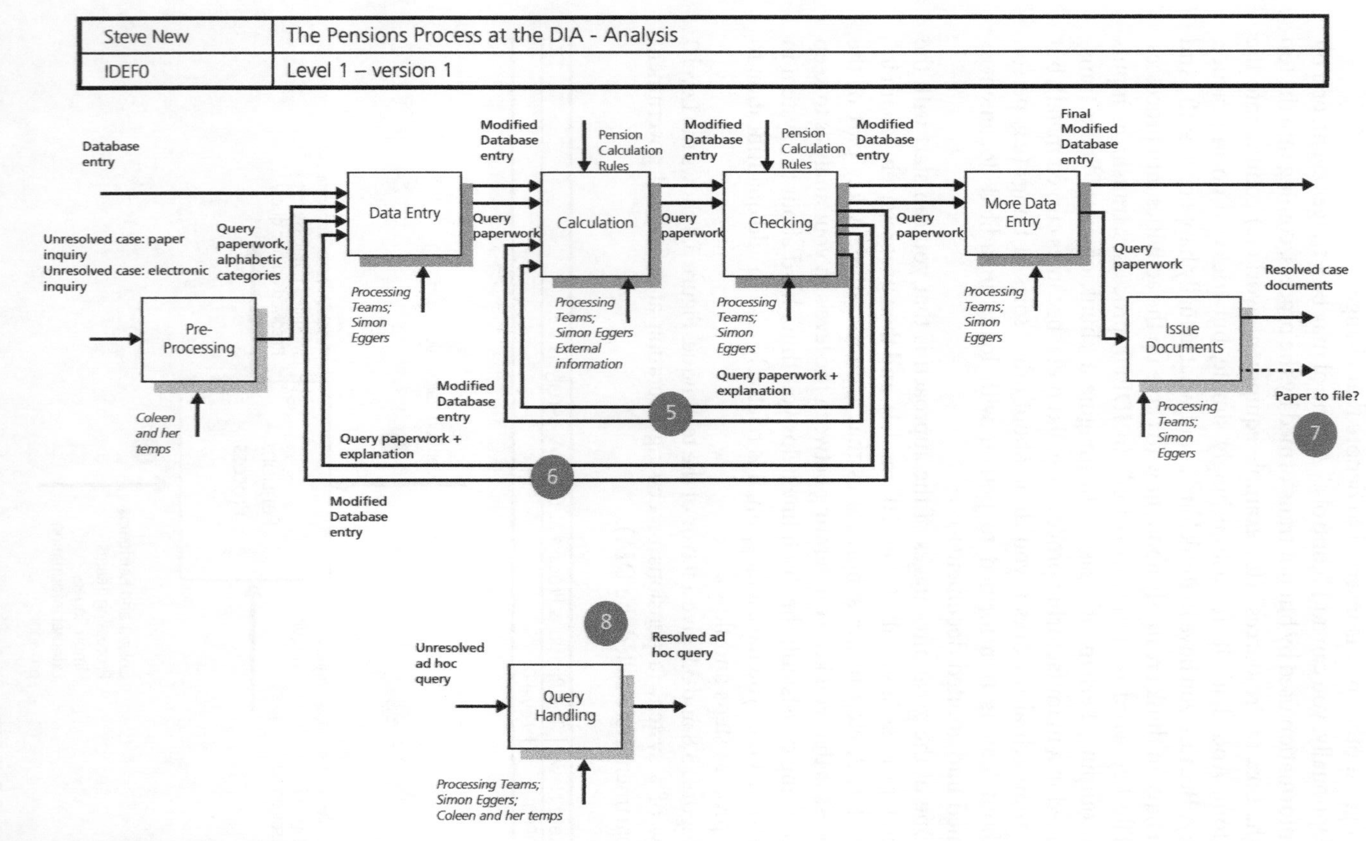

Figure 3.9 IDEF0 Level 1 map.

Source: M. Holweg and S. New, 2017. Process Mapping, Saïd Business School, Teaching Note.

Although superficially a Level 0 diagram looks rather uninformative, the key point is that it effectively sets a boundary on what is being considered.

The mapping task at Level 0 is really about determining what gets transformed into what. This is always more fiddly than it first appears; IDEF0 forces you to think about what's important and what's not. Here, we've chosen a small number of key **inputs** [(1) on the diagram in Figure 3.8] which are transformed into **outputs** [(3)]. We have assumed that the "inquiries" (both paper and electronic) are transformed into "resolved inquiries," with associated paperwork. It would be possible to draw the diagram with the inquiry as a "trigger"—and therefore coming in at the top of the box; however, it's shown as an input, to focus on the "transformation" of the inquiry as it flows through the system. The **controls** here are the "Pension Calculation Rules" [(2)]—it would be useful to see where this complex information is used in the system, especially as these may change over time. However, these rules themselves are not transformed by the process, and so they cannot be inputs. There's a small pool of **resources** [(4)]; the trick here is to see how the same resources might be called upon by different steps in the process.

The next diagram, Figure 3.9, shows a "Level 1" analysis; the advantage of the greater detail is that we can see a little more clearly how the different elements move through the system. In particular, in this case, it may be that the key things to think about are the "rework" flows [(5) and (6)]. Note that there's no need for the decision points used in conventional flowcharting.

The diagram helps raise some interesting questions: what happens to the paperwork at the end of the process [(7)]? And how does the processing of ad hoc queries [(8)] interfere with the main processes? These questions, in turn, guide the development of an improved process.

3.7 **Inventory "sawtooth" and inventory profile**

The inventory build-up diagram tracks the accumulation of inventory against time. It can depict how quickly, or slowly, inventory builds up under various assumptions of what can occur. While the process and information flow diagrams can help to visualize what is happening, the inventory build-up diagram can help to decide which course of action is the best to take.

Figure 3.10 is an example of an inventory build-up diagram, the so-called "sawtooth."

What can be seen is two types of stock, or inventory. Cycle stock "cycles" up and down over time—from receiving a new batch, to continuously withdrawing inventory, until the next batch arrives and replenishes the inventory. The other type of inventory is the safety stock, which does not change over time

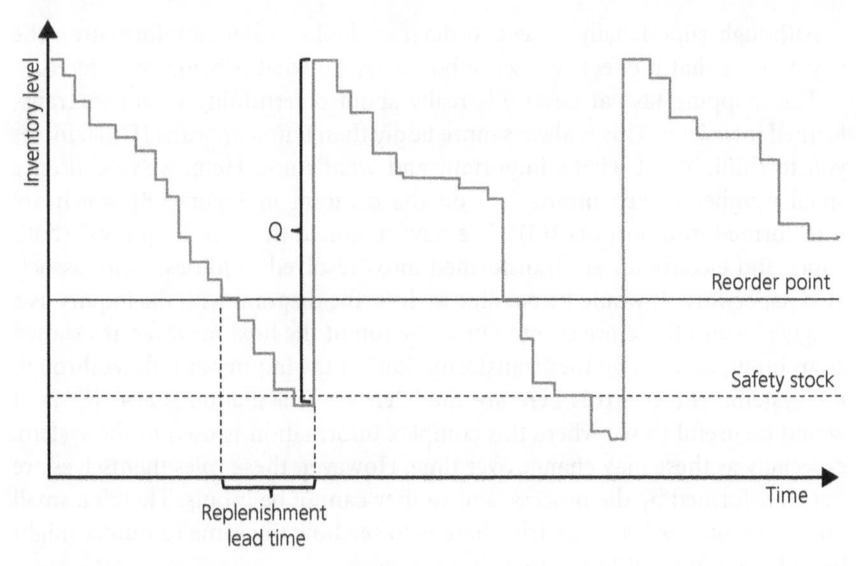

Figure 3.10 An inventory build-up diagram.

and is only used if the rate of depletion (demand) is higher than anticipated, at which point it serves as a (safety) buffer to make sure there are no stock-outs.

Note that the average cycle stock is equal to half the batch size (Q/2, if Q denotes the batch size), which is important as it shows that the average inventory level is effectively determined by a scheduling decision. Or, turned around, you cannot reduce average inventory levels below Q/2, unless you reduce the batch size Q itself!

3.8 Linking process maps to performance

The diagrams in Figures 3.2 to 3.10 can be very useful in capturing what is happening to a process and in visualizing that process and what can be done to improve it. More can be done, however, to understand exactly what is going on with a process, but it takes measurement. Some of the measures that have proven helpful are measures that can be attached—tagged—to diagrams like the process flow diagram.

There are a variety of measures that can be attached to the process flow diagram. The most fundamental ones are:

Time: An important metric to track is the time it takes materials or information to move through a process, from start to finish. This metric is usually termed the throughput time. When a process' throughput time is comparatively long, it is likely that something is amiss with the process—poor quality, a bottleneck of some sort, the need for overhead functions to spend time fixing the process, etc., unless of course there is a technological reason why the throughput is long. Thus, throughput time is an excellent proxy for the degree of non-value-added in the process. By finding where time starts to add up, one can uncover the weaknesses of the process and then work to remedy them. Reducing throughput time is one of the most effective ways to increase the productivity of a process.[2]

There are several ways in which time is relevant in a process setting, which makes it even more unfortunate that many diverging definitions are being used in practice. The main aspects of time in a process are as follows:

- **Cycle time** is the rate at which a process produces. Although called "time," it is actually a measure of throughput, defined as the rate at which a process produces. For example, in car assembly the cycle time is on average about 60 seconds. In other words, every minute a car rolls off the end of the assembly line. Cycle time thus is the time elapsed between one process cycle and the subsequent process cycle's completion. It is measured as time, but denotes a throughput metric. The minimum cycle time (i.e. fastest production rate) is limited by the bottleneck resource of the process.
- **Processing time** is the total time needed to complete the fabrication of one unit. It is generally deterministic and determined by the machine run speed.
- **Waiting time** is the time spent in WIP (work in progress) buffers before a process can take place. It is a stochastic component of the overall lead time of a process.
- **Throughput time** is the average time a part spends in a process, from start to finish. It contains both processing and waiting time components. You measure throughput time by observing a unit as it makes its way through the process.
- **Lead time** is the time required from customer order to delivery of the product or service. Typical lead time measurements are therefore "order to delivery," or "complaint to resolution" in a service setting. It is a customer-facing metric of how long the process takes from an "outsider's point of view."
- **Takt time** is a calculated value which describes the theoretical demand rate of the customer. It is the rate at which a process needs to produce to meet customer demand. This concept is closely linked to the Lean Production logic, which states that one should reduce *cycle time* down to *takt time*, to avoid overproducing. In other words, advocates of Lean state that it is wasteful to let processes run faster than the rate at which customers require the products.

Capacity: The most intuitive measure that can be tagged to the process flow diagram is capacity. From information on the design of equipment or from knowledge of its use or from industrial engineering studies of workers and/or equipment, capacities can nearly always be developed for each step in a process. Such information is, of course, most useful in determining where any bottleneck is, or could be expected to be. Simply being systematic in this way and being as precise as possible with capacity measures can uncover primary and secondary bottlenecks straight away. Such an analysis is naturally easier with well-delineated processes and ones where capacity is unambiguous.

In such well-delineated, unambiguous processes, the bottleneck is stationary. Work-in-process inventory piles up quickly behind it. Little gets through. Its cause is usually clear-cut. Perhaps a machine has broken down or key workers are absent, or demand has simply outstripped the clear, rated capacity of a particular machine. The remedy follows easily and logically. Such bottlenecks can occur in service operations as easily as in manufacturing, and they typically cause customers to wait.

More subtle are bottlenecks that shift from one part of the process to another or that have no clear cause. Inventories build up in different places and at different times. Such bottlenecks creep up on management and demand more thorough investigation. Perhaps they were detected as flaws in a product's quality caused inadvertently by workers trying to keep pace with unreasonable production demands. Or they may be caused by missing parts. They may be caused by a new product start-up or, frequently, by changes in the mix of products flowing through the factory. In such cases the remedies are less clear-cut, and some analysis is called for.

Such analysis is surely needed when less rigid production processes (such as job shops or batch flows) are involved. In such processes, not only are capacity figures potentially very volatile, but the process flow itself may be indeterminate, varying uniquely with each individual order. Identifying bottlenecks in these processes becomes a formidable task. Typically, ranges of capacity must be used and different arrangements of the process flow must be tried. Still, judicious and systematic use of a process flow diagram can be a valuable tool in identifying the process elements and conditions that account for bottlenecks and variability in process capacity.

Service operations are particularly ripe for such analysis. Their process and information flows are only seldom analyzed systematically, and seemingly minor adjustments in the service delivery process can frequently yield significant improvements. It is often very helpful to indicate where the customer interacts with the process and information flows. Thus, a service process flow diagram might include a lower half that tackles the "back-of-the-house" activities and an upper half that indicates when a customer has contact with the process.

The key metric in terms of capacity is utilization, which is defined through productivity metrics: what you get out of the resource, compared to what you put in. For example, labor utilization is the ratio of value-added work divided by the total labor time the firm is paying for.

Yields: Another measure that can be tagged to the process flow diagram is the yield of the process. With many types of process, as one progresses through it there is a gradual, although measurable, decline in the quality of the product, to the point where the fraction of output that is deemed good is significantly below capacity. Where yields suffer is typically somewhere well known. The process step in question is often considered problematic or the process itself is still under development. At such points in the process, it is often wise to put in an inspection step afterward so that more value is not added to units of the product that failed as a result of that low-yielding process step.

The key metric here is also a productivity ratio, namely what fraction of "good" parts you get as a fraction of the total parts produced.

Cost: Just as one can track the yield of the process as materials move through from process step to process step, so, too, can one track the cost of the product as more and more value and thus cost is added to it. That cost can be labor cost, materials cost, machine time, or the time spent by overhead functions such as engineering or quality control. At points where a lot of cost is about to be added to the product, it often makes sense to introduce an inspection step so that significant cost is only incurred for units of the product that are deemed to be good up to that point.

In terms of cost, many key metrics exist. At the highest level, the "unit cost" metric combines all direct costs incurred to produce one unit. This excludes any overheads, which of course need to be considered. It is also possible to measure the labor or material components in unit cost, for example by stating the "labor cost per unit," or "material cost per unit."

Inventories: Related to the metric of time is the metric of inventory. They are related because high inventory levels will lead to long throughput times. Diminish one and the other is also likely to drop. Tracking inventories, be they raw materials, work-in-process, or finished goods, can be a very useful endeavor to figure out what may be going wrong in a process. This can be done using a process flow chart, but, as we have seen, tracking the build-up of inventories with an inventory build-up graph can lead to other, important insights.

The key inventory metrics include physical counts of units held at the various stages of production, from raw materials, to WIP, and finished goods. When comparing the inventory levels to the average levels of customer demand, it is possible to calculate the "inventory cover" or "days of inventory" for each part of the process. In other words, you calculate how many days of production the respective inventory accounts for. Lastly, a financial metric that is very popular is the "inventory turn" or "stock turn," which divides the net sales (in $) over a given period by the average inventory valuation (also in $) for that period. This ratio effectively states how many times the items in that inventory "turned over," or were replaced, over the course of a period. While simple and popular, stock turns are based on arbitrary financial valuations and are often subject to manipulation, so need to be treated with caution.

We will return to measuring process performance in Chapter 7.

3.9 Industrial economics: processes and business strategy

So far in this book, we have explored the nature of different processes and certain important characteristics of those processes (e.g. volume and variety). We have noted that different processes have different strengths and weaknesses. It remains to marry these various processes that we have discussed to the needs of the company. Which processes should be used to produce particular products or to deliver particular services? Given the range of choice possible, the answers are far from obvious.

Analyzing this question opens up a wealth of issues about how profit is generated and what the role of the process is in generating that profit. Here is where company strategy meets process design. Understanding the *economics* of the industry is fundamental to the marriage of process to need. So, as economists would, we begin with a discussion of industry demand and supply.

Much of business strategy emanates from the economics of an industry. Consider Figure 3.11. The figure displays the demand and supply curves for an industry. The equilibrium price line assumes perfect competition.

The industry demand curve is the array of consumers who could potentially purchase some units of what is produced. At the upper left are those who are willing to pay a lot for the right to own a unit of production. At the lower right are those who do not value the output much at all. Similarly, the industry supply curve is the array of producers in the industry, with the low-cost producers on the lower left. As you progress rightward, the costs of production increase—secondary shift work, less productive capacity—until, at the right-hand end, costs jump up vertically because, in the short run, no more output is forthcoming, at any price.

The area below the industry demand curve and above the equilibrium price line is conventionally termed the consumers' surplus. It represents the value that consumers enjoy because they only have to pay the going price and they were all willing to pay more. The area above the industry supply curve and below the price line is similarly labeled as the producers' surplus. It captures the extra revenue that the lower-cost producers earn once their costs are covered. Think of it as profit. As output increases and the margin between

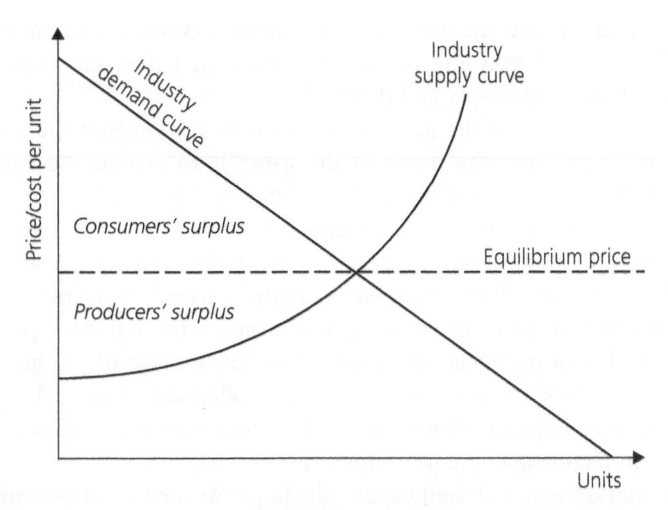

Figure 3.11 Industry economics and its impact on strategy.

supply and demand narrows, profit evaporates and the price and output of the industry are determined.

This figure can do much to characterize the dynamics of business strategy and its implications for operations management. The major area of contention is the producers' surplus. Naturally, a company wants the producers' surplus itself to be large and growing over time, and its share of that surplus to be as large as possible. Thus, being a low-cost producer and being in a growth industry with demand curves that are continually moving outward are obvious advantages. The former means more profit for the company and the latter means more total profit for all producers.

What are to be avoided, of course, are instances where the producers' surplus declines and situations where one's low-cost producer status is forfeited. The entry of new firms is the feared alternative. New firms can be lower cost and can thus displace the existing producers on the leftmost portion of the supply curve. And the entry of new firms shifts the supply curve outward and, depending on the slope of the demand curve, that may well squeeze the total area of producers' surplus, so that less total profit is enjoyed by ever more producing firms. No wonder that barriers to entry are prized.

Deregulation is a classic way by which the entry of strong new competitors can occur. Regulation, on the other hand, can lead to the opposite result. Regulation can help a firm lock into a good position within the industry supply curve and/or limit new entry. Regulation and deregulation can be very disruptive, however. They can alter the shape of the industry supply curve. Importantly, too, firms that were low-cost producers under one regime can wake up after regulation or deregulation and find themselves supplanted by other producers that are now the low-cost ones. Strongly competitive companies are vigilant about regulation and deregulation and what they can mean for the dynamics of industry supply and demand.

Much as the name of the game for operations is to exploit the producers' surplus, for marketing the name of the game is to exploit the consumers' surplus. Sometimes consumers can be isolated and induced to pay more for selected units of the good (e.g. revenue management for airline or hotel reservations). And sometimes market segmentation can shatter an industry demand curve into a host of smaller demand curves, where marketing can hope that different price levels can prevail. Industries that once produced a limited number of products now produce an entire range of products. Think of the proliferation of products or seasonal collections during the past few decades in any number of industries. The auto industry, fashion, or even drinks manufacturing come to mind here.

When market segmentation occurs, the hope for the operations function is that it is low-cost enough to find itself on the left-hand end of the new, segmented supply curve. There it can reap good profits. But, with segmentation, more may be demanded of the operations function than low cost. The market segment may emphasize customization. Or it may emphasize rapid delivery, or lots of product innovation. Just to be a "player" in the new segment may require considerable competitive skills that are different from the typical focus on just low-cost production.

Whatever the scope of the demand curve (industry-wide or market segment-specific), what is to be feared is the substitute good, perhaps from a new producer, that can shrivel the prevailing industry demand curve (or the particular market segment's demand curve), introduce an entirely new demand curve in its place, and shrink the total profit available for the established firms in the industry. The substitute product could also alter the slope of the original product's demand curve so that demand becomes more price elastic and the area of consumers' surplus declines.

Figure 3.11 shows the dashed line of price determined via perfect competition. With sufficient rivalry among the producing companies and limited bargaining power among all the economic actors involved, that line can be an appropriate estimate of the prevailing industry price. However, if the rivalry among competitors is not strong, or if the bargaining power of consumers (or, more likely, large, selected consumers) is great, then the price level that actually prevails can be lower than that implied by perfect competition, and a company's profit could suffer. Alternatively, if a company's suppliers have significant bargaining power, then the share of the producers' surplus retained by the company itself could be lower than expected, as more is taken by the suppliers. In such a situation, the value of vertical integration—being your own supplier—is enhanced.

Figure 3.11 can thus illuminate many of the scenarios where corporate strategy can be played out and can then affect a company's operations strategy. Here are some scenarios where a firm's share of producers' surplus can be greater:

- Where barriers to entry prevent new entrants, particularly new low-cost entrants, from coming into the industry
- Where the industry itself is growing rapidly (the demand curve is shifting outward)
- Where regulation has limited new entry and/or helped to guarantee a set producers' surplus
- Where regulation or deregulation has positioned the firm as a lower-cost producer along the industry supply curve
- Where the firm's command over new technology is significant and/or its management skills are substantial, so the firm can position itself on the lower portions of the industry supply curve
- Where marketing has successfully segmented markets so that the firm can become a low-cost producer in at least one of the new segmented markets
- Where the firm has strong bargaining power over its suppliers, or is itself vertically integrated backward, and thus can hold on to much of the producers' surplus that it wins for itself
- Where rivalry among firms in the market is not strong, and thus where the prevailing price can be maintained above the equilibrium price that perfect competition would ensure
- Where there are no strong substitute products that could shrink the existing demand curve (i.e. move it leftward) or establish another demand curve in its place, and thus reduce the size of the original producers' surplus
- Where there are no strong consumers whose bargaining strength could lower the prevailing price.

Similarly, of course, there is a mirror set of scenarios where the firm's share of the producers' surplus can decline.

The point of this economic analysis is that process choice can greatly affect the profitability of the company. Knowing what drives the economics of the industry and the company's place in the industry is critical to process choice and the management of operations generally.

NOTES

1. B.P. Shapiro, V.K. Rangan, and J.J. Sviokla, 1992. Staple yourself to an order. *Harvard Business Review*, 70(4), pp.113–22.
2. Throughput time reduction, together with the reduction of variation, is at the heart of the concept of swift, even flow, which is our Principle #8 (see Section 10.2).

FURTHER READING

Rother, M. and Shook, J., 1998. *Learning to See*. Lean Enterprise Institute (Cambridge, MA).

Schmenner, R.W., 1993. *Production/Operations Management: From the Inside Out*, 5th edition. Macmillan (New York).

Schmenner, R.W., 1998. *Plant and Service Tours in Production/Operations Management*, 5th edition. Prentice-Hall (Englewood Cliffs, NJ).

Upton, D., 1997. Why (and how) to take a plant tour. *Harvard Business Review*, 75(3), pp.97–106.

4 Variation, capacity, and throughput

With an understanding of what various kinds of processes are like and how they differ from one another, let us examine the design of processes, the first element in our structure of Design–Measurement–Improvement. The second principle, the first one that concerns process design, involves variation.

Before that, however, it is important to distinguish variation from a range of related terms—many of which are often used interchangeably. Variation is the measured deviation from an expected outcome. It is a statistical description of how likely an outcome is to deviate from the average outcome. Variability could be used as a synonym for variation, but in most cases refers to the upper and lower boundaries within which variation takes place. Uncertainty, on the other hand, does not carry the same statistical connotation, and describes the lack of confidence in expecting an event or change to take place. It is the most generic term of the three.

In relation to variation, we formulate our second principle:

Principle #2: Variation is inherent in all process inputs, tasks, and outputs.

Processes are awash in variation, and variation constrains any process that it touches. It is important here to distinguish two types of variation: common cause and assignable cause variation. This distinction is based on Walter Shewhart's seminal work from the 1920s, when he observed that variation in process outcome had two components: the first is *common cause* variation, which is random and cannot be predicted. It is noise, essentially. And then there is *special cause* or *assignable cause* variation, which is non-random variation caused by one or more identifiable factors with clearly defined characteristics. Such variation is eminently manageable. This is the signal in the system (see Appendix H for details on capability, control, and Six Sigma).

Variation can occur in three forms: *quality*, *quantity*, and *timing*. We will discuss them in turn below, and note a first subprinciple.

Principle #2: Variation is inherent in all process inputs, tasks, and outputs.
a. Variation can occur in quality, quantity, and timing.

4.1 **Variation in quality**

The quality of a product (either manufactured product or service product) refers to the degree to which its production conforms to predetermined specifications. As Chapter 1 related, the quest for quality over the years has been dominated by the search for ways to replicate a product's constituent parts perfectly. Completely interchangeable parts is a relatively new phenomenon, and it is only with the reasonable assurance of interchangeable parts in the early decades of the twentieth century that the statistical approach to quality that is now so widely practiced could come to the fore.

In this day and time, it is easy to treat quality management as a strictly statistical exercise, when in fact so much of quality assurance assumes that the basics of equipment operation and materials uniformity—what the pioneers of the modern corporation worked so hard to achieve—are well known and followed diligently. If they are not, the remedy to a quality problem is often a back-to-basics one where following the manual or other instructions and employing some common sense takes precedence.

This said, the statistical analysis of quality has reaped tremendous rewards. One should never take for granted the power of being able to distinguish random variation in the production of an item from an assignable cause for a quality problem. Hunches need never return to the realm of quality management.

There are a host of quality tools that can easily be adopted by both manufacturing and service processes. The key ones are well known, as shown in Table 4.1.

It is not the purpose of this book to expound on these well-known mechanisms to improve quality. They have been much written about. Suffice it

Table 4.1 A list of key quality tools

Quality tool	Application
Pareto diagram	Frequency diagram of the recognized problems. Shows what is important to work on.
Check sheet, histogram	Basic mechanisms to collect quality-related data and make sense of it.
Fishbone (Ishikawa) diagram	Systematic portrayal of potential causes for some effect (problem) so that more investigation can proceed.
Capability study	Analysis of the distribution of process results relative to the acknowledged specifications for the item, to determine if the process can create the item according to the specifications, without having to sort bad from good.
Control chart	Uses samples to determine whether the process is producing quality items. It can distinguish random variation in the process from unwanted variation that is due to some specific, assignable cause.
Experimentation	Scientific means by which the causes for particular quality problems can be isolated; the Taguchi experiment is one variant of the technique.
Analysis of variance	Statistical means by which data can be analyzed in order to attribute the variation experienced in a process to its various causes.

simply to observe how useful they have been in analyzing and then controlling quality in many different settings.

These quality tools, however, are data-intensive and operate after the fact. An alternative, lower-cost way to great quality is preventive in nature. Mistake-proofing, or poka-yoke in Japanese (sometimes ineptly called "fool-proofing"), is the low-cost way to achieve great quality and, regrettably, it is seldom used to its fullest. Making effective use of mistake-proofing often means incorporating it into the design of the product and into the process that produces it. That takes far-sightedness. But it is something that can yield benefits far in excess of its costs. Mistake-proofing often takes very simple forms: designs that are asymmetrical, highly visual layouts for tools/materials, checklists to follow, limit switches, electric eyes, vision systems, and other often low-tech mechanisms. The idea is to make sure that value is always added in the proper way, or that value is not added to something that is not in spec. It is an idea that will never go out of fashion.

A lot of mistake-proofing is seen in the daily workings of service operations. Table 4.2 contains a selection of examples of mistake-proofing, identified as either mistake-proofing directed to the process or mistake-proofing directed to the customer.

In many companies, these tools for assuring quality and for investigating quality problems exist within specific quality improvement programs. Quality management systems themselves are, however, subject to fashion, or so it has occurred over the years. In the period after World War II, the management of quality was frequently relegated to the quality control (QC) or quality assurance (QA) department. Quality was primarily seen as an exercise in inspection. Then, along came the Zero Defects program, where error prevention became important. After the rediscovery of quality by Western companies, around 1980, quality was seen to be so important that it needed to migrate out of the QC/QA department and be embraced by the entire company. People all around the company needed to be trained in the use of quality tools and put to the task of making improvements to company processes everywhere.

Table 4.2 Poka-yoke or mistake-proofing: examples

Process-based	Customer-based
French fry scoop	Reminder cards for appointments
Surgical trays with indentations	"Menu" boards
Color codes	Telephone menu prompts
Software prompts for data	Special uniforms as cues for customers
Sequential numbering of customers	Directions mailed ahead of time
Rehearsed opening lines for service encounter	Boarding passes etc. accessed online
Layouts that "force" people to move in one way	Different diameter nozzles for fuels

Thus was born the Total Quality Management (TQM) movement. The movement made much progress and became the inspiration for the Baldrige National Quality Award in the US and the European Foundation for Quality Management Award.

In the TQM philosophy, quality is everyone's responsibility. Everyone needs to be trained in the tools of quality. This view of quality follows very much the criteria for the awards. The EFQM Excellence Award structure is shown in Figure 4.1.

Since its heyday in the 1990s, however, Total Quality Management has waned as a movement. The number of companies applying for the awards has dropped. Yet, in its wake, another philosophy of quality has been in the ascendant: Six Sigma.

Although Six Sigma was originally developed by Motorola, an early Baldrige Award winner, there are some distinctions between TQM and Six Sigma that are worth remarking. While TQM suffuses the entire company with the mandate to improve quality, Six Sigma takes a more structured and centralized approach. At the heart of Six Sigma are the "black belts" and "green belts" that work on quality improvement projects. The statistical tools for both philosophies are the same. It is only the organization that differs.

For us, quality management appears to be on a pendulum that swings from more centralized control to more decentralized control and back. This may be

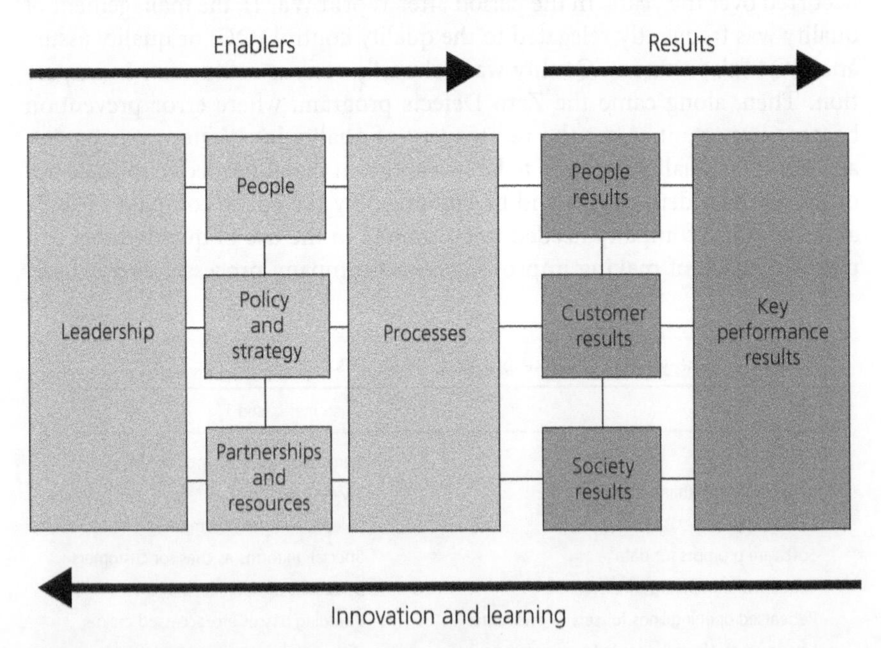

Figure 4.1 The EFQM Excellence Award structure.

an entirely understandable phenomenon. While we can acknowledge the logic that quality should be everyone's responsibility, getting things done often requires some delegation. And while delegation is often convenient, it risks being taken for granted. When too many people view quality as the realm of the black belts and not their own concern, it may be time for the pendulum to move back to a more decentralized approach such as TQM.

4.2 Variation in quantity and time

Less well appreciated than variation in quality is variation in quantity and time, which both have similar effects and thus we will discuss these conjointly. In its simplest form, this variation can be seen with two workstations, one passing on some work-in-process to the other. Assume a direct hand-off. If both workstations take exactly one minute to do the work, all will be well and the maximum output will be produced. However, if there is any variation at all in either of the workstations, the output produced will be less than the maximum. Why? The answer lies with blocking and starving. If the first workstation finishes its work before the second workstation, it will be unable to pass on its work-in-process. The enforced idleness that results can be termed blocking. The workstation is blocked from continuing. On the other hand, if the second workstation completes its work before the first one, it will have nothing to work on until the first workstation passes on the work-in-process. The second workstation is starved for work.

How much less than the maximum will be produced depends, among other things, on the degree of variation in the work times of the workstations. If the distribution of work times is widely spread, with no upper bounds, output will really suffer. The negative exponential distribution, which has no upper bound, is a frequently used, and naturally occurring, distribution that can sap considerable capacity from a process. (It is useful because it can describe many different business situations, such as customers entering a retail store.) If, on the other hand, the distribution is more constrained and tight, the drop in capacity will be less.

Variation in quantities and timing affect both the demand and supply sides of the operation. The customer's demands on the process can be variable, requesting quantities that can vary substantially from order to order and timing those orders in an erratic way, with delivery dates that can be erratic in themselves. Likewise, the process itself can suffer variation in quantities and timing. The output of the process may not be steady and may not produce predictable quantities. Yields might vary greatly and the availability of materials may itself be variable. And the work times for doing particular tasks that are called for by the design of the product can be a major source of variation.

Of course, some processes lend themselves to coping with variation in quantity and time more readily than others. The job shop, for example, is designed to facilitate such variation. Like equipment is grouped together so that product routings can easily return to the same sort of machine for work. All of the paperwork needed for guiding the job through the shop travels with the job. The workforce is skilled in setting up and running a wide variety of equipment. This is not so readily the case with the continuous flow process or the assembly line. Although some alterations in quantities produced and in their timing can be accommodated, this kind of flexibility needs considerable lead time.

The flexibility of the job shop comes at a price, however. That price is capacity utilization, as a later principle will make plain. For the job shop and other processes such as professional services to be as flexible as they are, there needs to be substantial spare capacity. A trip to a job shop should always reveal idle capacity. Having, and keeping, idle capacity on hand is a difficult concept for most managers to appreciate though. The inclination is always to squeeze in one more job, without reflecting on the consequences. Nevertheless, this inclination must be resisted if flexibility and good customer service are to be maintained.

The quest for flexibility is the province of production planning and control. Here the battle for reduced variation comes up against the massive leaps in flexibility that have resulted from technological progress in both equipment and software. Companies can now offer more varieties of their products at relatively lower cost than ever before. Moreover, it is now also easier for a company to alter its production plan at short notice. It is then obviously tempting to think that offering wide variety should be done routinely, and seemingly at the drop of a hat. Resisting this temptation takes real discipline. That wide variety can be offered does not imply that it should be offered. Although flexibility costs less than in the past, it still is more costly than standardization.

The more dramatic instance of variation in quantities and timing occurs in supply chains. Here, the ballyhooed bullwhip effect can cause frightful swings in the demands on the upstream portions of the supply chain. Small variations in the downstream elements of the supply chain, under the wrong conditions, can cause massive fluctuations for, say, the factory upstream. What is more, the wrong conditions—independence of the stages of the supply chain, orders that are bigger than they need to be, myopia that deals with one stage of the supply chain at a time and does not manage the supply chain as a whole—are easier to fall into than many suspect.

Variation in quantities and timing can be pervasive in services, and, furthermore, it can hurt service processes more because services typically cannot inventory product like a manufacturer can. To cope, many services try to manage customers instead. Reservation systems, peak and off-peak pricing, and complementary service offerings are all ways by which customers can be managed and the variation in quantities and timing lowered.

Of these two sorts of variation, variation in timing is the more troubling. It is more important that the process be regular in its timing than regular in the quantity it produces. Typically, the process can be scheduled to run a little bit longer, or a little bit shorter, so as to produce the quantities required of each of the products of interest. However, when the process' week-to-week and day-to-day schedule becomes more or less random, many critical aspects of the process can suffer (e.g. productivity, quality).

4.3 Coping with variation

There are a variety of coping mechanisms that have been developed to thwart the deleterious consequences of variation in quantities and timing. Buffers are principal ones. Buffers exist in three forms:

1. **Inventory**: holding more stock in the form of raw materials, work-in-process, or finished goods (or a combination of all these) provides the firm with a greater ability to respond to variation in demand.
2. **Capacity**: providing extra resources in terms of additional machine or labor capacity avoids holding excess inventory buffers, and allows the firm to respond to demand variation by ramping production up and down accordingly.
3. **Time**: using time as a buffer essentially means to use "slack" in customer due dates to pull orders forward and make them earlier when demand on capacity is low, or to postpone orders where possible, to times when capacity utilization is lower. In essence, flexibility inherent in the order profile is used to even out demand swings, to balance loads, and thus avoid situations of over- and under-utilization.

We note a further subprinciple:

Principle #2: Variation is inherent in all process inputs, tasks, and outputs.

a. Variation can occur in quality, quantity, and timing.
b. Variation in a process can be buffered by a combination of any of the following three means: time, inventory, and capacity.

Inventory buffers situated between workstations can lessen the impact of blocking and starving. The larger the buffer inventories, the less destructive the blocking and starving and the greater the capacity. However, it should be noted that a little buffering often goes a long way. Huge buffer inventories are not needed. There is a real diminishing marginal return to them.

Buffer lead times are also used, typically as part of the material requirements planning (MRP) modules of enterprise resource planning (ERP) systems. As will be plain once we address the issue of productivity, buffer lead times are much less desirable than buffer inventories. In addition, buffer lead times can contribute to increased variation in timing, and, as mentioned above, variation in timing is the more troubling source of variation.

Beyond buffering, there are coping strategies: aggregation and grouping, postponement or late configuration, and decoupling. Grouping like products/parts together and segregating them from others has been an effective way to cope with variation by reducing it. This mechanism has led to the creation of the "cell." The cell has helped to lower costs. Japanese manufacturers, in particular, have been leaders in its development. It has revolutionized our thinking about the common batch-line flow hybrid process.

A batch-line flow hybrid "decouples" the production plan for the assembly line from the production plan for the batch fabrication. The assembly line is typically planned to meet the market requirements that the company foresees. The fabrication operation, on the other hand, is not seen as flexible enough to be scheduled in the same way. Rather, the batches produced are large, to reduce the set-up/changeover time. And while, over the long run, the quantities produced and consumed are matched, over the short run they are not.

Cells concentrate on families of parts and put particular effort into set-up reduction so that small lot sizes of those product/part families can be run easily. By doing this, the decoupling inventory can be removed from the process. The demands of the marketplace can then trigger both the assembly line schedule and the part fabrication schedule. The cells can be married directly to the main assembly line. Sometimes the cells married in this way to the main assembly line are configured as U-shaped lines and sometimes they are configured as more conventionally straight lines.

Each cell typically has a mix of all the equipment needed to produce the family of parts or subassemblies. Some equipment will be used more than others; that is only natural. What is critical is that the cell, as a unit, keeps up with the speed of the assembly line. Cells force the re-layout of the operation. That, in itself, is often an effective way to cope with variation, simply by lessening the movement of materials through the operation.

VARIATION AND CAPACITY

It is essential to understand what variation does to the output of a process. Variation saps capacity from a process—any process. Quality problems, for example, often bog down a process as workers and managers try to figure out what is going wrong and then spend the time and resources needed to fix it. There may be rework to do, and that takes resources as well. Scrap may have occurred that needs to be removed and materials replenished. Waste of all sorts spills over the process.

Variation in quantities and timing also saps capacity from a process. When processes and their component process stages are subject to substantial variation, some stages within the process may be starved for work to do while other stages may be blocked from passing on their completed work. To cope with such variation, a process may be sized larger than it otherwise needs to be, with more space, inventories, and labor. Buffer inventories and buffer lead times may be ubiquitous. Such buffers may be needed. But their very presence indicates that output is likely to be less than it otherwise could have been.

Producing that output, despite the handicaps that might prevail, is central to operations management. Processes serve an important end, the production of goods and services. Getting more out of the process is the manager's constant goal. Although capacity can seldom be known precisely, the search for it is fundamental to operations management. With capacity, the needs of customers can be fulfilled. With enough capacity at the proper locations in the process, inventories can be avoided. Without capacity, markets may have to be abandoned and customers turned away.

The reason capacity is seldom known with precision is because so many things can influence the calculation (e.g. nature of bottlenecks, mix of products to be produced, yields, variability in quantities produced and in timing). Each stage of a process can have its own capacity, and every stage runs the risk of being the limiting constraint on the capacity of the entire process. Not only do the individual stages of the process pose limits to capacity, but how the stages interact with one another, given the variations each are subject to, can limit the capacity of the entire process. What is clear is that the actual capacity of a process is always less than the calculated average capacities that the various elements, or steps, of the process may show "on paper." Variation guarantees this result.

Although capacities cannot be known with precision, estimates of the capacities of process stages and of the entire process itself can be made and relied on for practical purposes. This is solace for the operations manager. More than this, the prospect of squeezing more output out of the process, and thus at the same time creating profit where none existed before, is an enticement with endless appeal.

4.4 **Inventory management**

INVENTORY: CAUSE *AND* EFFECT

Inventory is by default a visual representation of what is going on in the process, and therefore a common focus of attention in manufacturing.

The general notion is that inventory should be avoided where possible, as it causes costs and problems. For one, the capital invested in the inventory represents an opportunity cost, but furthermore, handling and quality problems quickly add to the cost of inventory (see Appendix C for more detail). So it is understandable that inventory reduction is such a prominent objective in manufacturing.

Yet it is important to understand inventory as both *cause* and *effect*: inventory is there for a reason. First and foremost, the amount of inventory is determined by scheduling decisions (see Section 3.7). The larger the batches one orders or manufactures, the larger the average inventory level will be. Furthermore, inventory is a common and effective buffer against uncertainty. The more uncertainty in terms of supply problems, machine breakdowns, or quality problems, the larger buffer inventory is needed. This effect is captured in the "rock–boat" analogy (see Section 8.3).

In essence, inventory is a cost driver, and excess inventory is to be avoided where possible. But before trying to reduce it, understand the reasons for it being there in the first place, and start attacking these. Inventory reduction without tackling the root causes is unlikely to be sustainable.

OBJECTIVES AND PHILOSOPHIES

Raw materials inventories, work-in-process inventories, and finished goods inventories all play different roles in the operation. As we have seen, the importance of those roles depends on the process. Managers should be clear about the major functions of these types of inventory for their particular processes.

The major functions of *raw materials inventory* are:

- To protect (as a buffer) against the unreliable or variable delivery of needed raw materials.
- To hold costs down if possible by buying large quantities or by buying raw materials at propitious times.

The major functions of *work-in-process inventory* are:

- To protect (as a buffer) against the unreliable or variable delivery of materials from elsewhere in the production process.
- To permit one segment of the process to operate under a different production plan and schedule from another segment of the process (a decoupling inventory).
- To permit individual workstations or machine centers to produce parts/assemblies/materials in sizable batches, rather than individually or in smaller batches. Such "cycle" inventories act to tide the process over until the next set-up.

The major functions of *finished goods inventory* are:

- To supply the product quickly to the consumer.
- To protect (as a buffer) against the uncertainties of consumer demand.
- To smooth (through the accumulation of finished goods inventory) the demands on the process even while demand is erratic or temporarily depressed.

At the same time, inventory of any kind represents a major cost—not just in terms of capital requirements and related opportunity cost (see Appendix C for an overview). Therefore, inventories of all kinds need to be managed.

The tools that production managers can wield in dealing with work-in-process inventories are frequently very different from the tools they can use to control raw materials or finished goods inventories. As we shall soon see, the available techniques for controlling either raw materials inventories or finished goods inventories are relatively well developed and widely known. Because of this, it is often taken for granted that these inventories are managed adequately; when many production managers think about managing inventories, they think about work-in-process inventories. Here the management tools are more ill-defined, since reducing work-in-process inventory generally means grappling with the production process itself and/or with the flow of information through it. To control work-in-process inventory levels, the manager might contemplate ways to shorten production throughput times (such as shortening process steps or coupling operations more closely), or ways to break existing production bottlenecks, or ways to improve the flow of information around the process. We will address the management of work-in-process inventories in Chapter 8 on process improvement.

So far, we have classified inventory solely according to its place in the process (raw materials, work-in-process, finished goods). There are other classifications possible. One useful one was developed by Joseph Orlicky, who distinguished between inventories of dependent demand items and independent demand items. Independently demanded items are typically finished goods or other items whose demands are unrelated to anything else produced or sold by the company (e.g. repair parts, production-related as opposed to product-related goods). Dependently demanded items, on the other hand, are those that can be directly linked to a specific product—typically, they are components and subassemblies that can be linked to an end item by a bill of materials. In such a case, demand for the end item automatically triggers demand for known quantities of the parts and materials that go into the product.

This distinction is useful because dependent demands fall out naturally from knowledge of their end items—there are no uncertainties—whereas independent demands are full of uncertainties as to both quantities required and timing desired. The inventory policies applicable to independently demanded items can be very different from the inventory policies applicable to dependently demanded items. For the most part, the management of finished goods inventories and, to a lesser extent, raw materials inventories is management of independently demanded items.

AN ANTICIPATORY APPROACH TO THE MANAGEMENT OF INVENTORIES: MRP

An anticipatory approach to inventory management has its most powerful application with dependent demand, although it can be used for end items as well as component parts and subassemblies. In this approach, commonly called material requirements planning (MRP), a company manages its inventories by anticipating their use and planning order sizes and timing accordingly to keep the stocks at some desired, low level.[1] One ideal for such an anticipatory approach to inventory is to have no finished goods inventory over and above that expressly planned for, and little or no raw materials inventory. Work-in-process inventories then would account for by far the greatest chunk of total inventory costs. What is needed to accomplish this anticipatory approach to inventory is a firm fix on exactly what products are to be produced and when, what materials go into making each product, when in the production cycle each part or material is used, and how long it takes suppliers to deliver these parts or materials. This is a lot of information, but every bit is needed if in fact inventories are going to be matched to a company's output. In more formal phrasing, such an approach to inventory management demands the following pieces of information:

- *Master production schedule (MPS).* When each product is scheduled to be manufactured. Usually the MPS is developed for either a month or a week. The firmness by which the schedule is held to can vary markedly from company to company and from time to time. These data "drive" the entire system. Often the system also keeps track of which orders are associated with which demands in the schedule ("pegging").
- *Bills of materials for each product.* Exactly which parts or materials are required to make each product. Each product variant needs its own bill of materials so that the demands for all the individual component parts can be detailed.
- *Inventory status of each component part.* How many of each part are on hand, and how many are scheduled to be received prior to use?
- *Lead times for all parts to be purchased or fabricated.* Their availability can then be timed exactly to meet anticipated needs.
- *Product construction standard times and schedules.* This information details how long (in standard hours) particular tasks can be expected to take and indicates when specific parts or subassemblies will be needed in order to

meet the established master schedule for the end product. This information is useful for scheduling materials as well as for assessing the capacity of the factory to produce the contemplated product mix.

- *Routings of parts to particular work centers.* These routings indicate which work centers (machine tools, assembly lines, departments) are involved in the manufacture of each product or product variation. This information is critical to the capacity planning function, for which an MRP system can be used. This adaptation of MRP is discussed later in this section.
- *Standard costs (optional).* Given standard costs for particular parts and subassemblies, an MRP system can be used to calculate inventory investments and to estimate product costs for any modification to the bill of materials' product structure. This adaptation of MRP is also discussed later in this section.

These pieces of information work together to determine what should be ordered and when. The MPS, together with the bill of materials, determines what should be ordered; the MPS, the production cycle times, and the supplier lead times jointly determine when the order should be placed.

These elements form an anticipatory approach to inventory management, which lies at the heart of MRP. MRP can become quite a bit more involved than this in actual practice, but at its roots lies this relatively simple notion of managing raw materials stocks by anticipating their use.

TIME-INDEPENDENT SYSTEMS

An alternative to the anticipatory approach of MRP is the more traditional time-independent systems. It is not too far off the mark to visualize the problem of managing either raw materials inventory or finished goods inventory as one of managing piles of "stuff" that either the process itself or consumers in the marketplace draw down. The objective of good inventory management in this case is to offer good service to either the process or the market at reasonably low cost. This objective, in turn, means deciding how many items should be in each pile, when orders to replenish the piles ought to be placed, and how much each of those orders should contain. Managing such inventory stocks (as opposed to managing work-in-process) essentially means deciding these three questions of pile size, order time, and order size.

Because the timing of independent demands is often so uncertain, the techniques typically used for managing inventories of such demands are themselves independent of time. These techniques are sometimes called non-time-phased inventory systems, meaning simply that they do not attempt to be so precise about timing orders to expected use. Their purpose is the same, however: to replenish a pile of items in timely fashion and at reasonably low cost. Retailing and distribution activities easily lend themselves to such techniques; in these areas, consumer demands are frequently variable and uncertain.

The two major non-time-phased techniques have these differing philosophies:

1. Replenish the pile on a regular basis (daily, weekly, monthly) and bring it back up to the size you want, usually enough to carry one to the next replenishment. The amount by which you replenish the pile may vary from one time to another, but you always replenish the pile. This basic strategy is often called a *periodic reorder system*.
2. Keep a constant watch over the pile. When its size dips to a predetermined level (typically enough to last until the next delivery), replenish the pile enough to bring it back up to the size you desire. Under this philosophy, the amount by which you replenish the pile stays the same, but the time spans between replenishments may vary. This basic strategy is frequently termed a *reorder point system*, the "reorder point" being the predetermined level that, once reached, triggers the replenishment of the pile by the same amount, typically computed as the economic order quantity (EOQ—see Appendix E for a general overview of trade-off models). The EOQ is frequently easy to compute, and hence it is overused. It is not a very effective way to develop lot quantities for production, but it is often used that way. It assumes instant replenishment, and, as noted earlier, regularity in timing (such as occurs with the periodic reorder system logic) is much more important than regularity in quantities (as is the case with the reorder point system logic of EOQ). As we point out in Appendix E, it has many flaws and should be avoided wherever possible.

4.5 Throughput rate, inventories, and throughput time

The throughput rate is the rate at which output is made. It is the speed of the process. Throughput time is the "clock time" it takes to journey from beginning to end of the process.

Throughput rate, work-in-process inventory, and throughput time are all related. The relationship is typically termed Little's Law, after John D. Little who advanced it in 1961, although in that context Little was interested in the queuing phenomenon, with its arrival rates, time in the system, and number in the system.[2] Little's Law is a relationship that is very common sense, and, importantly, it does not matter what the distribution of the throughput rate is.

This useful relationship forms our Principle #3:

Principle #3: Work-in-process is determined by throughput rate and throughput time.

Thus, if the throughput rate is thirty pieces per hour (one every two minutes) and it takes two hours for the product to flow through the production system, the quantity of work-in-process inventory will be sixty units. The formula can also be turned on its head to estimate the throughput time, knowing the level of work-in-process and the throughput rate. For example, if the work-in-process is 100 units and the throughput rate is twenty per hour, the throughput time will be five hours (see Appendix D for more detail).

Little's Law assumes that the process is stable. That usually means that the throughput rate is a stable rate. It may be subject to variation of one sort or another, but its output is produced at a fairly stable rate.

Naturally, managers may want to increase the throughput rate, say by adding capacity or by altering the process itself. For a time, then, Little's Law would not hold. When stability returns, however, Little's Law will reassert itself. If, for example, the throughput rate is increased, and work-in-process inventory is held the same, then it must be true that the throughput time drops. Materials must flow through the process quicker.

Similarly, if the throughput time is reduced and work-in-process inventory is held the same, then the throughput rate must have increased. That may be because equipment in the process now operates faster, but it may also mean that waste has been driven out of the system and the work-in-process inventory spends less time with nothing done to it. Many processes have been re-engineered in just this way, with waste driven out, even though the same equipment remains in place. Given that in many processes the actual value-added time is only 5 percent or so of the time that work-in-process inventory spends in the process, anything that eliminates some of the waste in the process will increase the throughput rate.

Little's Law also comes into play when managers seek to reduce inventory. Inventory soaks up working capital and is highly visible on the shop floor, so often simplistic objectives are given out, for example to "cut inventory by 50 percent." This is dangerous, as one can quickly cut below minimum work-in-process levels, and starve the process. As Little's Law states, the best way to reduce inventory is in fact not to reduce inventory, but to reduce processing time by cutting out waste from the process. Little's Law can thus tie together increases in the throughput rate (i.e. a gain in productivity) with decreases in the waste inherent in the process (i.e. things that keep the throughput time from declining). More will be said on this point when we discuss Principle #8.

THE SEARCH FOR THROUGHPUT

We have seen what it takes to squeeze more throughput out of a process. The resourceful operations manager is:

- constantly on the lookout for bottlenecks that can be broken cheaply, even if it means adding labor
- eager to remove non-value-added steps and any inventories that are clogging the process
- willing to rebalance a line, if need be
- willing to re-layout the process if that is found to be an obstruction
- willing to study the work to be done and the workstation that does it for improvements in the process (time and motion study)
- aware of which bottlenecks are stationary (and thus easier to deal with) and which are moveable (and thus a bit tougher); willing to coddle with material and labor the bottlenecks that cannot be broken
- committed to preventive maintenance
- sensitive to the production plan so that big fluctuations in the plan—fluctuations that could cause moveable bottlenecks—are reduced; more level production plans are valued, especially if those production plans mirror well the sales made
- willing to reduce the number of stock-keeping units, if need be, to trim complexity and cost from the system
- willing to create cells that can reduce the level of variation in the process and thus produce families of parts or products more productively than before
- attuned to the yields within the process and willing to invest in efforts to raise those yields when it is both feasible and cost-effective, and to otherwise improve quality so as to reduce scrap and rework
- attentive to variation that may be created by customers themselves, and thus willing to manage those customers and their demands, for instance by reservation systems or special pricing
- clear about the relationship between work-in-process inventories, throughput time, and throughput rate
- willing to hold work-in-process inventories low and at the same time to lower the throughput time, say by ferreting out waste in the process, so that the throughput rate can be raised.

Such actions are to be preferred to the more indiscriminate purchase of new equipment to raise the throughput rate. Resourceful operations managers squeeze their capital dry before they engage in the more costly purchases that raise capacity but may also raise costs to undesirable levels.

CUSTOMER WAIT AND THE KINGMAN FORMULA

None of us likes to wait, and some of us are even willing to pay more to avoid waiting. How long we have to wait is governed by a formula that is at once intuitive and profound. The time that customers wait for the output of a process can be reduced, but it means paying attention to the rate of production, the variation in the process, and capacity utilization.

What lies behind this truism is known as Kingman's formula, due to John Kingman, a British mathematician, who published it in 1966. It is an approximation for the mean waiting time in a single-server queue (see Appendix G for more details on the formula).

Kingman found that the waiting time in a queue depends on the product of capacity utilization, the variation affecting the process (demand and production itself), and the natural speed of the process (mean service time). The faster the process (i.e. the greater the rate of production and thus the lower the mean service time), the smaller the variability either of the demand striking the process or of the process itself, and the lower the capacity utilization, the shorter is the wait for the customer. These relationships have a lot of appeal. They can best be envisioned on a graph such as Figure 4.2.

Here the capacity utilization, ρ, is measured on the x-axis and the waiting time is measured on the y-axis. The precise dimensions of the waiting time depend on the speed of the process (the mean service time). Two curves are shown on the graph. Both Curves A and B demonstrate that waiting time can explode when capacity utilization gets close to 100 percent. Nevertheless, Curve A is at an advantage to Curve B, as its waiting time, for every level of capacity utilization, is less. The difference between the two curves is due to variation—either variation in the demand on the process or variation in the process itself.

An important consequence of this relationship between variation, utilization, and waiting time is that the waiting time is stochastic, and not deterministic. In other words, the actual wait cannot be calculated, but needs to be predicted as a function of the utilization of the system, and the variation in arrival and processing.

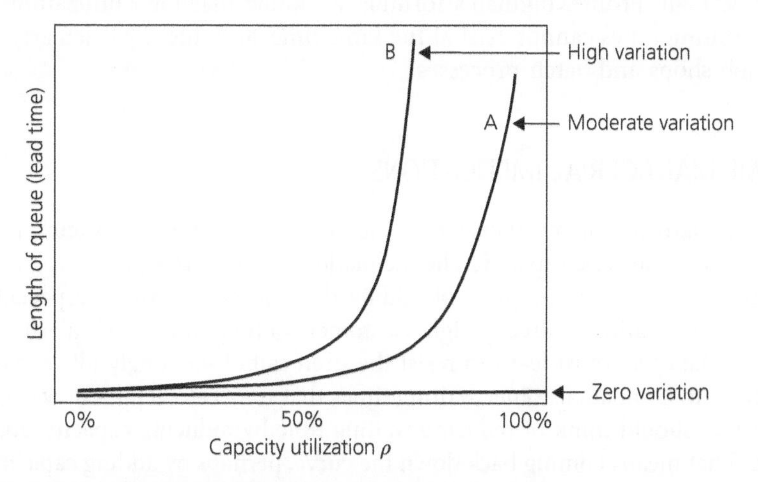

Figure 4.2 A visual representation of Kingman's formula.

We note an important subprinciple:

Principle #3: Work-in-process is determined by throughput rate and throughput time.
a. The throughput time of a process is stochastic, not deterministic.

What kind of process is captured by Curve A and what kind is captured by Curve B? Curve A may well be a continuous flow process or an assembly line. Curve B, on the other hand, may well be a job shop or a batch process. The job shop is the archetypal process that is affected by variation. Orders for jobs with lots of different characteristics for what is to be produced can come in at any time and can specify hugely variable due dates. The quantities in those job orders can be hugely variable. The process steps in a job shop can also vary dramatically. Materials can be routed to lots of different places in the job shop and the times spent at each workstation can vary greatly by job. Both the variation in demand on the process and the variation within the process itself are great in a job shop.

This is not the case with the continuous flow process. In comparison, there is not much variation to it. The continuous flow process is designed to produce nearly identical products in high volumes.

With this in mind, we should expect that the waiting times in job shops and batch processes will be considerably longer than the waiting times for continuous flow processes or assembly lines, for every level of capacity utilization. By the same token, for any level of waiting time for customers, one should expect that the capacity utilization of the job shop or batch process should be lower than the capacity utilization of the continuous flow process or the assembly line. This means that when you enter a job shop, you should expect to see idle equipment. If you do not, then waiting times will be high. From Kingman's formula we know that high utilization and low waiting times cannot exist at the same time, and this is particularly true for job shops and batch processes.

SOME MANAGERIAL IMPLICATIONS

This is hard for many managers to accept. Nature abhors a vacuum, and managers abhor idle capacity. The inclination is always to squeeze in just one more job. However, the price of adding that job can be steep, especially if capacity utilization is already high. Customer waiting time can climb dramatically. Managers must learn to resist the siren call of seemingly idle capacity. Instead, to combat customer waiting times that may be creeping upward, the manager should think of reducing waiting time by reducing capacity utilization. That means coming back down the curve, perhaps by adding capacity or perhaps by withdrawing work from the queue of work-in-process. Reducing variation will help, but it can be a costly option that will not have the impact on waiting time that reducing capacity utilization can have.

The Kingman formula does even more to call into question the use of a relative performance measure such as machine utilization. Utilization, we find from Kingman, provokes a trade-off with customer waiting time. A high value for a measure such as machine utilization may, on the face of it, seem to be a good thing. However, that high value implies a high value as well for the customer's waiting time, and that is not to be relished by management. Better not to think that machine utilization ought to be high. Better, in fact, to ignore it and to think instead of the customer's waiting time and what can be done to lower it.

The Kingman formula informs us that managers can aid themselves in the trade-off between capacity utilization and waiting time by reducing the variation that the process is subject to. Of course, this is often easier said than done—but it can be done. The manufacturing cell is a good example. Cells group together families of parts or products. By definition, variation within families is less than variation between different families. Having identified the families, cells then group together the equipment needed to produce them. Labor is assigned to the cells, and the tasks given to the workforce are frequently more encompassing than the tasks that they left behind in their former batch operation. These tasks can include inspection, materials handling, and maintenance. These are tasks that indirect, overhead functions might have otherwise performed. The operations of the cells are usually much more flexible than the operations of the previous batch processes ever were, and that means that the cells can usually be tied directly to an assembly line. The former inventory that decoupled the batch processes from the assembly line can be abolished and a single, all-encompassing production plan can be substituted for the pair of production plans that formerly controlled the filling of the decoupling inventory and the operation of the assembly line.

This kind of variation-reducing innovation repositions a curve such as Curve B to make it look more like Curve A. It is not a costless innovation by any stretch, but it can often be accomplished without too much investment.

This discussion has referred to variation in manufacturing. Of course, the same phenomenon exists for service operations. Indeed, variation is common in services. Customers interact with service processes all the time, especially in the professional service firm and the service shop. If such services are to be well managed, service processes need to cope with such variation. Service firms may not be able to remove much of the variation that occurs in the process itself; the splendid isolation of the factory has its advantages. However, with reservation systems, pricing to shift services away from peak times, and other policies, services can control at least some of the variation they face that can be caused by the demands customers place on them.

Unfortunately, these tactics do not always work. Services may have to target particularly attractive customers or redesign themselves if they are not to succumb to the harmful features of variation. Beyond this, services may have to increase capacity—this may be their only effective option. The capacity choice for the service firm is one of its most important decisions.

The Kingman formula urges caution upon us when comparing the throughput times of two processes or two series of processes (e.g. supply chains). One's throughput time (i.e. waiting time in the context of the Kingman formula) may differ from process to process. Our initial reaction might be to applaud the quicker one and to advocate that such a process be adopted more widely. Yet, before we do so, we should check to see that the levels of variation and the percentages of capacity utilization are effectively the same for the two processes or supply chains. The difference in throughput times may be due to differences in capacity utilization (e.g. the existence of bottlenecks) or to differences in the variation that the processes are subject to, and not to differences in their production rates.

Thus, the Kingman formula points out forcefully another argument for managers seeking out capacity wherever they can find it. Having capacity avoids stock-outs and the pain that they cause both customers and company, and having sufficient capacity means lower waiting times for customers, often a worthy goal in and of itself.

We will return to the Kingman formula in Chapter 8, as it is also fundamental to process improvement.

4.6 Getting the most out of the process: the matter of throughput

Whatever the design of the process, certain things can destroy its throughput or quality. If one is to get the most out of any existing process, a number of things have to be done well: the operation of the workstations in the process, the layout of those workstations, the balance of capacities represented by those workstations, the breaking of bottlenecks, and the production plans that call on the capacities of the workstations. Let us consider these elements in greater detail. We will focus on manufacturing in this section, simply because most of these concepts have been developed in manufacturing, yet of course they can be applied with some caution to the planning of service operations.

THE WORKSTATION

The building block for the process is the workstation, and this is the first place to examine. It is easy to take the workstation for granted. Because it is used all the time, it is easy to assume that the workstation is well laid out and that its responsibilities have been well studied. This is too often, however, not the case. Appeal to a variety of tools can dramatically improve the functioning of the workstation.

Methods—Methods improvement is too little appreciated in many companies, especially those in the service sector. It is frequently detailed, nitty-gritty work, but it can pay off handsomely. Methods improvement basically requires an open, inquisitive mind, an eye for detail, and a passion for keeping things simple. There are no pat solutions to apply in most instances. Methods improvements usually involve a systematic study of the current methods, an appreciation of what the job really calls for, and a disdain for any explanation that is not thoroughly persuasive.

Over time, many do's and don'ts have evolved about good methods practice, especially as regards the actions of individual workers. Good methods practice is always concerned with what tasks can be eliminated, simplified, combined with other tasks, or changed in sequence. While these kinds of change can frequently be accomplished with little or no investment in new tools, worker aids, or equipment, often methods study will lead to suggestions for capital investments of both large and small scale.

As with most jobs, when one attacks a task systematically, one's productivity is likely to improve. Systematic methods improvement calls for systematic methods study. Formal study of work methods—including concern for raw materials, product design, process design, tooling, plant layout, and the workers' interaction with all of these features—is sometimes referred to as motion study. While attention to methods has always existed, the formal study of work methods in operations is generally associated with the Gilbreths (Frank and Lillian), who in the late nineteenth and early twentieth centuries developed many of the techniques that have done much to improve worker productivity. The Gilbreths had a passion for describing methods precisely through the isolation, identification, and subsequent improvement of the elements of a task.

Paralleling the motion study pioneered by the Gilbreths was the time study of individual worker tasks. The pioneer in this study, as mentioned in Chapter 1, was Frederick Taylor. Much of Taylor's work had a similar intent to that of the Gilbreths—to improve productivity by looking closely at what workers did. However, rather than focus on the motions involved, Taylor broke down the job into elements and timed them. As in motion study, each element was studied to determine what should be kept and what should be discarded, but the stopwatch was the chief aid to the engineer rather than the movie camera or the process chart.

The time standards developed by Taylor have at least five broad applications. They can be used:

- for planning and budgeting
- to balance operations

- to improve performance
- to evaluate individual workers and to serve as a basis for wage payments
- to define the "efficiency" measure which is purported to capture labor productivity (more on this measure in Chapter 7).

Time standards can be developed in a variety of ways: history within the operation, time study by an engineer, predetermined motion time systems (that look at how tasks can be built up from specific actions), and standard data systems (that use large databases of tasks of different sorts). Cost and practicality typically determine which of these mechanisms to use.

Standard work—The concept here is simple but it requires great discipline to implement and to gain its many benefits. Toyota has been a big proponent of this practice. In contrast to the methods discussion above, standard work is not about setting standards for the work to be done. It is not about some industrial engineer rating a job. Rather, it is about the workers themselves documenting exactly what it is that they do in the time allotted to them so that they, and others, can review that work and determine what adds value and what may not add value. Standard work forms the well-understood, documented basis for considering change to the workstation.

Much of the huge leap in productivity that occurred with the creation of the moving assembly line at Ford's Highland Park facility in 1913–14 was due to study of individual workstations and standardizing the work performed in them. The constant experimentation that took place at Highland Park was, in large part, a search for ever better ways for each workstation to produce or to assemble the parts of the Model T. The discretion that a worker had under the former system of production was gradually but persistently removed as the work was made increasingly standard.

5S—The 5S or "housekeeping" system (Sort, Set in order, Shine, Standardize, and Sustain, also known as CANDO: Cleanliness, Arrange, Neatness, Discipline, Ongoing improvement) is a system that revolves around the workstation. It is devoted to making the workstation as efficient as possible by determining exactly what is needed to do the job and discarding anything that is not needed, assigning a rational place for all the tools and other materials used by the workstation, and keeping it all clean and ready for work. Every workstation doing the same job should look and operate the same way. And, importantly, there should be a systematic and periodic review of all of the elements of every workstation, with the intent to improve each workstation continually. The 5S system focuses relentlessly on the workstation.

Quality tools—One of the most effective ways for a workstation to become more productive is to improve its quality. Through better conformance to the requirements set for the product produced, a workstation can avoid a slew of costs such as scrap, rework, and warranty charges. As the discussion in

Chapter 2 related, there are a host of quality tools, many specific to the workstation, that can easily be adopted and have proved themselves over time.

Equipment—The heart of most workstations is the equipment within them. While quality tools can be applied to such equipment, simply making sure that the equipment is up to specification, as determined by the equipment manufacturer, and that the operators of the equipment are running it according to its design can be easy to do and a low-cost way to improve the operation.

THE LAYOUT

The spatial aspects of production—how materials and products move from point to point in the operation—are too important to ignore. Poor layouts can:

- interrupt the physical flow of materials
- add direct labor time to the product
- introduce excessive handling, with the risk of damage and loss
- cause queues of work-in-process inventory to proliferate
- keep workers and/or managers at a distance from one another when in fact they should be close
- increase the time it takes to manufacture the product or deliver the service
- increase set-up time unduly
- add to overhead
- crowd departments into too little space
- contribute to poor housekeeping
- make any space expansion more difficult to accomplish
- otherwise add costs to the operation.

Some poor layouts are born, but most are made. That is, some poor layouts are bad designs from the beginning, but most poor layouts develop bit by bit over time, as one change after another is made in an incremental way. New products get introduced, and the space they need is hurriedly assigned. New equipment is purchased, and a place is quickly found for it so that the rest of the process is not disturbed while it is debugged. The space is expanded, but to avoid disruption a completely new layout is not designed and implemented; only a few areas are redone. In these ways, over time, bottlenecks are built into the process and its layout. It is naturally difficult for many companies to "bite the bullet" and completely refashion the layout of the process, but that is what is called for in most situations.

Generally, layouts can be classified into three major categories—job shop, line flow, and fixed position—although several offshoots are possible.

The job shop (or process) layout—The job shop, or process, layout, as noted briefly in Chapter 2, groups similar equipment together. Such a layout makes sense if jobs are routed all over the place, there is no clear dominant flow to the process, and any tooling and fixtures need to be shared. Maintenance and set-up equipment can be stored nearby. And operators, without thorough cross-training, can run two or more pieces of equipment to enjoy the productivity gains inherent in such a scheme. On the other hand, the job shop layout does make production control, inventory control, and materials handling more challenging.

The job shop (or process) layout is attractive when routings are unique to each job, a situation that would create chaos in a more line flow layout.

The line flow (or product-specific) layout—If there is a discernible, dominant flow to the process, then a line flow, product-specific, layout has tremendous advantages over a job shop layout. Materials handling can be greatly simplified because materials "live" at the same sites along the line. With the product moving from workstation to workstation in a regular pattern, the space necessary for production can be reduced, often dramatically. Production control is easier; the paperwork trail to each job in the job shop can be largely abandoned. In effect, the layout itself acts to control priorities. Work-in-process inventories can be shrunk to a fraction of what they would be in a job shop layout. Production cycle times can be similarly reduced, making the feedback of quality information that much quicker and more effective as well.

The fixed position layout—A layout in which materials are brought to a stationary product is termed a fixed position layout. It is common when the product itself is so massive or awkward that transporting it through the process is unreasonable. Construction and shipbuilding are readily recognizable examples of fixed position layouts, but so too is the typical auto repair operation.

Fixed position layouts are typically chosen by default, and for good reasons, yet there are several potentially detrimental aspects of fixed position layouts that one needs to be aware of. First, they make materials handling more difficult because the space- and time-saving delivery of materials in bulk cannot be accomplished. Rather, a "kit" of the required parts has to be assembled and distributed at the proper time to a variety of products-in-process rather than delivered to a single point along the line. Second, workers of different types and skills have to move from product to product, or else a single set of workers has to remain with the entire job. In the former case, scheduling worker movements becomes a chore, while in the latter case training workers to do the entire job takes time and resources. Third, quality control becomes more problematic in fixed position layouts. Inspectors often have to roam, and that may waste operators' time as they wait on inspection. Moreover, one does not have the luxury of evaluating the process capabilities of just one machine or one workstation along the line; there are many stations to evaluate, as many stations as there are stalls filled with work-in-process.

Hybrid layouts—Each of these layouts has advantages but also downsides. For example, the downside of a line flow is that the content of the job in a particular workstation can become very limited and therefore highly boring. The worker may not really understand anymore what his or her contribution to the final product is all about. While the downside of the fixed position is the lack of specialization and the inefficiency of the materials handling, it does have the advantage of greater fulfillment for the skilled worker, who may be able to accomplish a "complete" job, repair a car, or produce a subassembly. In particular, in line flows with a high level of demotivation of the workforce or high absenteeism there have been many experiments in industry with hybrid layouts whereby one keeps the principle of the line flow, but increases the number of tasks carried out in one workstation.

Diversity in goals for the design of the layout—Optimizing the layout is of course about increasing productivity. One often thinks about enhancing the output by smoothing the flow or increasing the pace of the production line. But there may be other goals. There have been interesting experiments in the German automotive industry (Daimler Benz and BMW) to design the layout in order to cope with an ageing workforce. Productivity enhancement in automotive assembly is not necessarily about increasing the pace, but often about reducing the defects at a constant pace of output. In experiments with layouts designed by the workers themselves, it turned out that a team of workers aged above 60 could be equally productive as, if not more than, a team of younger workers. The layout improvements were aimed at compensating for diminished physical capabilities—e.g. additional tools to lift heavy components, larger screens to compensate for the reduction of eyesight, wooden floors which are more gentle for weaker joints, etc.

BOTTLENECKS

Bottlenecks are the classic reason why processes do not realize the throughput they could. In his famous book, *Theory of Constraints*, Eli Goldratt stated that the bottleneck governs throughput of the operation. Simply stated, the slowest process in the sequence of processes determines the throughput, as working faster than this bottleneck process will only lead to inventory piling up elsewhere in the system, or more specifically before the bottleneck operation.

We note another important subprinciple:

Principle #3: Work-in-process is determined by throughput rate and throughput time.

a. The throughput time of a process is stochastic, not deterministic.
b. Bottlenecks govern the throughput of a system.

In fact bottlenecks will govern the maximum throughput of a system that theoretically can be achieved. Of course there will be variation in inputs into the bottleneck resource, as well as variation in the conversion at the bottleneck resource itself. So, in practice, the actual throughput achieved in the system will be *strictly less* than the bottleneck capacity.[3]

Sometimes the bottleneck is a one-time occurrence. Perhaps a machine broke down (which often highlights the importance of preventive maintenance), or perhaps there are material shortages or labor shortages (e.g. unexpected absences). More troubling over the longer term are chronic bottlenecks, ones that recur. They can either be:

- *stationary* (permanent) bottlenecks, which do not move and exist irrespective of the production schedule, or
- *moving* (floating) bottlenecks, which shift over time depending on the production schedule or demand pattern.

The stationary bottleneck is the easy one to spot, where everyone is clear that it is the limiting aspect of the process. Work-in-process inventory stacks up in front of it and breaking it immediately results in increased output. Often, breaking a stationary bottleneck means adding equipment or refurbishing existing equipment.

Stationary bottlenecks demand constant attention because any loss of output from them is output lost to the process as a whole. They need to be scheduled completely and any downtime has to be thought through carefully so that it is minimized. Stationary bottlenecks should be lavished with resources like labor and maintenance to make certain they produce as much as they possibly can.

Moving bottlenecks are more problematic. They shift around the process and can elude identification. They may be caused by persistent quality problems, or perhaps routinely missing parts. Often, however, the moving bottleneck occurs as a result of scheduling a particular mix in the products planned for the process. Some product variants place especially high demands on certain pieces of equipment or on certain stages of the process. If too many of these product variants are scheduled, a bottleneck can ensue. Change the production plan, however, and the bottleneck can disappear or resurface elsewhere.

Breaking a moving bottleneck is not as straightforward as breaking a stationary one. While permanent bottlenecks are a capacity problem, moving bottlenecks are a scheduling problem (the waste associated with moving bottlenecks is sometimes referred to by the Japanese term, *mura*, as distinct from the other seven wastes, *muda*). So first and foremost an analysis of demand is needed, to understand what scope there is to alleviate the problem by changing the product mix. Only then does one ask whether more capacity may be needed. Adding capacity indiscriminately can be very costly. Often a solution stems from eradicating the cause, be it a quality problem, missing parts, or the production plan itself. The production plan may have to be adjusted in advance so that it does not place too taxing a load on any one portion of the process.

Load Balancing

Bottlenecks restrict the throughput of processes. Increasing throughput is often an exercise in isolating bottlenecks and then systematically breaking them. Good operations are often those that are diligent and resourceful in identifying bottlenecks and breaking them in creative ways. Ideally, one wants a process with no bottlenecks, or, more precisely, a process with every workstation the bottleneck. In that instance, there would be perfect balance among the workstations.

Assembly line balance is the archetypal vision of workstation balance. A good line balance assures the process of output near its theoretical maximum. Achieving such balance is usually not assured; often trial and error has to be pursued. The goal, however, is clear: to assign the various operations that define the process in such a way that the actual cycle time for the process meets the calculated ideal of the control cycle.

On Breaking Bottlenecks

Ferreting out where bottlenecks exist and then breaking them in clever, often low-cost ways is the under-appreciated nitty-gritty of good operations management. The very best operations are relentless about it. Arguing for the latest technology, for new equipment, or for additional workforce is often the easy way out. Squeezing the existing capital stock and workforce for every last bit of output is tougher to do, but often it is the most productive and profitable way to proceed. Managers who excel at this do not neglect what the latest technology and equipment can do and they are not averse to hiring, but these exemplary managers do not propose significant expenditures without first assuring themselves that they have done all they can with the resources they already have.

At the same time, many companies do not value bottleneck breaking as much as they should. They systematically undervalue what the breaking of a bottleneck does for the company's economics. Indeed, when a company is short of capacity, the full value of the contribution that it is forgoing should be assigned to the bottleneck. Consider the following example.

A plant that produces instruments can be divided into three areas: fabrication, assembly, and test. The accounting system routinely assigns cost and value-added in the following way: fabrication 30 percent, assembly 40 percent, and test 30 percent. Suppose that the plant could produce more but is constrained by a lack of fabrication capacity. Indeed, suppose that the plant could earn an additional $100,000 net present value of contribution if the bottleneck in fabrication could be broken. Suppose that breaking that bottleneck costs $50,000. Should the plant proceed with the bottleneck breaking?

In the accounting that prevails in some companies, the additional $100,000 of contribution would be divided up by area, much as a general overhead would be spread across them. Thus, the fabrication area would be accounted for providing $30,000 net present value of the $100,000 of net present value of contribution to be enjoyed. Spending $50,000 for a benefit of only $30,000 would not be looked upon favorably. Such thinking neglects, of course, the fact that the $100,000 of added contribution would not be possible at all without breaking the bottleneck in fabrication. The traditional spreading of cost has to be ignored. All $100,000 in added net present value should be assigned to fabrication, easily justifying the breaking of the bottleneck.

This is only good economics, and it is consistent with what the shadow price in a linear program would reveal were the constraint to be relaxed. Bottleneck breaking can be a very profitable activity.

Balance and Excess Capacity

When bottlenecks are broken, the process comes into better balance. And when the balance in the process is good, production closer to capacity is possible. Balance can be tighter with processes that are on the right side of the process spectrum, because capacities can typically be more precisely defined for those processes. The continuous flow process is typically designed with great attention to the balance of its equipment. The assembly line does much the same but with tasks that often require human effort. For batch and job shop processes, however, capacities are usually more ambiguous and thus balance becomes a looser concept.

If balance cannot be absolutely perfect, it brings up the question of where one might want to hold any excess capacity. Indeed, having excess capacity may be a very useful thing. You may not, in fact, want perfect balance. Think, for example, of an integrated steel mill. The process, in gross terms, consists of blast furnace, steel making, casting and semi-finishing, and lastly finishing. Does it matter where the excess capacity is held?

In this steel mill example, holding excess capacity at the end of a process permits the early portions of the process to continue to produce no matter what the final product mix is. That can be very beneficial.

There are several reasons for holding excess capacity in particular locations in a process:

- Holding excess capacity in the early stages of the process:
  - If yields drop off the further one goes in the process, having excess capacity early on can be useful to help provide enough output.

  - If changes to the product, or to the product mix, are easy to make late in the process, excess capacity earlier may be desirable.
- Holding excess capacity in the later stages of the process:
  - If changes to the product, or to the product mix, are hard to make late in the process, excess capacity later is desirable.
- Other reasons for holding excess capacity anywhere in the process:
  - Often capacity additions entail large, fixed-increment ("lumpy") investments. This is a very common reason why excess capacity may exist in a process.
  - Sometimes capacity is cheap to build. If growth is expected, often it makes sense to hold excess capacity for what is cheap to build. This can work especially well if, over time, the bottleneck segment of the process can be broken by taking small, incremental steps.

Yields

Process yields that are less than 100 percent are technically a sort of bottleneck. Increase the yield and the process' output surges. Nevertheless, yields may not be as readily augmented as a run-of-the-mill-type bottleneck can be, where an equipment purchase remedies things right away. The work needed to increase a process yield can take a long time and is much more inherently uncertain. It typically requires a revision to the process. All this said, increasing yields is a splendid way to raise output and to cut costs.

PRODUCTION PLANNING

Production planning is all about getting the most out of the capacity that the process has. The goals of production planning are straightforward: figuring out which products to produce, when to produce them, and how much of each. Nevertheless, accomplishing this task effectively can be devilishly difficult.

An effective production plan meets its demand obligations on time and at low cost. Being on time with production requires management to know what the process capacity is and not to promise deliveries for which it does not have the capacity. Keeping costs low requires a match of resources (workforce, equipment, materials) to obligations that neither unduly stretches those resources nor leaves too much excess capacity. Short-term capacity can be augmented in several ways—adding extra workers, scheduling overtime or extra shifts, and placing auxiliary equipment into service. Sometimes, companies can subcontract with others for extra production. All of these options, however, raise costs. Extra workers are frequently more costly to secure and less productive than regular workers. Overtime and extra shifts add costs to direct labor bills, maintenance, and overhead. Auxiliary equipment is typically less efficient and more expensive to operate and maintain. The production planner is justifiably loath to force short-term capacity increases by these means. However, the production planner also inflicts extra costs on the company if too much excess capacity is held. These costs are opportunity costs, the revenues forgone by failing to produce output that could have been sold. Striking a balance between resources and demand obligations is what production planning is all about.

In all processes, there is a sincere desire to produce to exact customer specifications and to ship precisely when the customer indicates. This goal is not fully achievable in all processes because of some inherent constraints. In those that do achieve this goal, various policies are adopted:

Modulating capacity—The timely delivery of a customer's precise order can be ensured by continually varying labor and materials resources and "rebalancing" the process if need be. Scheduling overtime is the classic version of this approach. Modulating capacity is a common production planning policy in service industries because many services cannot be inventoried; thus, demands must be met primarily by adjusting the workforce and materials available on any given shift.

Inventory buffers—Some processes fill their orders out of finished goods inventory.

Managing demand—Reservation systems are a classic way to manage demand, especially in services. Price can be another way. Some job shops, for example, adjust their bids for work. In times of high demand on capacity, bids for business could be on the high side to help choke off the business a process would have trouble delivering on time; similarly, in times of excess capacity, lower bids can hope to draw in more business.

Sometimes processes cannot adopt these policies successfully. In such cases, the operation may have to defer production for a particular order until room appears in the schedule. The time deferred may not be particularly long, but these delivery dislocations are an inevitable consequence of the rigidity in some processes. For example, if the demand for, say, paper was particularly strong, not all deliveries would likely be made. Carrying spare pulp and paper capacity is an increasingly expensive undertaking, and so the capacity utilization of pulp and paper mills is generally high to begin with. A peak demand situation is likely, then, to imply a rationing of paper to customers.

Another interesting, and common, process is the hybrid process, such as a brewery, where the beer is brewed in batches and the bottles and cans are filled in a continuous flow operation. It offers an example of another means by which deliveries can be met effectively. This type of process is interesting precisely because it mixes production planning systems. The first portion of many hybrid processes is triggered by either a sales forecast or the level of work-in-process inventory held; the latter portion of the process, on the other hand, is generally triggered by actual orders. What permits the company the luxury of planning production and managing materials in two different ways is the existence of the work-in-process inventory that separates the first portion of the process from the second. This inventory "decouples" one from the other. Without an inventory that functions in this manner, the latter portion of the process would probably have to be geared to the sales forecast, not to actual orders, and the company would probably have to store more in finished goods inventory, at higher cost, than it would ordinarily. Alternatively, incentives would have to be introduced to lock customers into longer lead time orders than is now the case, so that both portions of the process could be done to order.

The key advantage of such a decoupling inventory is that it breaks up the information and materials management needs of the entire process into pieces that can be managed more easily on their own. There is a cost, of course, because the decoupling inventory must be financed, but the cost can often be substantially lower than the financing of increased finished goods inventories.

In almost all cases, the mix of resources capable of meeting the prevailing demand obligations is not perfectly balanced between the workforce and the available equipment. Either the workforce will be the scarce resource and there will be idle equipment, or equipment will be the scarce resource and workers will be left idle. What the scarce resource is has a critical impact on how production is planned. Is the production plan designed to keep the equipment loaded (long production runs), or is it designed to keep the workforce busy (perhaps through many set-ups and shorter production runs)?

Because more workers can generally be added to any process, low-cost production plan design is essentially concerned with the economics of the process. Is equipment cheaper to hold idle than labor, or is the reverse true? The question is easy to state, but in practice it may be very difficult to answer. On the one hand, it is easy to see why a paper company might devote its talent to a careful scheduling of all the papermaking machines that it owns—an unnecessarily idle paper machine costs the company a bundle in forgone revenues. In cases like this where idle machinery is very expensive, we often see that these companies work two or three shifts a day or even a 24/7 work schedule.

On the other hand, it stands to reason that a job shop would house a number of machine tools that would lie idle a good deal of the time. Some machines have specialized uses and remain idle for that reason, while others can pay for themselves by being used strictly for sporadic in-tandem jobs with another machine or for addressing chronic bottlenecks. At many companies, especially job shops, holding equipment idle is cheaper than holding labor idle; production planning could call for a schedule of short runs if they would lead to on-time delivery and fewer bottlenecks.

These two examples are polar cases; in between is a sea of gray. For processes that are mostly batch and line flow, it is not always clear whether it is cheaper to hold idle some equipment or some labor, and thus whether the long production run is to be valued above a series of smaller runs. The decision depends on factors such as the costs of equipment, labor, inventory carrying, and inventory stock-outs, and on production speeds, prices, and quality levels.

If the full range of a company's product mix cannot be produced on time, which of the product mix ought to be produced? The production plan should be sensitive to those products or services that earn more profit or contribution per unit of time or per unit of some other scarce resource. Production plans—particularly at the end of a month, quarter, or year—are often weighted heavily towards high-contribution items or towards those that can easily be completed and billed. In many companies, the great end-of-month scramble to push product out the door is a scramble to push out the "winners," leaving poorer-selling or poorer-earning products until the next month. This kind of scheduling, of course, is more prevalent in job shop and batch flow processes; the more inflexible processes follow more rigid production plans.

Developing a Good Match between Resources and Demand

The development of a lowest-cost production plan depends not only on identifying the most valued resource and how that scarce resource should be scheduled, but also on the specific techniques that can be brought to bear on the match between resources and demands. An effective production schedule is the heart—or at least the pacemaker—of many operations. Constructing one is an important but involved task. Figure 4.3 shows a generic framework for how production planning and control works in a manufacturing context.

The final production schedule for a plant is developed bit by bit, in stages, as more definite information on demands, materials, and capacities becomes available. Figure 4.3 depicts these stages. The first cut planning of production is generally concerned only with broad aggregates—entire product lines, gross materials needs, rough estimates of labor and machine availabilities—for time periods that can stretch twelve to eighteen months into the future. This is long enough that all materials needs can be planned for but not so long that production cannot be regarded as significantly constrained by the present facility and any changes already in the works for it. Because it deals with broad aggregates of resources, this stage of production scheduling is frequently termed *aggregate planning*.

The aggregate plan serves as the first alert for marshaling resources—getting initial commitments from suppliers, checking whether more (or less) labor is

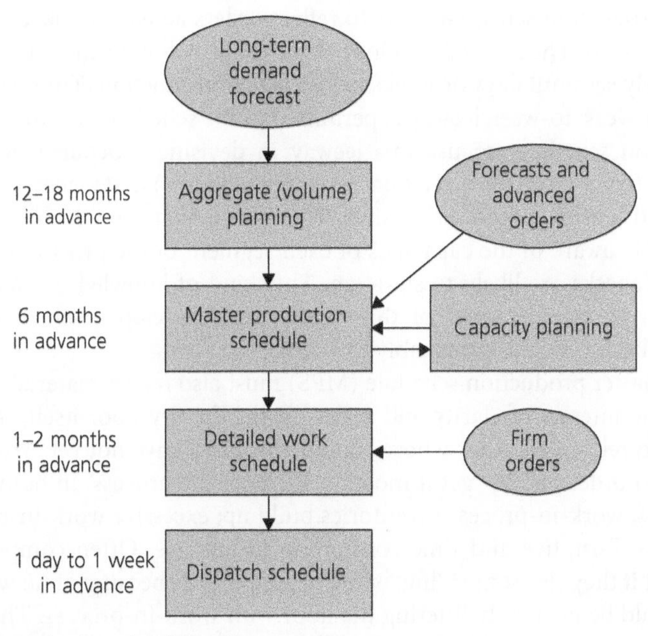

Figure 4.3 Production planning: a framework.

needed, ensuring that inventories on hand are adequate to meet demands, determining whether machine capacity is adequate. Given this alert, the managers responsible can go about securing the resources needed to meet the plan. Decisions can also be made about how production is going to vary to cover the expected pattern of demand. Should production remain "level," building up inventories to cover anticipated peaks of demand? Or should production try to "chase" demand, with little or no accumulation of inventory? Or should some mixed, in-between strategy prevail? It is in assessing the aggregate plan that decisions of this type are generally first made.

Since the aggregate plan is associated with marshaling resources, it inevitably becomes entwined with the budgeting process for the plant and the company division it reports to. It also becomes a prime battleground between marketing—with its forecast of sales and any plans for product changes or new products—and manufacturing.

As demand firms up, the broad outlines of the production schedule, as determined by the aggregate plan, can be filled in with greater detail. Broad product line demand forecasts are replaced with more detailed forecasts of specific products, and eventually with specific product variations. Material supply capabilities and lead times are known with more certainty. More specifics are known about actual labor and machine availabilities. The aggregate planning stage gives way to successive stages of more detailed scheduling, generally termed *master production scheduling* (MPS).

The production schedule starts to reflect orders actually booked as well as those expected. The schedule begins to become firm, but it generally cannot be completely set until days or weeks before actual production. Thus, some day-to-day or week-to-week leeway is permitted in the schedule; it is the job of the production scheduler to use this leeway in devising a detailed production schedule (sometimes termed a final assembly schedule) that places as balanced a demand on the process as possible. This means that the scheduler must be thoroughly aware of the capacities of each segment of the process and where any bottlenecks are likely to show up. This kind of knowledge often leads a scheduler to concoct rules of thumb that help develop a schedule that is feasible, balanced, and reasonably low cost.

The master production schedule (MPS) must also reflect material availability. In the interest of clarity and order on the factory floor itself, it is often unwise to release an order whose component parts have not yet arrived or to release an order just to "get it moving" through the process. In both of these situations, work-in-process inventories build up; excessive work-in-process is often too disruptive and time-consuming to manage. Often companies are better off if they risk some idling workers temporarily because of no work than they would be purposely littering the floor with work-in-process. The hidden costs of work-in-process induced inefficiencies are frequently greater than the highly visible costs of idle labor. Yet, of course, many plants feel compelled to get something going in order to accommodate sales pressures, even if it means provoking inefficiencies in the process.

The goal of capacity planning is to estimate how much process capacity will be taken up by any proposed level and mix of product demands. Effective capacity planning can indicate whether a proposed production schedule is feasible; thus it is an important tool for the scheduling process. There are several useful capacity planning techniques that companies use. These techniques vary in their sophistication, specificity, and data requirements. Some are part of the companies' computer systems, and some stand apart.

Master scheduling is a process—an ongoing activity—that melds forecasts, booked orders, and knowledge of the effective capacity of the factory. It is a process that periodically and systematically "publishes" a document—the master production schedule—that indicates how many of each product the factory will produce for a specified time period or succession of time periods. The MPS is stated in physical units for every end item for which there is a bill of materials, or more often, for a readily recognizable aggregation of end items that could be termed a model, style, series, product line, or something similar.

If an aggregation of end items constitutes the MPS, then a more precise schedule must be developed for the specific end item variations that will actually be produced. Often this more precise schedule is termed the *final assembly schedule* (FAS). The final assembly schedule paces the flow of products and materials through the process. It acts as both a planning tool and a control document against which actual performance can be measured.

The MPS is a key bridge between manufacturing and marketing/sales because it is with the MPS that manufacturing commits to making what marketing/sales has either forecast or actually booked as orders. Typically, manufacturing's commitment takes the form of a due date for the completion and shipping of the product in some agreed-upon quantity. For this order promising to proceed smoothly over time, manufacturing has to keep track of the production quantities that are available or could be expected to be available, and also how much of any of those quantities could actually be committed for shipment.

The "Level versus Chase" Strategy Choice

Perhaps the key choice that production planners face is that of which strategy to lean towards, a "chase" or a "level" one. These two strategies are the polar extremes that anchor production planning. Recall that the chase strategy eschews the build-up of inventory in favor of matching production in each period as closely as possible to the sales for that period. The level strategy, on the other hand, tries to avoid the ups and downs—hires and layoffs, overtime, subcontracting—that are frequently part of a chase strategy, in favor of letting inventory be a kind of shock absorber for the factory. Rarely do companies follow either a pure chase or a pure level strategy; they usually employ a mix of the two. Still, it is always useful to understand the forces that can, and should, cause a company to lean one way or the other in devising its production plans.

Choosing between a chase and a level strategy is essentially an exercise in comparing relative costs. What kinds of costs are important? The costs of carrying inventory, the costs of (re)hiring and laying off workers, the costs of producing on overtime, the costs of subcontracting work to other producers, and the costs of not making the product on time and thus of stocking out, to name the main ones. It is the comparison of these costs relative to each other that is key in determining which strategy is more attractive to follow. Naturally, the higher are the costs of hiring, layoff, overtime, and subcontracting relative to the costs of carrying inventory, the less attractive the chase strategy becomes and the more attractive is the level strategy. In addition, the chase strategy risks stock-outs somewhat more than the level strategy, because it is frequently difficult to augment capacity fast enough. Thus when stock-out costs are relatively high, the level strategy is preferred. Alternatively, it may also be difficult to scale back production quickly enough to match sales exactly. This may lead to overproduction and the need to throw away part of the production. In the case of high-value products the chase strategy may run the risk of expensive write-offs.

As economic conditions change, the advantages of chase versus level will also change. For example, as interest rates rise, inventory becomes more expensive to carry and the chase strategy becomes more attractive. On the other hand, company commitments to no-layoff policies or new union contracts that make layoffs more difficult or expensive to institute naturally favor a level rather than a chase strategy. Production planners need to scan the economic horizon periodically for changes in the relative costs with which they have to work.

NOTES

1. MRP systems were once stand-alone computer systems. Today, they are modules within larger enterprise resource planning (ERP) systems.
2. J.D. Little, 1961. A proof for the queuing formula: $L = \lambda W$. *Operations Research*, 9(3), pp.383–7.
3. W.J. Hopp and M.L. Spearman, 2011. *Factory Physics*. Waveland Press.

FURTHER READING

Goldratt, E.M. and Cox, J., 2016. *The Goal: A Process of Ongoing Improvement*. Routledge (Abingdon).

Hopp, W.J. and Spearman, M.L., 2011. *Factory Physics*. Waveland Press (Longrove, IL).

Kingman, J.F.C., 1966. On the algebra of queues. *Journal of Applied Probability*, 3(2), pp.285–326.

Little, J.D., 1961. A proof for the queuing formula: $L = \lambda W$. *Operations Research*, 9(3), pp.383–7.

Silver, E.A., Pyke, D.F., and Peterson, R., 1998. *Inventory Management and Production Planning and Scheduling*. Wiley (New York).

Vollmann, T.E., Berry, W.L., and Whybark, D.C., 2005. *Manufacturing Planning and Control Systems for Supply Chain Management*. McGraw-Hill (New York).

5 Scale, scope, and complexity

So far we have discussed processes in steady state, how to analyze them, and how to manage their performance. As Chapters 1 to 4 have made plain, processes differ from one another but they can be characterized with some general elements. For the most part, operations management—in practice—is concerned with managing existing processes within an organization. It is of course also possible that a process must be designed from scratch, for example in a growing start-up or a new business unit in an established company. We have reflected on the design of processes in the light of the previous chapters on process types, analysis, and performance. In this chapter we consider the changes that occur when operations grow in volume, scope, or most often both. Consider, for example, a growing start-up. Its initial success is likely on the back of one breakthrough product or service offering. Over time, the single product that made the company great tends to become several products or even product lines. The once leading-edge technology matures and the product architecture settles on a dominant design. Competitive priorities also evolve. Rather than competing on features and customization, quality and delivery speed may become the order winners, until eventually the product becomes commoditized.

As the operation grows, one has to think differently about product or service delivery. Customer requirements become less about innovative features, and more about operational factors such as quality, delivery, and reliability (along the product–process matrix discussed in Sections 2.5 to 2.8). Complexity in tasks is likely to rise, as will complexity in relationships with stakeholders. So the nature of the operation also needs to change. The key challenge becomes managing this complexity, driven by growth in scale and scope. The way in which a process is designed can make it simple or increasingly complex. This brings up our fourth principle.

> **Principle #4:** Complexity in process design amplifies managerial challenges.

One might argue that complexity arising from scale and scope is inevitable for any operation that grows from a start-up to a successful firm. Exposure to complexity is inevitable, but it is the managerial response that determines how the organization performs. Let us consider scale, scope, and the ensuing complexity challenge in more detail.

5.1 The role of scale

It is frequently stated that large companies enjoy a competitive edge over small companies because of the inherent advantages of economies of scale. The phrase has a strong appeal, and large companies with sizable operations have a certain aura about them. The phrase draws nods of recognition, yet few people can define it and fewer still have thought critically about it. The original definition of "economies of scale" discussed four basic scale-related effects, which lead to a reduction in unit cost: (1) if the production volume (throughput) increases, (2) if the capacity utilization increases, (3) when process repetition leads to learning, and (4) when process repetition leads to a reduction in stochastic effects (e.g. defects, breakdowns).[1] In short, arguments around economies of scale rest on the assumption that the more that is produced, the better existing fixed costs can be spread across the units produced, and that the more often the process is repeated, the more efficient it becomes. This is the theory.

In practice, however, all too often you hear a company president nonchalantly say something like, "If we increase the size of our operations here, we'll naturally enjoy some economies of scale." There is nothing natural about economies of scale, and certainly nothing to be nonchalant about. Confusion about the term is understandable because it serves as an umbrella for a number of real, but quite distinct, concepts. Because it is an umbrella term, "economies of scale" often loses its usefulness in making management decisions on plant size and capacity.

In fact, the term "economies of scale" suffers from irredeemable ambiguity. As we have said, it is based on "levers" that are very different depending on one's interpretation of "scale" as volume, capacity, or process technology. Even then, there are a variety of ways to effect these economies. Instead of inviting confusion by using the term "economies of scale," we argue that operations managers should think of volume, capacity, and process technology separately. Learning curve effects due to the repetition of the process, in our view, are matters of process improvement and not economies of scale. They are dealt with in Chapter 8.

Moreover, as we will discuss in Section 6.2, there are diseconomies of scale, as well as these economies of volume, capacity, and process technology. With scale come complexity challenges that can escalate. The levels of management can multiply and, with that, control can become more difficult. The ability to be nimble in reaction to competitors' initiatives, or even to enact a company's own initiatives, can diminish. Logistics becomes more complicated and inventories can balloon. Small can be beautiful and big can be ugly.

But first, we will discuss the three specific types of economies: volume, capacity, and process technology.

THROUGHPUT (VOLUME) EFFECTS

As a general rule, higher-volume plants will enjoy lower unit costs than smaller plants because they can spread their fixed costs (overhead, capital costs) over a greater number of units. If by scale we mean volume, then the difference in unit costs can be an economy of scale. For some people, however, this "spreading of fixed costs" seems too trite an example to be labeled a "scale economy," so they dismiss it.[2] These people then modify the definition of a scale economy to exclude economies that are really economies of volume.

Also it should be noted that the relationship between volume and unit cost is not entirely linear—as volume rises, an extra shift, a new production line, or even an entirely new production facility may be needed. This introduces discrete "steps" into the unit cost function that can be significant.

CAPACITY EFFECTS

A related and similar effect is based on the utilization of production assets: a higher utilization not only spreads existing fixed costs across more units, it also permits the company to carry proportionately less raw materials inventory. This may be due to the familiar "economic order quantity" result that optimal inventories need increase only as the square root of volume and not proportionately with volume (see Appendix E, where we discuss basic trade-off models).

Another capacity effect relates to changeovers. Suppose a plant makes two different products. If it has only one production line, then it must change over from one product to the other, and consequently builds up proportionately more finished goods inventory to cover its demand. On the other hand, if it has two lines, the plant can afford to manufacture each product on a separate, dedicated line without interruption. In the first instance, the plant needs to carry enough cycle stock inventory of its first product to tide itself over while it makes its second product. In the second instance, one need not worry about this problem. It is instructive to think about the changeover problem in light of Toyota's "90/10" rule, whereby equipment should run 90 percent of the time, while 10 percent is spent on changeovers and maintenance. So if you want to produce more product variants on the same line, or reduce batch sizes, you have to cut down the changeover time (this is, of course, where Shingo's famous SMED = "single minute exchange of dies" approach comes in).

In addition to these inventory-associated economies, increased capacity allows the luxury of more redundancy, such as spare equipment and maintenance capabilities, or of additional and useful overhead functions. If scale means "capacity," then any differences in unit costs can be appropriately called economies of scale.

TECHNOLOGY EFFECTS

Technology, or more specifically the nature of the production assets, can also provide economies of scale. The choice of equipment is in fact a large determinant in the unit cost of production. Larger equipment aimed at achieving higher throughput provides a capital-for-labor substitution, and in turn leads to labor specialization. "Automation" is the term commonly used here, whereby manual tasks are replaced by mechanized or robotized tools that perform the same task. This substitution of capital for labor generally leads to a drastic reduction in unit cost, which is a technology-related economy of scale. There are, however, obvious downsides.

A higher degree of automation increases the rigidity of the plant, as the equipment is dedicated to one or just a few products. Automation will reduce flexibility of the plant's technology and approach to performing the tasks, although in many cases it can also increase the capacity to produce product variety. Equally, increased automation requires an increase in capital that alters the process. Often a company cannot make small additions to its plant's stock of equipment and space; large additions have to be made and are perhaps the classic explanation for economies of scale. Such investments are usually substantial alterations to a plant's process technology and so are more than just scale changes. They are changes in process technology, and should be recognized and managed as such.

One particular substitution of capital for labor merits special mention. The geometry of processes that deal with free-flowing materials, like chemicals or liquids, often permits output to vary according to the volume of its capital equipment, while the costs (construction and/or operating costs) vary according to surface area. This is the "6/10 rule," which argues for large-process technologies. The rule is so named because it was found that, for chemical plants, a doubling of volume leads to only an approximately 6/10 increase in surface area, and thus in costs. An oil refinery is one such example. Output depends greatly on the sizes of tanks and pipes, but construction and maintenance costs depend more on the surface area of the material that holds the oil. For most other (non-free-flowing materials) operations, however, such cost advantages are much less significant.

More automated plants may have lower unit costs because they have altered process technology to specialize labor for particular tasks. In order to make the process more continuous, jobs may have been "deskilled." That is, instead of large numbers of highly skilled workers, each performing a number of operations to form the product, the process may be organized to link together less skilled workers, who carry out a small number of specific operations. The time and responsibility any one worker devotes to a particular product may be reduced in an effort to increase productivity through repetition and specialized competence. The pace of the production process shifts from worker discretion to management option. The car assembly line is a classic example of labor specialization and management (that is, mechanical) pacing.

To reiterate, both capital-for-labor substitution and labor specialization alter process technologies. Thus, if by scale we mean "process technology," then we can appropriately call these two means of cost reduction "economies of scale."

In sum, "economies of scale" is a vague enough term to provide easy justification for any number of decisions on plant capacity. However, because it is so vague, its usefulness to managers is minimal. Moreover, as we will see later, speed (quick throughput time) is nearly always more powerful than scale, and more to be feared in a competitor. Thus, two areas should be carefully scrutinized: (1) the cost reductions a company claims it can achieve through specific changes in a plant's volume, capacity, or process technology, and (2) what those changes may actually mean for management control, logistics, inventories, or the ability to respond to product or process innovations.

5.2 The role of scope

New firms often grow on the back of one successful product. As the firm grows, product or service lines are extended and broadened to serve a diverse set of customer segments. This proliferation of offerings is important for growth and generates volume within and across product lines. However, as the scope of the firm grows, so does the required managerial effort.

Yet scope is not all bad. As several products are produced in the same factory, or even on the same production line, they share the overhead for the entire facility. In some cases one product variant may even offset low demand for another, so the combined volume leads to a higher level of facility utilization. While product changeovers will reduce efficiency, product variety or scope does bring advantages in the form of increased total volumes, and the potential of offsetting or leveling demand, and thus increased utilization. These advantages are economies of scope.[3]

Product variety effectively comes in two forms—*external* variety, which is the level of variety the customer sees and chooses from, and *internal* variety, which is the complexity caused within the manufacturing operation to deliver the external variety offered in the marketplace. For many firms, particularly those pursuing mass customization strategies, the level of external variety is considerably greater than the level of internal variety to be managed. Modularity, component commonality, and postponement are each levers to reduce the challenges of complexity in providing the requisite product variety to customers.

Consider the power of modularity for a manufacturer of industrial trucks. The manufacturer may offer customers a choice of three use types (medium, heavy, and extra heavy duty), five engines, four axles, four gearboxes, and five cabin configurations. Externally, this variety is multiplicative, with the customer able to select from 1,200 unique combinations. Internally, variety is additive in nature, with modularization enabling the firm to plan and build any finished product using just twenty-one modules. Internal complexity and the associated managerial challenges are greatly reduced.

5.3 The complexity challenge

Complexity is a word that is used often, yet generally poorly understood. Often it is used synonymously for "difficult," whereas in fact it is a well-defined concept. Complexity exists at two levels: static complexity, which denotes the number of nodes and connections in a network, and dynamic complexity, which describes the interactions that take place between nodes in that network. Both concepts directly apply to process design, whereby a process can become complex in a variety of ways.

Static complexity is caused by:

- different inputs
- different outputs
- process steps that may lead, also, to long throughput times
- inventories of one type or another.

Dynamic complexity is caused by:

- customer interaction with the process
- different suppliers with a wide variety of different supply contracts
- different components to the products and complex "recipes" for how they combine to produce the products.

We note:

Principle #4: Complexity in process design amplifies managerial challenges.

a. Complexity is a function of the number of static elements (structure) in a process, their heterogeneity, and their dynamic interactions.

This fundamental distinction is based on the works of Simon and Weaver, who discussed structure and interaction in complex systems.[4] A key aspect in this complex system is the *indecomposability* of elements. In other words, all elements need to be present for the whole to work; no one element is redundant or tangential. Most subsequent definitions of complexity are based on this fundamental distinction, in one way or another. We can talk about organizational complexity, describing how the firm is structured, or cultural complexity induced by working across many countries and contexts.

We can also directly link this definition to process and process design. Within the organization, and given the products to be produced, the question is: are our processes effective and efficient in delivering our products and services? In this context the key drivers of complexity link back to scale and scope. In the broadest sense, scale relates to how many production lines or facilities we operate, and scope relates to how many product variants we produce. Process complexity is co-determined by the scale and scope of the operation, and there are ways to manage it.

5.4 Managing complexity

Complexity develops naturally in the context of the growing operation, so it is by no means all bad. Some complexity is needed to satisfy the diverse customer needs—the key is therefore not to eliminate all complexity, but to balance its benefits with its cost by focusing on eradicating unnecessary or non-value-adding complexity. Complexity increases coordination cost, and reduces managerial span of attention, which is an opportunity cost. When complexity occurs, the management systems that spring up to care for it can, in themselves, be complex and expensive. For example, the enterprise resource planning (ERP) systems that cope with these many differences in inputs, outputs, and tasks can be huge and demanding to maintain. Bills of materials can explode, with many levels. Products can be interrelated in many ways. Product routings can direct materials all over the operation. Process sheets can be very involved.

Two main ways exist to deal with complexity: (1) to simplify and thus reduce complexity in the first place, and (2) to increase the organization's ability to cope with the complexity at hand. The difficulties that complexity brings to various operations have triggered numerous mechanisms for simplifying and/or coping. Consider some of them. For one, there can be limits on product proliferation or on customization. Here the company realizes that it incurs significant costs to offer a wide choice to the marketplace, and that restricting that choice may in fact lead to higher profits. Also, there can be restrictions on customer interaction. Customer interaction is a major source of additional cost, particularly with service operations. Coping with it may necessitate limiting the degree to which the customer is permitted to interact with the process and what that interaction can consist of. Consider Amazon versus a traditional bookstore. A traditional bookstore offers personal service, but interaction with customers introduces variation and limits the efficiency of any one worker. By contrast, Amazon buffers the workers from the customer. Workers operate efficiently in fulfillment centers, while customers are able to choose from a huge amount of product variety, and arguably the rating system provides even more feedback on potential books than is available in many bookstores.

Other mechanisms include changes to layout, make-or-buy decisions, and factory focus. First, consider improvements to the shop-floor layout. We introduced the concept of the cell in our earlier discussion of different types of processes. Cells group families of similar parts or products together and, in so doing, limit the variation within that specific production process. Change-over costs can be reduced and tasks can be better balanced when families are dealt with individually. Another option is subcontracting: if the alternative is vertical integration, where the company takes on the responsibility for producing all aspects of the product, then subcontracting can be the simpler solution. Subcontractors are typically the experts when it comes to their limited responsibilities and their costs can be lower. Finally, the concept of cells and subcontracting are part of the larger aspect of factory focus. Factory focus can be viewed as the cell writ large. Focused factories deliberately limit what they do and seek a simpler organization to do it (we will discuss "fit" and "focus" in detail in Chapter 6).

Other opportunities to reduce complexity also exist. Let us look at some of the most common approaches to managing complexity in more detail.

POSTPONEMENT AND LATE CONFIGURATION

Postponement or late configuration follows the idea of delaying the point of commitment to the latest possible point in time. For example, manufacturers will seek to delay the final configuration of a product until a customer requests the product. The main benefit is simply to reduce internal variety without compromising external variety. Until that customer order is received, the materials or components remain fungible and can be used for any other order. The labor needed to finalize the product will only be invested once the sale is certain. Often this approach is called the "vanilla strategy," using the ice cream parlor as an analogy, where many products use vanilla ice cream as a base, to be augmented with other flavors, fruit, and sauces. And even sprinkles.

Postponement greatly reduces the coordination effort. It simplifies the internal planning process by reducing the number of items to be considered, and improves the ability to generate forecasts. Rather than predicting every single product variant, the aggregate "vanilla" component can be estimated. By aggregating, any forecast will improve.

MODULARITY

Modularity is a closely related concept, or, more accurately, an enabler of postponement. The main idea in modularity is to segregate the product into exchangeable parts, or modules. For modularity to work two things are needed: (1) standard dimensions, so different parts can fit, and (2) defined interfaces and protocols so that different parts can fulfill the same function. The desktop PC is the classic example here, whereby memory chips, hard drives, and graphics adapters can be freely interchanged without worrying about functionality. As discussed earlier, modularity strategies allow the firm to offer high levels of external product variety, but minimize the associated internal variety.

A modular product design can enable a great deal of responsiveness to customer orders too, whereby the configuration of the final product is delayed until the customer order is received. The manufacturer would hold component inventory and then assemble the product to order, once the customer's order has been placed. Dell is a good example of this strategy, yet it is also used by other firms, such as opticians, to customize frames and lenses to order. This approach comes close to what Stan Davis in 1987 proposed as "mass customization" (an amalgam based on "mass production" and "individual customization"). He wanted to challenge manufacturers to provide individually customized products to their customers, yet produced at the same level of efficiency as in mass production of standard goods.

Despite its benefits, modularity has downsides too. First, any modular product design is in effect suboptimal, as it needs to make compromises to ensure standard dimensions and interfaces are maintained. In contrast to *integral* products, designers of *modular* products need to make some concessions. Modularity hence often is not used for high-performance products, where these concessions are not considered acceptable.

Modularity is mostly linked to product design, but can also be applied to process design. Not unlike object-oriented programming in software development, distinct subprocesses or "modules" of a process can be reused, replicated, or replaced without redesigning the whole process. As with product modularity, process modules need to be clearly defined, and standardized, with specific (but limited) functions. Modular processes can be managed autonomously, yet function together seamlessly within the whole operation and can facilitate the understanding of complex processes by stakeholders.

Modularity can increase both the rate and ease of change to the process, as well as allow both customization through the coordination of modules and scaling through replication across teams, production sites, and services. The use of modular processes can be a key practice for managing increasing complexity in an operation.

HIGH-RELIABILITY ORGANIZATIONS

So far we have discussed "traditional" manufacturing and service processes, where organizations often have a choice as to how much complexity to allow, and some ability to control the drivers of variation that underlie dynamic complexity. This ability to influence the level of complexity is not always possible though, so it is insightful to also consider process design in so-called "high-reliability organizations" (HROs)—a term coined by a team around Todd LaPorte at Berkeley in the 1980s. LaPorte and his team studied aircraft carriers, and defined HROs as organizations where failure may have far-reaching, potentially catastrophic consequences. Other examples include nuclear power plants, nuclear submarines, and commercial aviation. Such organizations are typically characterized by high dynamic complexity and high component interdependence. Dynamic complexity is high due to the interaction among system components being unpredictable and/or invisible, while a "tight coupling" among a system's components (including people, equipment, and procedures) leads to a high degree of interdependence.

Many obvious features characterize effective HRO management: a fair culture where everyone has the psychological safety to report deviations and problems, a learning organization which seeks to improve continuously, and of course containment and anticipation mechanisms. Strikingly, HROs exhibit highly defined processes and procedures for normal operations, as well as for exceptions. For any foreseeable event there are clearly defined procedures, responsibilities, and actions that are to be executed in case the event takes place. As the processes in any HRO take place within a complex network (high static complexity), such specificity allows a reduction in both static and dynamic complexity: static complexity is reduced by assigning clear roles and responsibilities, therefore reducing the number of linkages in the network, while establishing clear procedures and rules in both normal operations and in case of deviations drastically reduces the dynamic complexity in the network.

HROs also have a particular approach to quality management. Rather than the assembly line approach to quality, where failure at any one task on the line leads to a defect, HROs adopt a "swiss-cheese" approach to quality. Imagine layers of Swiss cheese slices. Each hole is an opportunity for a defect or failure to occur. Layering multiple slices of cheese on top of one another greatly lowers the risk of failure, as the holes across these multiple layers of "defenses" are highly unlikely to align. HROs implement multiple layers of safeguards to limit the ability of complexity to create an adverse outcome. Some safeguards are engineered (like alarms or automatic shutdowns), some rely on people (such as pilots, surgeons, or operators), while others rest in the procedures and administrative controls themselves. The extremely low level of failure in such systems points to the success of such practices.

SIMPLICITY WINS

Complexity is a natural phenomenon that is driven by growth and expansion—as scale and scope increase, the managerial effort to coordinate processes increases. Much of this complexity is needed, but not all. The key is to identify and eradicate unnecessary and non-value-adding complexity by simplifying the process or increasing its ability to cope with this complexity. Postponement, modularity, and high-reliability organizations together provide a generic lesson about the design of any process, namely that a comparable, yet simpler solution will always outperform a more complex one in the long run. This is an important aspect of process design, especially as there is a common tendency in humans to over-engineer processes. The latter is generally done with good intent, yet also amplifies managerial challenges. In short, simplicity wins.

We conclude with a further subprinciple:

Principle #4: Complexity in process design amplifies managerial challenges.

a. Complexity is a function of the number of static elements (structure) in a process, their heterogeneity, and their dynamic interactions.
b. A comparable, yet simpler solution will always outperform a more complex one in the long term.

NOTES

1. J. Haldi and D. Whitcomb, 1967. Economies of scale in industrial plants. *Journal of Political Economy*, 75(4, Part 1), pp.373–85.
2. R.W. Schmenner, 1976. Before you build a big factory. *Harvard Business Review*, July–August 1976, pp.100–4.
3. J.C. Panzar and R.D. Willig, 1981. Economies of scope. *The American Economic Review*, 71(2), pp.268–72.
4. See H.A. Simon, 1962. The architecture of complexity. *Proceedings of the American Philosophical Society*, 106(6), pp.467–82, and W. Weaver, 1991. Science and complexity. In G. Klir (ed.), *Facets of Systems Science* (pp. 449–56). Springer.

FURTHER READING

Baldwin, C.Y. and Clark, K.B., 1997. Managing in an age of modularity. *Harvard Business Review*, 75(5), pp.84–93.

Chandler, A.D. and Hikino, T., 1994. *Scale and Scope: The Dynamics of Industrial Capitalism.* Harvard University Press (Cambridge, MA).

Gilmore, J.H. and Pine, B.J., 1997. The four faces of mass customization. *Harvard Business Review*, 75(1), pp.91–101.

Haldi, J. and Whitcomb, D., 1967. Economies of scale in industrial plants. *Journal of Political Economy*, 75(4, Part 1), pp.373–85.

Rochlin, G.I., La Porte, T.R., and Roberts, K.H., 1998. The self-designing high-reliability organization: Aircraft carrier flight operations at sea. *Naval War College Review*, 51(3), p.97.

Simon, H.A., 1962. The architecture of complexity. *Proceedings of the American Philosophical Society*, 106(6), pp.467–82.
Starr, M.K., 1965. Modular production—a new concept. *Harvard Business Review*, 43(6), pp.131–42.
Voss, C. and Hsuan, J., 2011. Service science: The opportunity to re-think what we know about service design. In H. Demirkan, J.C. Spohrer, and V. Krishna (eds), *The Science of Service Systems* (pp. 231–44). Springer US (New York).
Weaver, W., 1948. Science and complexity. *American Scientist*, 36(4), pp.536–44.

6 Aligning operations

6.1 Fit and focus

As is plain from examining the economics of an industry, much of the size of a producer's surplus is determined by the demand curve. Exploiting the demand curve, or at least coping with it, lies at the heart of much of business strategy. Operations management and its strategy can only be determined, however, once the business unit strategy has been set. Once that strategy is set, it must be interpreted to discern what it implies for operations. The competitive priorities and key performance metrics effectively translate the firm strategy into an operations strategy. In essence, operations strategy is the set of rules, policies, and restrictions used to decide how to allocate operational resources to fulfill demand. Operations strategy chooses its processes and the metrics on those processes so as to *fit* best with the business unit strategy. Fit, or alignment, between firm or business strategy and operations is achieved when operations supports firm-level objectives to the best possible degree. *Focus*, in turn, is the notion that operations cannot achieve all performance aspects simultaneously: lowest cost, highest productivity, best quality, lowest lead time, greatest flexibility, best service, etc. It needs to focus on the key competitive priorities set by firm strategy. Combined, fit and focus form the operations strategy of a firm.

This operations strategy process is not one-way, however. While old-school thinking would argue that operations must always follow strategy, this view is in fact limiting. It effectively relegates operations to simply executing strategy in the most efficient way, making "cost-efficiency" the dominant metric. This view misses the opportunity of allowing operational capabilities to challenge and inform the strategy formulation process. Think about Toyota—in its early days, its strategy was to develop affordable passenger cars for the domestic market. Given the constraints imposed by US administrators in the post-war years in Japan, it had to adapt Ford's mass-production methods. For example, the *just-in-time* (JIT) principle was developed to limit capital expenditure and material inventories. Coupled with the *jidoka* principle, which dates back to Toyota's loom manufacturing days, the Toyota Production System (TPS) gradually took shape. TPS in turn provided Toyota with leading productivity and quality outcomes, which then became core to its strategy (the "Toyota Way"). For many successful firms such as Dell, Wal-Mart, and Amazon, operations has contributed considerably to their success, and has become integral to their strategy.

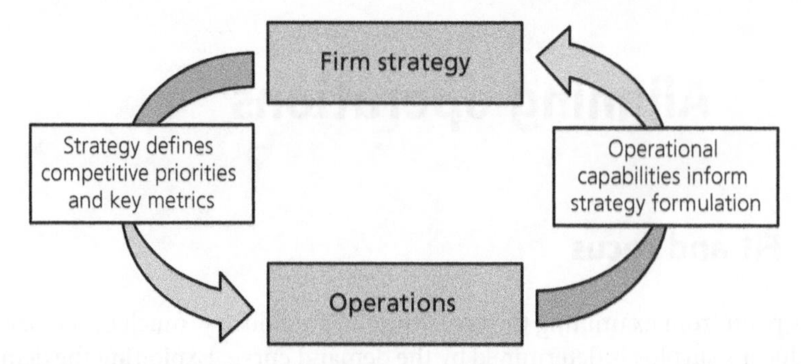

Figure 6.1 Strategy and operations: a two-way process.

Figure 6.1 captures this relationship between firm strategy and operations. The operations task is effectively the translation of the firm unit strategy into terms that operations people can use. It answers the question of what operations must do well in order for the business unit strategy to succeed. The operations task may be consistent with the classic industry demand and supply curves and thus the task may be to produce the standard product at a low price. In that way, cost reduction could be the critical goal. Alternatively, the operations task may be tied to particular market segments and, for example, it could be to stay state-of-the-art, with the ability to adjust to demanding changes in the design and production of the product. Or the task may be to offer the market quick and sure delivery. Perhaps multiple tasks are required by the business unit strategy. All of this depends on the character of the demand curves that prevail in the market segments in which the company wants to participate. Operations' strategic importance can be much more than simply clinging to low-cost producer status.

This understanding brings to the fore our next principle:

Principle #5: Process choice requires fit between the task and the external requirements.

We have covered a key aspect of process choice in Section 2.4, where we introduced the product–process matrix. In essence, there are two main dimensions that determine which types of processes are economically viable, and which ones are not. These are *volume* and *variety* for manufacturing processes, or *labor intensity* and *degree of customer interaction* for service processes (several other ways to describe this have been used also). Common to all these descriptions are the notions that the volume of the process and its variation determine which types of processes are economically appropriate and feasible.

This distinction is also of the essence in operations strategy, as the nature of the task that is to be conducted changes as volume and variety change. The higher the volume, the more a firm is able to split the tasks at hand into smaller, repetitive tasks. This has three main advantages: first, a smaller task that repeats often is easier to define, measure, and improve. Frequent repetition allows firms to exploit the learning curve more easily, and productivity should increase. Second, the skill level required reduces, as simpler tasks require less skilled and thus cheaper labor. Third, splitting tasks into small subtasks allows for a better load balancing across workers, which also increases productivity by minimizing idle time.

We formulate this as our first subprinciple:

Principle #5: Process choice requires fit between the task and the external requirements.

a. The higher the volume/lower the variety of the process, the more segregated and specialized tasks will become.

An increase in volume or reduction in variety also changes the equipment or production assets that are commonly used. As the volume increases, there is a much greater scope to invest in dedicated and automated equipment. Automation, for example through robots and conveyor or transfer systems, tends to become economical only where tasks are repeated continuously. Robots can handle some variety, but on balance still work best in high-volume, low-variety environments. As a downside, then, a higher degree of automation is also likely to increase the rigidity of the plant.

We formulate this as our second subprinciple:

Principle #5: Process choice requires fit between the task and the external requirements.

a. The higher the volume/lower the variety of the process, the more segregated and specialized tasks will become.
b. The higher the volume/lower the variety of the process, the more dedicated the assets it uses will be.

The choice of process to be employed by a company thus depends on the needs of the product or service to be marketed and the fit of that need to the marketplace, to technology, to any regulations, and to the environment.

Let us consider manufacturing first.

6.2 Manufacturing (and) strategy

As should be clear by now, manufacturing managers have a wealth of choices as to the means by which they can influence the manufacture of goods. These choices are encountered everywhere, especially where there is no consensus on the best way to do things and where practice is itself diverse. We review the matter by providing some major headings that help to define how a process is designed and within which there can be disagreement. Some potentially critical questions are offered under each heading.

Operations choices can be segregated into three broad categories: (1) technology and facilities, (2) operating *policies*, and (3) operations *organization*. Let us review these categories and choices in turn.

TECHNOLOGY AND FACILITIES

These choices frequently involve large capital expenditures and long periods of time. These are the big decisions that do much to define the type of process employed.

- Nature of the process flow—which type of process (e.g. job shop, assembly line) makes the most sense to institute.
- The degree of vertical integration—what does the company do for itself and what is it most appropriate to have others do for it; this is sometimes called the make-or-buy decision.
- Types of equipment—to what degree is general-purpose equipment called for rather than more special-purpose equipment.
- Degree of capital or labor intensity—how much equipment should be purchased and how much of any workforce should be displaced by it.
- Attitude towards the process technology—should the company invest its own resources in process technology advance, and to what degree.
- Attitude towards capacity utilization—how much spare capacity ought there to be.
- Plant size—at what point should any expansion in the size and employment at a facility be stopped and an entirely new facility be sought.
- Plant charters and locations—what should a particular plant be charged to produce (e.g. product range, process to be mastered) and what should the geographic dispersion of the various plants look like.

OPERATING POLICIES

Once the process technology and facilities have been selected, management must still decide on a host of features concerning how the process technology is used. Three broad segments of such operating policies present themselves: loading the factory, controlling the movement of goods through it, and distribution.

In terms of loading the factory, consider the following:

- Sourcing—how many different suppliers ought there to be and what should the contracts with them look like.

- Supply logistics—to what extent does the company provide its own logistics for supply and to what extent does it contract with others.
- Raw materials inventory system—what quantities of raw materials are kept and how are those raw materials monitored so that there is always enough when and where needed.
- Production planning—to what extent are level production strategies pursued and to what extent are chase strategies pursued.
- Maintenance—how much preventive maintenance is engaged and what does that maintenance look like.

In terms of controlling movement through the factory, consider:

- Production scheduling and inventory control—what acts as the trigger for production (e.g. ERP system decisions, signals from downstream customers), and how much work-in-process inventory is kept and how is it tracked.
- Pacing of production—is the pace of production determined by workers themselves, supervision, signals from the marketplace, machines, or another method.
- Production methods—typically different methods can be used to produce a particular product, some more expensive than others, some with better inherent quality, some with more or less waste of materials, etc.
- Production control—to what degree are items tracked and how is this done.
- Quality control—how much investment in inspection and in prevention is made, and what types of quality improvement program are engaged in.
- Workforce policies and training—who is thought to make up the ideal worker, how are such workers recruited, how are they paid, how are they trained, how much cross-training is done.

In terms of distributions, consider:

- Distribution—what are the levels of the distribution system, how many of them are there, and where is that distribution to be.
- Logistics—how is the product transported through the distribution channels and to the marketplace.

ORGANIZATION OF OPERATIONS

Here two key decisions or choices are important in relation to:

- Operations control, measurement, and evaluation—what measures of the process are consistent with the corporate strategy and what measures would be counterproductive; how are those measures captured and used.
- Where talent is placed—which talents are absolutely critical to the operation and thus must be managed well (e.g. supervision, planning, technology).

These choices—and all operations must make them, either explicitly or implicitly—define to a great degree the design of the company's production process—what it looks like and how it operates. Furthermore, these choices are a significant determinant of how well an operation is running or could be expected to run. This is an important point; let us consider it in greater depth.

We have discovered that for each broadly defined type of process (job shop, batch flow, line flow, continuous flow), certain characteristics of the process hang together and define what that process is. For example, one would expect a job shop to be characterized by such operations choices as general-purpose equipment, broad work content of the jobs workers perform, production to order, and lots of information flowing within the shop. If these features were not all present, one would have good reason for suspecting that the particular process being investigated was not a pure job shop. Similarly, one would expect a continuous flow operation to be characterized by operations choices such as special-purpose equipment and capital intensity, production to stock rather than to order, machine pacing of production, and at least some dependence on the forecasting of demand. Deviations from this list would also raise questions about whether this was a pure continuous flow operation.

We can proceed a step further. Not only do certain broad characteristics of any process hang together, but they should hang together. The operations choices we have outlined should be carefully matched up to be consistent with one another. In most instances, deviations from the model and consistently defined process should be avoided because they run a serious risk of acting at cross purposes to the other elements of the process. For example, a "job shop" whose workers are limited by their training or by management edict to perform only a few, very specific tasks risks losing a great deal of flexibility and scheduling ease compared to a job shop where workers have a broad work content to their jobs. Such a process choice risks establishing workers as well as machines as regular bottlenecks to the shop capacity. Clearly, in this case, worker tasks ought to be expanded.

To cite another example, a line flow operation that permits many or significant engineering changes on a regular basis risks losing the benefits of production speed, lower labor value in the product, and low work-in-process inventories. The products of a line flow process should be fairly standard; if they cannot be, the other elements chosen for the process ought to be seriously examined and the process altered to make it less line flow and perhaps more batch flow.

Consistency in the choice of process characteristics is the essence of Principle #5 and of what has come to be known as manufacturing strategy. Let us explore it in more depth.

To say that certain broad characteristics of any process should hang together as a consistent whole is not to say that every operations choice mentioned can be unambiguously assigned to a specific process. Picking the process does not at the same time mean that all of the operations choices we discussed are automatically determined. A company typically can exercise a great deal of latitude in selecting the specific elements of its production process. The job shop and the continuous flow process, which lie at either end of the process spectrum, are probably more constrained to specific choices of process elements than are batch or line flow operations. In other words, the job shop and continuous flow processes must, in general, be consistent over a greater range of process element choices than either a batch or line flow process. Nevertheless, considerable choice is possible in defining almost any process. Recall also that different challenges to management are inherent in different types of production processes and in the process elements that make them up. Here, too, the job shop and continuous flow process are more clear-cut in what they demand of management. For the job shop, scheduling workers and machines, bidding for new jobs, handling materials, and maintaining the flexibility to manufacture a great variety of goods are paramount to management. For a continuous flow process, management's challenges are completely different: care with the planning of capacity and new process technology, and with the management of materials from suppliers to the plant and from the plant to the customers. The challenges to management for batch or line flow operations are less well delineated, since both must be concerned with the balance of capacities within the process, product flexibility, worker motivation and training, and product design. There are shades of stress on these challenges, but the distinctions between them are more blurred and less clear-cut.

Too many managers falsely believe that manufacturing's goal should be low-cost production in every instance. As the discussion earlier of industry economics and company strategy indicates, being the lowest-cost producer is often a very advantageous position, but market segmentation requires many other ways to compete successfully. Products can be differentiated from one another too readily and markets have too many niches in which companies can position their products. In one sense, this marketing diversity takes the heat off operations people to cut costs continually; but in another sense, it broadens the role of operations in the company, because operations must now react to different sets of competitive demands.

What is more, the competitive demands that can be placed on manufacturing are diverse and numerous. Eight major competitive demands, sometimes termed manufacturing tasks, come to mind. They can be organized into three distinctly different groups: (1) product-related concerns, (2) delivery-related concerns, and (3) cost concerns.

Product-related concerns

- *Product performance.* Whether the product's design or engineering permits it to do more or better than comparable products.

- *Product reliability and workmanship.* Apart from differences in product design, whether the quality of materials and workmanship enhances the product's value and increases its durability and reliability.
- *Product customization.* How adaptable the operation is to meeting special customer specifications.
- *New product introduction.* How readily the operation can bring out product variations or completely new products.

Delivery-related concerns

- *Speed of delivery.* The time between order taking and customer delivery.
- *Delivery reliability.* Apart from the speed of delivery, how close actual delivery is to any quoted or anticipated delivery dates.
- *Volume flexibility.* How readily the operation can switch production rates on some or all of its products.

Cost concerns

- *Cost to produce.* The traditional burden on manufacturing to become the lowest-cost producer, generally related to higher volumes and less customization.

Which of these competitive demands takes priority at a company depends on several forces: the economics of the industry, particular competitive pressures, government mandates and incentives, the company's own resources, and the company's culture and attitudes. What is important to recognize is that operations can be subject to different, and changing, competitive demands. Determining priorities for competitive demands frequently is challenging. Marketing managers typically want the company to compete on all aspects. They can recognize competitors that cater to each "manufacturing task," although no one competitor competes across all dimensions. Determining the competitive demands the firm will concentrate on (essentially, translating the business unit strategy into clear manufacturing tasks) often is very difficult.

All of this said, manufacturing has more to offer the company than what some business strategists thought, not so long ago, were the strategy elements of manufacturing: economies of scale and the learning curve. For these strategists, manufacturing benefits a company when it can increase its scale and lower its cost, and when, through experience, manufacturing can move down the learning curve ahead of other companies. What is significant here is that the notions of economies of scale and learning curve are both cost-related. What those strategists neglect are the many other ways by which manufacturing can be strategically important to the company. Good manufacturing strategy can highlight the importance of these non-cost-related factors.

TRANSLATION: THE TOUGHEST THING

From our experience, the toughest aspect of the manufacturing strategy process is making the translation from business unit strategy to a set of manufacturing tasks. The translation has to be in plain language so that manufacturing can discern what its true priorities are, and also understand how it is to be measured against those priorities. The sad fact of the matter is that the numerous manufacturing choices listed earlier in this chapter will be made by the company by one means or another. If neither manufacturing nor general management become involved in setting tasks and in making these choices, they will be made by people lower in the organization, including workers and foremen. If companies do not engage in a dialogue about these priorities, they risk inconsistencies all across the board. For general management, the question is a very real one: who do you want to run the company? Do you want general management to run the company, or do you want foremen's and workmen's decisions on strategic matters to hold sway?

Not falling prey to this problem takes concerted action. What is needed is a determination from top management of what corporate strategy means for manufacturing—an evaluation of the importance of the eight "manufacturing tasks" cited earlier. Once manufacturing is clear about what is demanded of it, it can go about choosing the technology, facilities, operating policies, and organization that are at once internally consistent and consistent with the declared corporate strategy and competitive priorities. The importance of these consistencies has been argued forcefully and persuasively by Wickham Skinner, the acknowledged "father" of manufacturing strategy.[1]

For Skinner, good manufacturing strategy must start with an explicit statement of the corporation's objectives and business unit strategy. This statement must then be translated into "what it means for manufacturing," and the existing operation must be examined, element by element, in a kind of manufacturing audit of the existing facilities, technology, and operating policies. Only then can the company think of altering any of the elements that do not mesh with the explicit statements of corporate strategy and its meaning for operations. The goal is to have all of the operation—right down to the first-line supervisors and all of the workforce—pulling in the same direction, the direction implied by the proclaimed corporate strategy. Manufacturing should be well coordinated with marketing, finance, personnel, engineering, R&D, and other departments. Naturally, this takes a substantial amount of communication and discussion among functions and between levels of the organization.

THE FOCUSED FACTORY REVISITED

Skinner is also the original advocate for the "focused factory."[2] The focused factory concentrates on a limited range of products or processes, knowing that the factory cannot do everything well. Typically, a focused factory is a factory devoted to a single product line. It is a particularly compelling design for many situations.

Focused factories have a number of things going for them:

1. **Factory focus reduces the impact of variation.**
   Factory focus is a strategic way to reduce the impact of variation. Focused factories resemble manufacturing cells, only writ large. They contain a broad cross section of operations and support functions (e.g. engineering, quality, production planning and control, accounting)—everything required for the production of the product assigned to them. They reduce the impact that variation can have on all of a company's manufacturing.
2. **Factory focus allows flows to surface, to be studied and improved.**
   By segregating products (or processes), focused factories isolate flows effectively and this can accelerate the rethinking and redefinition of those flows. When the complications of other products (or processes) are removed, often those close to the process can see the next logical steps much more clearly. Bottlenecks can be determined and broken. Waste can be more easily identified and removed. Quality-related feedback loops are shorter and less convoluted and this, too, can help.
3. **Firms learn more quickly in focused factories.**
   Learning can be quicker in a focused factory, not only because the flows of materials and information are readily identified and clear to all, but also because of two other factors:
   - First, focused factories tend to have fewer layers of overhead personnel, largely because the flow of the product is more visible and comprehensible and fewer overhead people are needed. More people are thus directly placed into situations where they can learn and experiment, and this helps the learning process.
   - Second, because most sources of cost are directly attached to the focused factory (and thus to the product line it produces) rather than allocated to it, product costs are better known. Accounting and performance measurement are simpler, less arbitrary, and thus typically more effective in a focused factory.

Skinner, in his classic article, argued that: "Focused manufacturing is based on the concept that simplicity, repetition, experience, and homogeneity of tasks breed competence."[3] Learning is breeding competence.

MULTI-PLANT STRATEGIES

Focused factories are usually part of a portfolio of factories that a corporation controls. Equally, there are often portfolios of operations units for services, such as for example bank outlets. That portfolio has its own logic. Analysis of company branch plants and of the base, or "mother," plants from which they typically spring reveals that branch plants fit into a prescribed place in a multi-plant company's scheme of things. Four general types of multi-plant manufacturing strategies seem to prevail in the operating divisions of large companies. Behind each one are some compelling cost or managerial reasons.

The product plant strategy—Perhaps the most popular strategy is the product plant strategy, where distinct products or product lines are manufactured in separate plants, each plant serving the entire market area (e.g. Europe, North America, Asia, or even the world).

The product plant strategy permits each plant to concentrate on a limited set of products, generally within a well-defined market niche. This concentration has the advantage of permitting the plant management to select the process technology, equipment, labor force, manufacturing policies, and organization that are consistent with the particular competitive priorities (e.g. cost, performance, product flexibility, speed of delivery, or quality and reliability) associated with the plant's products. In this way, the company can avoid much of the complexity and congestion that plague many oversize, multipurpose factories. In addition, if there are any economies of scale to be reaped, a product plant strategy can take advantage of them. Product plants can also take advantage of any raw materials or worker expertise that are specific to particular geographic areas.

Within such a strategy, a significant challenge to management lies in recognizing when a plant has become too large, and *diseconomies of scale* or volume may creep in. What constitutes "too large" varies from industry to industry, technology to technology, and company to company; but the most frequently quoted figures lie between 500 and 1,000 employees, with few studies stating figures in excess of 2,000.

Companies in many industries can divide operations according to a product plant strategy because their products are many and varied. It is particularly popular for fast-moving consumer goods or electronic products. Also many chemical processing companies follow product plant strategies. It is a popular multi-plant strategy for both large and smaller corporations.

The market area plant strategy—Under this strategy, plants are designated to serve particular market areas. The plants themselves manufacture all or most of the corporation's product line. When freight costs are important because of high product weight or volume relative to value, it makes sense to spread plants apart geographically. This is all the more true if products are consumed over wide areas, and if the market requires a quick response by manufacturing.

The market area plant is perhaps the classic notion of a branch plant. It was the strategy that prevailed in many companies in Europe before the establishment of the Single Market, when many countries were hiding behind tariff and non-tariff barriers. At that time, many companies had multi-product plants sited in each of the major countries of Western Europe. Those plants would have been overseen by a country managing director. Since 1992, however, many companies have changed from a market area plant strategy to a more efficient product plant strategy. As a result, country managing directors are less numerous, replaced simply by plant managers who report to a headquarters, either regional or international in character. With the growing reaction against globalization we may see the rebirth of some of these market area plants, trading in some efficiency in exchange for higher national control.

The process plant strategy—Rather than separate their products into individual plants, some companies, notably those with complex products, separate their production process into various plants. These plants are often viewed as feeders to one or more final assembly plants. A process plant strategy is less prevalent than either the product plant or market area plant strategies.

Like the product plant, the process plant exists to simplify an inherently complex and confusing managerial situation. For complex products like airplanes, large machine tools, and computer systems, a number of plants become involved in making components of the completed product. The manufacturer typically faces a rash of make-or-buy choices for many of these components, but to be able to produce one or another of these components competitively may require different raw materials, labor skills, control systems, or management skills and organization. This difficulty, coupled with the already discussed diseconomies introduced by large size, argues for a division of the complete manufacturing process into stages, with separate plants for each stage. This stage-by-stage division may lead to many feeder plants shipping to one or more assembly plants, or to one or a few feeder plants (for a critical component, say) shipping to many other manufacturing plants. German chemicals producers are known for what is sometimes called a "Verbund" or an association of many chemical plants that feed into each other. The output or a by-product from one plant becomes the input for another one. BASF has actually reproduced this concept all over the world. In Singapore the government has created an island reclaimed from the sea, Jurong Island, which offers a similar network for petrochemical plants of different companies. For other industries, e.g. machinery or textiles, this has sometimes been described as an "industrial commons."[4] In any event, the concept of plant separation to simplify operations persists.

The general-purpose plant strategy—Some companies do not establish specific plant charters. Rather, plants are prized for their flexibility in adapting to constantly changing product needs. Defense contractors, among others, are typical companies following a general-purpose plant strategy.

GLOBAL NETWORKS OF PLANTS

In recent years Vereecke et al. and others have argued that we need also to analyze the role a factory plays in a larger network of operational units.[5] Their focus is on the network of factories and the flows between those factories: flows of capital, goods, people, and knowledge. Focusing on the knowledge-generating role of a factory for the overall company, they make the distinction between four types of plants:

- **Isolated plants**, which are almost outside of the knowledge network; their main role is to produce according to a blueprint. Many of them are "footloose," i.e. they have no real connection to the local community and can easily be closed or transferred.
- **Receiver plants**, which are well integrated but do not produce (process) knowledge and simply receive the knowledge from other units.
- **Hosting network factories**, which play a key role in receiving and sending people from all over the network; they play a significant role in the dissemination of know-how throughout the network. Often they are close to the headquarters of the company or have played a significant historical role in the development of the firm.
- **Active network factories**, which are at the edge of know-how production for the whole network.

This classification has a significant impact on how you manage the individual factories and the network as a whole. Isolated and receiver plants do benefit from a low-cost environment, but from Vereecke et al.'s empirical analysis it is clear that such considerations are far less relevant for hosting and active network factories. They also suggest that senior operations managers who oversee the portfolio of plants need to preserve the balance between the different types of factories. They followed the evolution of a few factory networks over a period of twenty years and have been able to document the dynamics in these networks. As one would expect, there has been a clear geographical shift towards East Asia. But an interesting observation was that through dynamic management of the network the companies were able to preserve a balance of the different types of factories.

In more recent work, Ferdows et al. observe that some of the networks of multinational corporations have become so complex that perhaps there is a need to cluster them in groups of plants.[6] They propose that global operations managers should group their different plants and factories in "focused clusters," based on three criteria: the extent to which process knowledge is proprietary or standardized, the degree to which the products produced in the plants are unique or standardized, and finally the degree of rootedness (i.e. to what extent is the factory rooted in the local industrial networks of

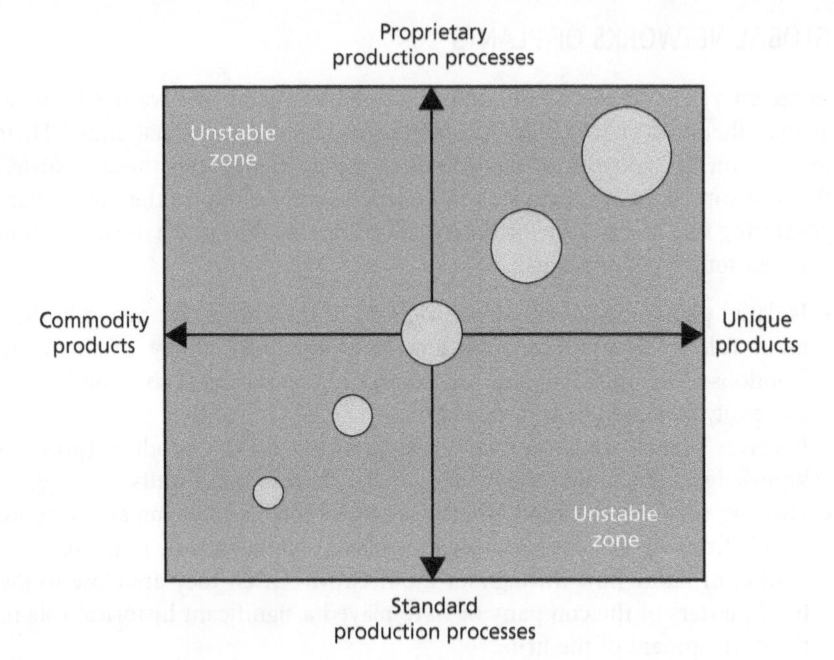

Figure 6.2 Focused clusters; the size of the circles indicates the rootedness.

Source: Ferdows et al. (2016).

suppliers, technology providers, educational institutions, etc.). They suggest that, based on this classification, global operations managers should map their clusters of factories on the matrix proposed in Figure 6.2. Ideally, clusters should be on the diagonal of the matrix, and the size of the bubbles, representing the degree of rootedness, should increase towards the upper right corner of the matrix. Deviations from these ideal configurations can exist, but need to be strategically justified.

6.3 **Service (and) strategy**

THE SERVICE ENCOUNTER AND WHAT SURROUNDS IT

In the provision of services, it has been noted that there is often a "moment of truth"—a phrase usually associated with Jan Carlzon, former CEO of SAS, the Scandinavian airline—where the service process comes face to face with the customer, and where the customer can easily confront his or her willingness to purchase the service or to continue an association with the company.

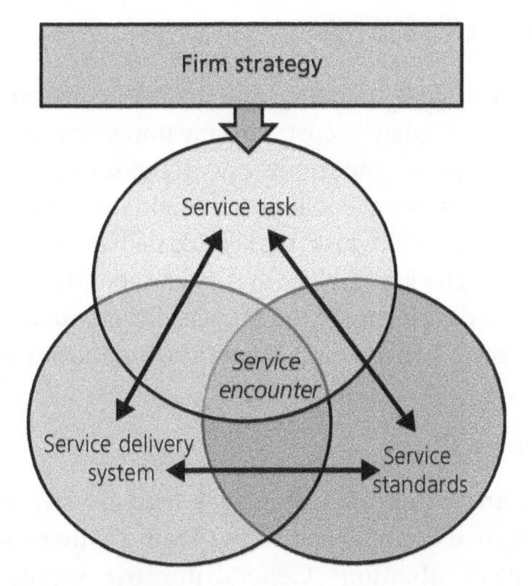

Figure 6.3 Service strategy framework.

This occurs during what is termed the "service encounter," when the customer and the service meet and interact. Surrounding and supporting the service encounter, where this "moment of truth" flourishes, are three attributes of service management that need to be clearly defined, and that permit the service encounter to be a pleasant one for all concerned (please refer to Figure 6.3).

SERVICE TASK

The service task states why the service exists in the marketplace and what the customer truly values about the service. It is a statement that conveys the essence of what the service provides to the customer, and thus provides both management and the workforce with a goal to achieve. In more fashionable terms, it is the "voice of the customer" in how the service is delivered. Note that the service task is always defined with reference to the customer; a service task that ignores the customer is almost invariably from a service business that is suffering, or at least on the verge of a downturn.

SERVICE STANDARDS

Service standards define what is effective provision to the customer. The standards are the controls, the guardians of quality and cost-efficiency in the service firm. Standards are measurable. Thus, one should be able to go down a checklist of standards or audit the service to determine how well it is being delivered.

THE SERVICE DELIVERY SYSTEM

The service delivery system specifies how the service is produced, including how it is controlled for quality, cost, and customer satisfaction. The service delivery system needs to be synchronized with the service task and the service standards so that the service encounter remains a pleasurable one for all concerned. With a clear service task, the service delivery system can be selected with more assurance. The key choices that most types of service business have to think through and decide on are the same as for manufacturing: technology and facilities, operating policies, and operations organization.

Technology and Facilities

- Type of facility and equipment (Are they used by customers themselves? How? How attractive do they have to be? How are they used during a peak versus a non-peak situation? General-purpose versus special-purpose equipment? Anything proprietary about the equipment or its use?)
- Layout (Job shop-like? Fixed position? Other?)
- Location (How critical is it to attracting customers?)
- Size of the facility
- Geographic spread of any multiple facilities
- Degree of labor intensity
- Attitude towards capacity utilization (Facility for the peak demand or not?)

Operating Policies

A. Planning the operation
  - Forecasting (Extent required? Type used?)
  - Sourcing of any materials needed
  - Logistics and inventory system used for materials employed
  - Manpower planning (How many needed? Where? When?)
  - Schedule setting (Can service provision be "leveled" in any way?)
  - Demand management for peak and off-peak times (Can customers be shifted to off-peak times with either price or non-price incentives?)

B. Controlling the operation
  - Labor issues (Hiring, training, skill levels required, job content, pay, advancement, unionism)
  - Controls used (For materials, for demand management...)
  - Checklists developed (typically for quality)
  - Foolproofing designed into the layout and the equipment
  - Quality control audits and policies
  - What triggers provision of the service and the pace of the operation? (Customer? Forecast?)

- Production control (How does the information flow within the operation? What is on track? What is not? How can anything gone amiss be fixed? How can any changes be implemented?)

Operations Organization

- What is kept at the individual unit level, and what is centralized?
- Where is talent held in the organization?

STRENGTHENING THE SERVICE ENCOUNTER

The service encounter is strengthened when the three attributes—service task, service standards, and service delivery system—that surround the service encounter are mutually consistent. Service operations tend to lose out if these three compete with one another or if one or more of them is neglected.

Just as manufacturing choices work best when they are consistent with each other and with the competitive priorities implied by the business strategy, so do service operations choices. Service business competition can be as cutthroat as any, perhaps more so, because barriers to entry are frequently lower for service businesses. The service business with inconsistent operations choices is often quickly weeded out.

Service businesses can no more be all things to all customers than can manufacturers. The concept of "factory focus"—which argues that factories perform better when their goals are limited—has easy parallels in the service arena. A number of the criticisms leveled at various service companies reflect concern over too many different kinds of services offered or a failure to achieve the operational synergies touted when a merger or acquisition was first undertaken. One cannot assume that the "formula" that has been so successful in one service business will necessarily carry over to another service business, even if that business is merely a segmentation of the old one. An interesting example of this is the airline industry: in most cases the established airlines like Singapore Airlines (SIA) had to spin off their low-cost airlines, because there was an inherent conflict in having the same organization delivering very different levels of service. In the case of SIA they even developed separate airlines for regional service (Silkair), short distance low-cost service (Tiger Airways), and medium to long distance low-cost service (Scoot). United Airlines had a very similar experience with its low-cost arm, Shuttle by United, earlier on.

Think about the service companies with great reputations and strong financial performances. They are absolutely clear about why customers come to them rather than the competition. They measure how they provide their services and what their levels of quality and cost are. And their service delivery systems are well conceived and understood.

Defining the service task is tough. A lot of services have a wishy-washy, me-too type of character; they are services with not very well-defined service tasks. They lack a clear vision as to why a customer might choose them over somebody else. These wishy-washy, me-too services often earn returns below their potential; some do not last long at all in the marketplace. On the other hand, if the service task is well defined, it can help to separate that service in the customer's eyes from the run-of-the-mill. Well-defined services thus stand a much better chance of making money. The resurgences of some firms have in large measure been stimulated by rethinking and restating their service tasks. The current malaise at other companies has been attributed, in part, to a lost appreciation for their customers and how those customers think. Stating the service task clearly, using fifty words or fewer, can help a company latch onto what it must do to keep its customers coming.

If the service task can be stated extremely clearly, say in twenty words or fewer, it is more likely that that service task can become engrained in the workforce. Every worker then knows what he or she has to do to fit into a grand scheme that the customer values. The service task becomes a part of the corporate culture, a motto, creed, or slogan that everyone respects and follows, almost instinctively. If that occurs, then you are much better off, and stand a still better chance of making a lot of money. Thus, the simpler the statement of the service task, the easier it is for the workforce to provide the company with a real advantage.

NOTES

1. See Wickham Skinner, *Manufacturing: The Formidable Competitive Weapon*, Wiley, 1985, which brings together a number of Skinner's articles that appeared first in the *Harvard Business Review*.
2. W. Skinner, 1974. The focused factory. *Harvard Business Review*, 52(3), pp.113–21.
3. See p.115 of Skinner, Focused factory.
4. The notion of an "industrial commons" was introduced by G. Pisano and W. Shih, 2012. *Producing Prosperity: Why America Needs a Manufacturing Renaissance*. Harvard Business Review Press.
5. A. Vereecke, R. Van Dierdonck, and A. De Meyer, 2006. A typology of plants in global manufacturing networks. *Management Science*, 52(11), pp.1737–50.
6. K. Ferdows, A. Vereecke, and A. De Meyer, 2016. Delayering the global production network into congruent subnetworks. *Journal of Operations Management*, 41, pp.63–74.

FURTHER READING

Ferdows, K., Vereecke, A., and De Meyer, A., 2016. Delayering the global production network into congruent subnetworks. *Journal of Operations Management*, 41, pp.63–74.

Hayes, R., Pisano, G., and Upton, D., 1996. *Strategic Operations: Competing through Capabilities*. Free Press (New York).

Schmenner, R.W., 1982. Multiplant manufacturing strategies among the Fortune 500. *Journal of Operations Management*, 2(2), pp.77–86.

Schmenner, R.W., 1995. *Service Operations Management*. Prentice-Hall (Upper Saddle River, NJ).

Skinner, W., 1969. Manufacturing—missing link in corporate strategy. *Harvard Business Review*, 47(3), pp.137–45.

Vereecke, A., Van Dierdonck, R., and De Meyer, A., 2006. A typology of plants in global manufacturing networks. *Management Science*, 52(11), pp.1737–50.

7 Measuring performance

We have already noted that various measures—capacity, yields, inventories, cost, and time—can be tagged to a process flow diagram. Such measures are very useful for locating bottlenecks and for determining where processes can be improved. The realm of measurement, of course, spills over to a much larger canvas. Whole operations need to be assessed and their problems identified and evaluated. With this chapter, we move from *design* to *measurement*.

7.1 Why measure?

Measurement is the empirical assessment of a given characteristic, in our case a specific aspect of the input, conversion, and predominantly outcome of a process. Measurement forms the fundamental basis on which managerial decisions are made, and validated or refuted. It has been often said that "You cannot manage what you cannot measure." Without measurement it is impossible to design and validate effective managerial interventions.

There is a wide range of process measurement schemata available; before going into detail on what these may entail it is important to outline the key dimensions or types of measurements. Most importantly, there is the time dimension: is the metric forward-looking, or is it a retrospective measurement? Forward-looking metrics cover what should happen in the future, such as the number of new products under development or offer letters sent to prospective clients, while retrospective measures cover what has happened in the past, such as number of units built or number of defects observed. A second key dimension or type is financial versus non-financial metrics. Financial metrics include all costing data, including stock or inventory turns (as this is based on a financial valuation of inventory), versus operational metrics such as number of units in inventory, lead times, defect rates, and the like. At firm level it is generally good practice to combine both forward- and backward-looking metrics, as well as financial and non-financial metrics. Established combinations of such metrics include Kaplan and Norton's "Balanced Scorecard" and Neely's "Performance Prism."[1]

For the purpose of measuring a process, there are two critical questions for which we need measures:

1. Is the process performing well? This is a routine, everyday type of question to ask.
2. Is the process doing for us what we need to do to be competitive? This, in contrast, is ultimately a very strategic question to ask.

We will address these critical questions in turn, along with the principles allied to them.

7.2 **Is the process performing well?**

A process is a complex entity. Like another complex entity, the human body, there is no single measure of the health of the "organism." The body can be sick, yet its temperature may still be normal. So it is with processes. The "dashboards" for many companies consist of a variety of measures, testament to the fact that no one measure adequately captures everything that one needs to capture to manage a process well. The major performance measures are of several types.[2] We will include only a fraction of all of the measures that companies have devised; these are the measures that we find most persuasive.

Our first measurement principle, number six in our list of ten, therefore is this:

Principle #6: No single measure can capture the performance of a process.

The two most basic categories of performance are the *effectiveness* and *efficiency* of a process.

Effectiveness describes the process from the customer's point of view: does the process deliver the expected cost, quality, and lead time required by the customer? This is the outward-looking view of process performance. It considers how well the process meets the objectives of those consuming its products and services.

The inward-looking metric is looking into how *efficiently* the process converts resources into outcomes. Both effectiveness and efficiency are necessary, while neither is sufficient: an effective process that meets customer demand but is inefficient in its resource utilization will mean that the company is uncompetitive and will go out of business sooner rather than later. Equally, an efficient process that does not meet customer expectations will not support a firm in the long run. One always needs both: effectiveness in meeting customer needs, and efficiency in resource utilization.

Let us consider both in more detail.

EFFECTIVENESS: THE EXTERNAL VIEW

The external view of process performance considers the voice of the customer, asking a simple question: does the process fulfill the requirements set by the customer? Common metrics include the basic QCD metrics: quality (does the product or service meet the quality standard?), cost (does the product or service meet the cost expectations, e.g. agreed price?), and delivery (was the product or service delivered within the expected lead time?) These can be complemented by measures regarding service (how quickly was a complaint resolved?), flexibility (to what degree can volume or specifications be changed?), sustainability (e.g. energy consumption, carbon footprint), and the like. The effectiveness of a process can only be assessed by the customer, and the customer alone.

EFFICIENCY: THE INTERNAL VIEW

Efficiency considerations assess to what degree the process uses resources well. These metrics are generally based on the notion of productivity. Very often productivity in operations is narrowly defined, most commonly as labor productivity—how much output the operation generates for the amount of labor that is applied. This certainly is an important metric and easily measured, but it is also a limited one. In like fashion, productivity metrics can be applied to any resource: labor, machinery, energy, or materials. A more complete measure but one that is harder to measure is *total factor* productivity, defined as the ratio of all outputs to all inputs:

$$(Total\ factor)\ Productivity = \frac{\sum outputs}{\sum inputs}$$

This measure of productivity thus includes both labor *and* capital as factor inputs. Because it is a ratio, one can increase productivity either by increasing the outputs for a set of given inputs, or by reducing the inputs needed for a given output.

MEASURES OF VARIATION IN THE PROCESS

As has been discussed, variation can be the bane of any type of process. Three sorts of variation are of interest: quality, quantities, and timing. A variety of measures can be associated with each.

Quality—Quality has been much studied and there are a host of metrics that can be used to diagnose quality problems and then to remedy them. This book is not the place to examine these quality metrics in detail, but a quick overview of the most important quality metrics is merited.

- Customer complaints—This is a classic measure. Often the complaints need to be categorized, as not all complaints carry the same weight.
- Scrap and rework—These are fairly easily quantified measures of quality and indicative of selected problems with the process.
- Warranty costs—These costs are easier to gather than many other costs.
- Control chart—The classic contribution of Walter Shewhart uses samples and the central limit theorem to identify when a process is in control (i.e. only random variation present) and when the process is out of control (i.e. the process cannot be counted on to produce product within specifications, due to an assignable cause). The control chart can then trigger when one needs to intervene in order to fix a process whose quality is suffering from an assignable cause. (See also Chapter 8 on Six Sigma.)
- Process capability chart—A tool that can demonstrate which machines, or subprocesses, are capable of holding the necessary tolerances without producing units that are out of specifications.
- Yields over time—A document of what yields have been at specific points in time.
- Frequency distribution of defects over time—A document counting defects of various types over time, used to help find out where any problems may be located.

Quantities—The variation in quantities produced can be significant.

- Stock-keeping units (SKUs)—The number of different models or variants for the product lines produced.
- Production plan variation—A measure of the dispersion of production quantities for key products over time. This measure could be the range (maximum less minimum) for a product over the time period (a fairly simple measure), or the standard deviation of the distribution of production quantities (a more sophisticated measure).
- Deviation of actual from plan—A difference measure of actual sales (or production) from the planned production of the item.
- Percent of orders shipped complete—This is one of the classic measures of actual performance versus what the customer ordered. The measure should not solely list the number of items shipped versus the number ordered. Rather, it should capture whether the customer received precisely what was ordered, both what was ordered and how much was ordered.
- Inventories—The extent to which inventories accumulate (either inventory counts themselves or inventory as a percentage of sales) can indicate whether production matches sales well or not.

Timing—Variation in timing is even more problematic than variation in quantities. It can be more disruptive to the process.

- Degree of expediting—This is a measure of how much expediting has been accomplished in order for customer needs to be fulfilled. A typical measure is the percentage of orders expedited.
- Percentage of orders shipped by customer-defined due date—This is a measure of how on-time production has been, using the customer's preferred due date as the reference.
- Time from order to delivery—This measure shows (in days) how long it takes to satisfy the customer with the product ordered.
- Extent of any backlog—This can give one an idea of how much still needs to be done, measured in units.

MORE SPECIALIZED METRICS

There are a variety of more specialized, and often sector-specific, metrics. This section lists some illustrative ones.

Supply Chain Metrics

- Throughput time—The total time it takes to produce the product from scratch. This includes both the value-added time and the non-value-added time. It can be defined for a factory operation or for the entire supply chain.
- Supplier on-time performance—This metric should be gauged from the point of view of the customer. It can track the fraction of the materials needed that arrived on time.
- Time from order to delivery—This is a time measure that is most relevant to the customer, although for the supply chain itself the more challenging metric is the throughput time measure. The time from order to delivery can be lessened to the extent that delivery is from inventory, either finished goods or work-in-process. Throughput time, on the other hand, requires tracking the complete process from start to finish.
- Degree of any bullwhip effect—To measure the bullwhip effect one can track the quantities at different stages of the supply chain and also track, over time, the variability of orders from each stage.
- Stock-outs—These can be stock-outs at the finished goods level, but the measure could also capture stock-outs from within the supply chain at levels lower than the finished goods level.

Environmental/Sustainability Metrics

- Waste generation—How much waste is generated in the process? How does it compare over time?
- Recycling—How much of the waste that has been generated can be recycled?

- Energy use per unit of output.
- CO_2 use per unit of output.

Product Development Metrics

- Time to develop new product or model—What is the calendar time from initial product conception until ramp-up and delivery? A historical perspective/comparison is often required to appreciate this metric fully.
- Number of new products introduced to the operation in the past period(s).
- Percentage of the products that have been introduced recently (e.g. over the last two years).
- Percent/days late for new product introduction to market.

Safety

- Number of lost-time incidents.
- Time since last major accident.
- Total time lost to accidents or other safety incidents.

7.3 Interdependency of measures

Effectiveness and efficiency are two key metrics of a process. However, it is important to state that they are not perfectly correlated with each other. Or, in simple terms: a productive resource is not necessarily an effective one.

Principle #6: No single measure can capture the performance of a process.
a. Performance metrics are not necessarily independent of each other.

Our Principle #6 acknowledges that there is no one single measure that can capture a process' performance. Multiple measures are required. This raises the question, then, whether some measures are somehow more fundamental than others. If a process is to perform well, should it concentrate on certain measures first, or does it not make any difference?

The ascent of successful Japanese manufacturers in the 1970s and 1980s brought this issue to the fore. Prior to that, many people were willing to think that low-cost producers could not at the same time be producers of high-quality products. Or that a company could not at the same time offer customized products and deliver them in timely fashion. People were resigned to a realm of trade-offs. With the major Japanese manufacturers of that era, however, it seemed to be possible to purchase high-quality goods at low cost, and for those goods to be delivered in a timely manner. The old realm of trade-offs was under threat.

A solution was discovered that resolved this seeming contradiction. Research, most prominently that of Ferdows and De Meyer,[3] suggested that capabilities such as low-cost or high-quality production could be "cumulative." That is, capabilities could build on one another rather than always be at odds with one another. Their "sandcone" model (discussed in detail in Chapter 8) posited a progression of capabilities that began with quality and then progressed to delivery, then flexibility, and finally cost-efficiency. By working on specific capabilities, hanging on to those gains, and working on new capabilities, companies could accumulate capabilities and become better along multiple dimensions at the same time.

This suggests, then, that quality measures may be in an important sense more fundamental than others. Getting quality correct may be the best first step that a process can make. Likewise, cost may be more of a result of doing other things well.

7.4 Absolute vs. relative performance measures

The performance measures listed above are absolute ones. Each of them can be tracked over time and it is unambiguous whether there has been progress or not.

Such is not the case with the relative measures of a process. These are the measures that depend, to one degree or another, on a standard of some kind. Unfortunately, they have enjoyed a long history with managers and are widely used. Labor efficiency is a classic one. It is typically defined as standard labor hours divided by actual labor hours (times 100, to get a percentage).

Labor efficiency is a measure that goes back to the days of Frederick Taylor and his followers and the initial setting of labor standards for jobs. The labor standard, of course, is the time in which the process' engineers think that a worker, working with proper methods and diligently, should be able to do a particular job, at a pace that can be maintained throughout the day.

If the worker works to standard, the labor efficiency measure reads 100 percent. If the worker can "beat" the standard and perform the task in less actual time than the standard allows, the labor efficiency measure reads greater than 100 percent. Likewise, if the worker cannot maintain the standard, the labor efficiency drops below 100 percent.

As is plain to see, the labor efficiency measure depends crucially on the setting of the time standard. A time standard that is too generous leads to labor efficiency that is high. On the other hand, a time standard that is too tight leads to labor efficiency that is low. One can naturally understand why workers do not like such measures and why, when an industrial engineer comes to study a job, they might want to "sandbag" in order to get a more favorable standard. This then sets the industrial engineer to craft more and more sophisticated ways to avoid this problem—measuring jobs from a distance, rating how diligently the worker is working, using technologies such as video to study the job, using work sampling techniques, etc.

This uncertainty in establishing the standard contributes to questions about the validity of the labor efficiency measure itself. More than this, the usefulness of the measure can be called into question. Ordinarily, labor efficiency is thought to relate to labor productivity. The reasoning is that higher effort by the worker will result in both better productivity and a higher value to the labor efficiency measure.

Principle #6: No single measure can capture the performance of a process.

a. Performance metrics are not necessarily independent of each other.
b. Absolute measures are preferred to relative ones because of their greater explanatory power.

The problem with this thinking is that the labor standard at the root of the measure can just as readily describe a process that adds little or no value to the product as it can describe a process that is critical to the product. Having high labor efficiency is not a guarantee that the process itself is well designed and productive; it could be riddled with waste. Or the process could be reimagined, perhaps with the introduction of new or different equipment.

Focusing on labor standards, and perhaps trying to establish an incentive wage scheme that pays the workforce according to their performance against the standard, smacks of the scientific management movement championed by Frederick Taylor. With such a view of the workplace, the job is seen as well defined and the issue is studying it so that the workforce can accomplish the job in a very efficient manner. This is not the only way to look at the workplace. As David Hounshell makes clear in his history of Ford Motor Company's early years, the engineers at Ford were continually trying to discover how work could be moved from labor-intensive steps done by the workforce to machines that could perform things more quickly and reliably.[4] More will be said about labor efficiency when we introduce Principle #8.

Machine utilization suffers from the same kinds of complaints as labor efficiency. Machine utilization is conventionally defined as the percentage of time that a machine that is available for work is actually run. The higher the machine utilization, the more effective the process is thought to be. After all, when machines are running, output is produced.

The flaw in this thinking is that the factory only gets paid when it ships completed products. It does not get paid when any particular machine runs, unless as we argued earlier that machine is the bottleneck machine of the process and thus the one that defines whether the product can be completed. If it is the bottleneck, then management needs to lavish attention on it so that it runs for as much of the time as good maintenance permits. A general measure of machine utilization, where all machines are considered, is thus not particularly closely related to productivity. From our examination of production processes we know that machine utilization should be low for job shops. Only for the high-volume, continuous flow operation that, in essence, operates as one big machine does machine utilization make any sense as a performance measure.

As a measure, machine utilization only helps to assess whether new equipment is needed, or conversely if old equipment needs to be retired. That is, if machine utilization is high, it might argue for more investment in equipment, and if machine utilization is low, it might argue for divesting some equipment.

Similarly, the debate on product cost has raged for years. Should one try to measure product costs, or not? There remain advocates for direct costing, where individual product costs are not calculated, but where instead the overhead remains unallocated to products. However, most operations allocate overhead to their different product lines in an attempt to isolate those products that are high-margin ones from those that are low-margin ones. Decisions about the process itself can hang in the balance.

It should not be so. In many instances, the allocation of overhead to a particular product line relies on the direct labor content of that product line. Product lines with relatively more direct labor content get allocated more overhead than product lines with relatively less direct labor content. But what does direct labor have to do with the overhead? Under what logic does greater direct labor content correspond to greater use of or dependence on overhead? The notion that overhead expenses actually get saved when direct labor is removed from the process strains credulity for many operations people.

Research by Miller and Vollmann has shown that overhead is better identified with transactions than with direct labor.[5] Free the factory of transactions (order entry, inventory control, production control, quality control, purchasing, and the like) and you free it of overhead expenses. Direct labor is not at all a good proxy for the number or extent of transactions in the process. Highly labor-intensive products should not, on their own, generate more transactions than less labor-intensive products.

By calling into question the flaws in using direct labor to allocate overhead, one calls into question the construction of product costs as a whole, and certainly their use in assessing operations.

Many projects that can affect operations of all sorts are evaluated using the expected cost savings that those projects are estimated to enjoy. Such cost savings anchor many capital appropriation requests as well as the improvement projects undertaken in Six Sigma programs and others. Using such cost savings as performance measures, however, is fraught with difficulty.

For one thing, these cost savings are typically estimates in anticipation of some alteration to the process. Rarely are there thoroughly objective follow-up analyses of the actual savings realized. Many suspect that, if some thorough follow-up studies were done, the actual reduction in costs that a company realizes would have little relationship to the expected project savings that were argued for beforehand. Cost saving estimates are not themselves trustworthy performance measures.

In summary, processes can be measured in many different ways. Some of these measures are absolute in character and some are relative. For us, the best performance measures are those that capture absolute measures that can be traced directly to things that matter to processes and the variations of different types that affect them. Those measures capture real improvements to processes of all types and do not reference anything else.

Thus, a process can be determined to be "efficient" by the relative measures often used, but it need not be very productive or it need not be producing quality products. Better to stick with absolute measures to answer the critical question of how well the process is performing.

7.5 The strategic view: is the process making us competitive?

We have addressed the question of whether the process is performing well. The other critical question is whether the process is making the firm competitive. This is far from a routine question. Indeed, it takes us to the heart of operations strategy. As the old adage goes: "What gets measured gets managed." In fact, as obvious it may seem, it needs to be stated that you cannot manage what you do not measure. Without having a detailed empirical understanding of how a process is performing, any process improvement is effectively like wandering in the dark.

So we need to understand first what needs to get managed. That fundamental and strategic issue was the province of Chapter 6 and its focus on the operations task and operations choices. Such choices are at the same time large-scale and sweeping, and small-scale and subtle. They forge the distinctions that can help a process deliver on the operations task.

Whatever the operations task set for the firm and the operations choices made to complement that task, the next step is to decide on the process metrics that are consistent with the operations task. If operations choices and metrics are not both compatible with the operations task, then the strategy will suffer. This brings us to our next principle:

Principle #7: Process metrics can drive unintended behavior.

and an important subprinciple:

Principle #7: Process metrics can drive unintended behavior.
a. You cannot manage what you do not measure.

Metrics are not universal; neither are the routine metrics that describe how well a process is doing nor the strategic metrics that determine how the process is to compete within its industry. Too often, we think that metrics are standard and that we should be able to compare any two operations using standard, off-the-shelf measures. However, metrics, whatever their origin, that are inconsistent with either the operations tasks or the operations choices of the business unit can be devastating for the realization of that unit's strategy. Indeed, the easiest way to ruin a good operations strategy is to use the wrong metrics. Managers respond to metrics, and if they are inconsistent managers can be pushed to do things to or for the process that on reflection they would never otherwise do.

Recall the eight competitive demands from Chapter 6:

Product-related concerns

- *Product performance.* Whether the product's design or engineering permits it to do more or better than comparable products.
- *Product reliability and workmanship.* Apart from differences in product design, whether the quality of materials and workmanship enhances the product's value and increases its durability and reliability.
- *Product customization.* How adaptable the operation is to meeting special customer specifications.
- *New product introduction.* How readily the operation can bring out product variations or completely new products.

Delivery-related concerns

- *Speed of delivery.* The time between order taking and customer delivery.
- *Delivery reliability.* Apart from the speed of delivery, how close actual delivery is to any quoted or anticipated delivery dates.
- *Volume flexibility.* How readily the operation can switch production rates on some or all of its products.

Cost concerns

- *Cost to produce.* The traditional burden on manufacturing to become the lowest-cost producer, generally related to higher volumes and less customization.

In the typical industry, one can usually point to competitors that are stronger in one or more of these dimensions, but not universally strong across all of them. Thus, the weights given to these metrics will differ from company to company.

Too often, the metric that grabs attention at headquarters is cost. Yet cost is the headline metric much more often than it appropriately should be. If what is truly needed is speed of delivery or product customization, but instead cost is the headline metric, then the company may suffer. Company managers who are attentive to how headlines read at headquarters will either deliberately, or perhaps inadvertently, make decisions that reduce cost but that, at the same time, may also delay delivery of the product or hinder customization. The result could then be a company that ends up pulling in diverse directions and attenuating its impact on the marketplace.

In fact it is human nature to respond to the metrics used to measure individual or collective performance, so the choice of metrics drives both focus and behavior.

We add a second subprinciple to our Principle #7:

Principle #7: Process metrics can drive unintended behavior.
a. You cannot manage what you do not measure.
b. What you get is what you measure.

The weights given to various metrics should differ from facility to facility within a company, depending on the array of capabilities at the facility (people, talents, equipment, processes mastered), the multi-plant strategy of the company, and the charters that have been given to each facility (including the understanding of the marketplace and the customers for the facility). For example, many manufacturing companies have specific plants that have been assigned the highest-volume production that the company does. Often, the mandate, derived from the economics of the industry and the perceived needs of the marketplace, is for at least one plant to produce that high volume with the lowest cost possible. The factory would typically have been designed to keep costs low. Thus "cost to produce" may be especially apt for such a plant.

Other plants within the same company, however, may be dealing with lower-volume products whose position in the market does not depend so much on low cost but on some other dimension, be it product-related or delivery-related. This may be particularly true for plants that deal with new product introductions (e.g. "mother" plants) or for plants that deal with the company's low-volume or fading products (e.g. "junk" plants). Indeed, many manufacturing companies can cite instances where their plants have progressed through a life cycle, gathering skills and capabilities, but at the same time accumulating responsibilities and becoming more subject to variation in the products and processes in their portfolios. At each stage of these life cycles, different metrics were probably called for. Unfortunately, in many companies, neither the metrics nor the weights attached to them are permitted to vary, either across units of the company or across time. Inconsistencies among tasks, metrics, and choices are thereby introduced inadvertently and can be allowed to persist. A company's competitiveness can be steadily and silently eroded in this way.

In the past couple of decades, a broader approach to performance measurement has become increasingly popular.[6] It is known as the "balanced scorecard" and it offers an array of different measures that incorporate four major perspectives: financial (How do we look to our shareholders?), customer (How do our customers see us?), internal business (What must we excel at?), and innovation and learning (How can we continue to improve and create value?). The balanced scorecard has been influential in elevating operating measures to the attention of general managers who ordinarily might have been fixated on financial metrics to the exclusion of broader measures of the company's performance.

7.6 Measuring gemba: taking a plant or service tour

Those of us in operations management often have the opportunity to visit an organization's operations. What should we be looking for? What can or should we counsel our students to look for on such visits? How can we best analyze a process on the fly?

We can, of course, lapse into a non-critical frame of mind, but a plant or service tour gives us the opportunity to sharpen our understandings of process. To make the most of such an opportunity, we need to gauge things in real time. The visit is an exercise in measurement, albeit of a very particular kind.

What we should look for in a plant or service tour depends at least in part on the reasons for the visit, but some general observations can be made. Permit us to present some of our own views about what we generally look for in a tour and what we advise our students.[7]

BEFORE YOU SET FOOT IN THE FACILITY

The tour begins before you set foot inside the building. You can gain insight into the company from outside the facility.

- How old is the facility?
- How well maintained are the grounds?
- Is there room for expansion, or is the site as built-up as it will ever be?
- Are there designated parking spaces for management?
- Is there an egalitarian feel to the place, or not?

It is helpful to know ahead of time what the character of the process is likely to be. For manufacturing, is it a job shop, batch, line flow, or continuous flow? For services, is it a service factory, service shop, mass service, or professional service? It may not be possible to know in advance, but having some idea of what to expect can help to frame the visit.

THE PROCESS FLOW

We prefer to follow the flow of materials (or elements of the service) through the process. For manufacturing, that means starting at the receipt of raw materials and then progressing from stockroom to factory floor to loading dock for the finished product. For services, it may mean following the order from receipt until the service encounter is complete. Here are the kinds of questions to which we seek answers:

- How often are materials delivered to the operation?
- How much is delivered at any time?
- How does it arrive?
- How frequent are orders? How variable are those orders?
- Is there incoming inspection?
- How quickly do materials flow to the operation?
- In what quantities do they flow? Are they grouped with other materials or parts?
- What happens to the materials once they are delivered? Are they taken up by the process immediately or do they wait?
- How do the materials progress from one operation to the next?
- Is the flow interrupted for any reason? What might cause an interruption?
- What "checkpoints" exist along the path of the materials or of the order?
- How complicated or simple is the flow of materials or of the order?
- How long does it take to produce the product or service?

THE LAYOUT

- Is the layout logical? Or is it confusing to follow what happens to the materials or the order?
- What would the spaghetti diagram look like?
- Does the character of the process change at all as materials or orders progress through the process? Are there stockrooms in the middle of the flow of materials?
- How compact is the layout?
- How unobtrusive is the materials handling system? How much material appears to be around the process? Does it seem excessive?
- Is there a lot of work-in-process inventory around?
- How is the housekeeping?
- Are items labeled clearly and prominently?
- Has the layout been reconfigured recently? Has space been freed up in the process?
- How much space is dedicated to repair and rework?

THE WORKSTATION

- Is the layout of workstations logical?
- Is there evidence of 5S activity?
- Do the workstations appear to be in balance with one another, or are some obviously more overloaded than others?
- How are any changeovers from one product/service to another accomplished? How quickly are any such changeovers done?
- How do workers know what to work on? Can they exercise choice about what to work on?
- How do workers know what to do to any unit/order?
- How evident is paperwork—process sheets, routing sheets, engineering changes?
- Is any expediting evident? How much, if any?
- What steps affect quality and how is quality managed? Are the tools of quality readily seen? Are quality measures posted?
- How labor-intensive is the process?

INVENTORY

- What does the stockroom look like? How orderly? How full? How fancy?
- What is the level of work-in-process inventory? Of raw materials inventory? Of finished goods?
- What kinds of buffer inventories have been created?
- How is work-in-process inventory stored? What controls are in place? How visual are such controls?

EQUIPMENT

- How much equipment is there to the process?
- How much is specially designed and single-purpose? How much is generally available?
- How new is the equipment? How sophisticated?
- Is any equipment grouped into cells? How are any cells performing? What are the results?
- How is the equipment maintained?
- How easy is it to change over?

MANAGEMENT

- Where are management offices in relation to the operation?
- What hierarchy of management exists? How many levels?

- How has the facility changed over time? What has changed?
- What is management most proud of? What is management least proud of?
- How are people treated? What can be gleaned about HR issues such as morale?
- Is the operation unionized? What is management's stance towards any union?
- Is the operation evaluated as a cost-center or as a profit-center?

One could, of course, ask more questions of the process, but these, we have found, are helpful ones for analyzing a process being visited.

NOTES

1. See R.S. Kaplan and D.P. Norton, 2005. The balanced scorecard: Measures that drive performance. *Harvard Business Review*, 83(7), p.172, and A.D. Neely, C. Adams, and M. Kennerley, 2002. *The Performance Prism: The Scorecard for Measuring and Managing Business Success*. Prentice Hall Financial Times.
2. For an exhaustive survey of the many issues surrounding performance measures, see A. Neely, M. Gregory, and K. Platts, 2005. Performance measurement system design: A literature review and research agenda. *International Journal of Operations and Production Management*, 25(12), pp.1228–63. This article is a reprint of a 1995 article in the same journal.
3. K. Ferdows and A. De Meyer, 1990. Lasting improvements in manufacturing performance: In search of a new theory. *Journal of Operations Management*, 9(2), pp.168–84.
4. D.A. Hounshell, 1984. *From the American System to Mass Production, 1800–1932*. Johns Hopkins University Press, pp.249–53.
5. J.G. Miller and T.E. Vollmann, 1985. The hidden factory. *Harvard Business Review*, 63(5), pp.142–50.
6. R.S. Kaplan and D.P. Norton wrote the two seminal articles on the idea: The balanced scorecard—Measures that drive performance. *Harvard Business Review*, 70(1) (January–February 1992), pp.71–9, and Putting the balanced scorecard to work. *Harvard Business Review*, 71(5) (September–October 1993), pp.134–47.
7. D. Upton, 1997. Why (and how) to take a plant tour. *Harvard Business Review*, 75(3), pp.97–106.

FURTHER READING

Johnson, H.T. and Kaplan, R.S., 1991. *Relevance Lost: The Rise and Fall of Management Accounting*. Harvard Business School Press (Boston, MA).

Kaplan, R.S. and Norton, D.P., 1996. *The Balanced Scorecard: Translating Strategy into Action*. Harvard Business School Press (Boston, MA).

Neely, A.D., Adams, C., and Kennerley, M., 2002. *The Performance Prism: The Scorecard for Measuring and Managing Business Success.* Prentice Hall Financial Times (London).

Neely, A., Gregory, M., and Platts, K., 1995. Performance measurement system design: A literature review and research agenda. *International Journal of Operations and Production Management*, 15(4), pp.80–116.

Upton, D., 1997. Why (and how) to take a plant tour. *Harvard Business Review*, 75(3), pp.97–106.

8 Improving processes

So far, we have introduced seven principles that define the *design* and *measurement* dimensions of our process theory framework. There remains *improvement* to discuss, and the next three principles deal with how operations of all sorts can improve.

8.1 The perennial need

In practice, process improvement is one of the key tasks in operations management, alongside planning and resource allocation. The reason is simple: once set up, most operations run for a considerable time, and change little as new product generations are introduced. As fancy as it may seem to design an operation from scratch (the proverbial "greenfield"), the reality is that most operations design takes place in established settings (the proverbial "brownfield").

With brownfield settings, process improvement becomes a recurring activity—not because firms want to, but because their competitors force them to. Think of the Red Queen race in Lewis Carroll's *Alice in Wonderland*. If you and your competitor are both running, "it takes all the running you can do, to keep in the same place. If you want to get somewhere else, you must run at least twice as fast as that!" So, process improvement is not something you opt to do; it is a perennial need enforced by the market the firm operates in.

It is also important to note the effect of entropy in processes, as unmanaged processes deteriorate over time. In other words, unless specific attention is paid to maintaining standard operating procedures that underpin a process, gradually non-standard activities and workarounds will creep in. As a result, variation will increase, and in the long run performance will decrease.

The second law of thermodynamics states that entropy, a measure of disorder in the universe, always increases, and consequently that the potential to do work—that is, to transfer heat from hotter to colder objects—declines with time. A similar phenomenon appears to be present in companies. Although this phenomenon cannot be captured in a formal law, there is a distinct tendency for variation and complexity to creep incessantly into a company's operations, and for good reasons. All the good things that you'd like to see happen to a company—more customers, growth in sales, new products, new locations—contribute to increasing the variation and complexity with which the operation has to cope. And that variation and complexity reduces an operation's productivity and thus its potential to do work.

Think of it. When customers are added and when sales grow, the number of transactions that the operation has to perform increases. Moreover, customers invariably request special favors—an early delivery here, an expedited delivery there—that stress the operation. Growing sales typically mean growing inventories, and that threatens throughput times. New products and new options on existing products are developed. Some of them may sell well and others may languish. In either case, variation and complexity have increased. New locations, either new sales locations or new operational locations (e.g. factories, warehouses), also add to the variation and complexity that the company must deal with. The irony of this operational entropy, this increasing disorder, is inescapable. In the growth that a company longs for lie the seeds for the very operations headaches that can stall that growth.

Any process improvement is essentially a change project, and needs to be managed as such. There are three stages in process improvement, as defined by Kurt Lewin and many others. First, it is important to measure the baseline, as the actual improvement will be measured against this. Second, the process is "unfrozen" and the actual changes are made. Third, the new process is enforced by developing new standard operating procedures ("refreezing"). As such, process improvement forms a special case of change management, while all the theoretical models of motivation, ownership, and sustainability of change apply. Here, the world of operations and organizational behavior intersect.

As shown in Figure 8.1, there are two basic types of process improvement: continuous improvement activities (also known as kaizen) and breakthrough or radical improvements (or kaizen blitz, kaikaku, or rapid improvement events). Like yin and yang, these two forms work together, and neither is sufficient on its own. Kaizen refers to worker-led activities that—on a continuous basis—review and improve the actual process through quality circles, daily team meetings, and the like. However, these improvements may hit a "glass ceiling" when major changes such as modifications in layout, IT system, or otherwise are required. At this point a kaizen blitz or radical change is needed, to address a focal problem that prevents further process improvement. Kaizen blitz events are fun and hugely motivating, as the results can be seen straight away. Simply relying on them, however, without the structure of kaizen, is not sustainable. Firms that conduct many rapid improvement events in isolation are very unlikely to be able to sustain the improvements made, and will eventually do the "bunny hop" but not move ahead.

Think of the old fable of the tortoise and the hare. In that fable, the hare brags about its speed and ridicules the slow-moving tortoise. The tortoise is provoked to challenge the hare to a race. The hare quickly takes the lead, but, well ahead, pauses to nap. Meanwhile, the slow but steady tortoise keeps moving to the finish line, and crosses it before the hare wakes from its nap.

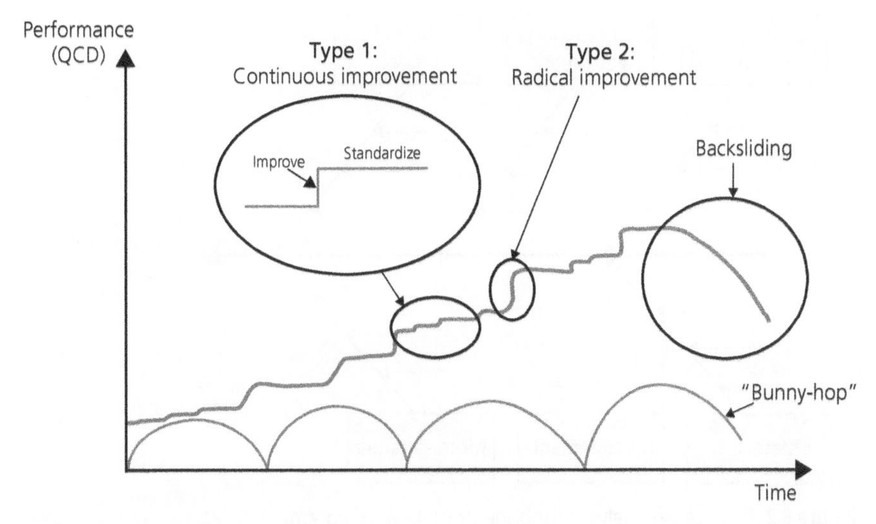

Figure 8.1 Process improvement.

Suppose that the tortoise and the hare owned factories. How would the hare's factory differ from that of the tortoise? For one thing, the hare's factory is filled with new and fast equipment but it is not well maintained. Quality is iffy. Set-ups and changeovers take time. Materials wait a long time before they are worked on. The layout is a scattered one, with much movement into and out of the storeroom. The production schedule is replete with interruptions for expediting and engineering change. Rework is common. Work-in-process inventory is everywhere.

The tortoise's factory is not at all the same. It is slow but steady and always in motion. Value is constantly added. The process works faultlessly. Quality is exceptional. The equipment is probably run at slower than its rated capacity. It is well maintained. Set-ups and changeovers are studied and quick. Materials do not wait long to be worked on. Layouts are compact. Materials move economically between operations. The production schedule is smooth, with few interruptions. Little rework is required. Work-in-process inventory is low. We would be proud to have Aesop as our plant manager.

The hare scampers all over its factory. There seems to be lots to do, and certainly lots of troubleshooting. The tortoise does not have to scamper at all because its factory is all about swift, even flow. The non-value-added steps have been eliminated. Everything is rational. In essence, the tortoise gets to run a much shorter race than the hare.

We will return to the challenge of sustaining process improvement below. But before we do, we need to define another key term in process improvement: "root cause." When problems occur in a process, symptoms will generally sprawl up in many places. Consider for example an unstable manufacturing

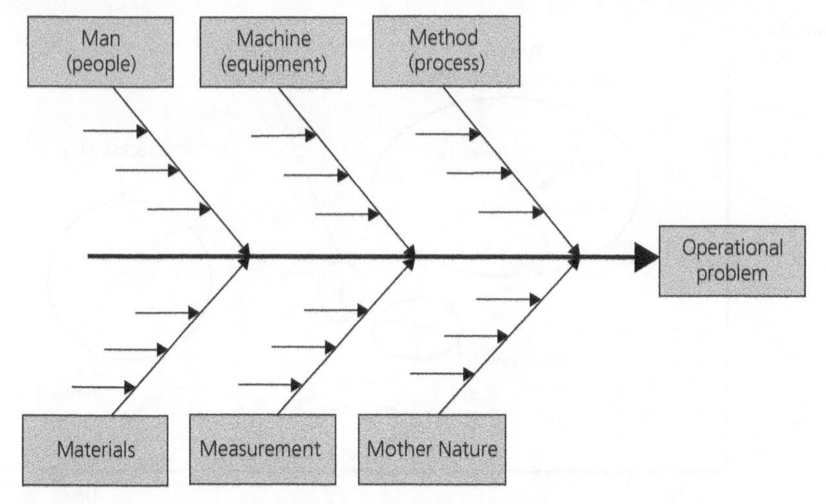

Figure 8.2 Root cause analysis: fishbone or Ishikawa diagram.

process, which could lead to increased product returns as defective parts are being shipped to the customer, higher scrap rates, and increased machine downtime due to breakdowns and higher maintenance effort. All of these effects are important symptoms of the process' failure, but to eradicate them it is necessary to identify the root cause that is causing these symptoms. Fixing the symptoms will generally only lead to short-term relief and can waste valuable time in dealing with the underlying issue.

To get to the root cause, a range of tools are used widely: the "5 Whys" that ask "why" up to five consecutive times to get from observed problem to root cause; the fishbone or Ishikawa diagram (named after its inventor, Kaoru Ishikawa, shown in Figure 8.2), which can graphically illustrate the findings of the "5 Whys" exercise; or the Current Reality Tree (CRT) tool popular in Six Sigma. The key is to distinguish recurring symptom from underlying cause, and to focus on eliminating that very root cause.

8.2 **The essence: swift, even flow**

Operations managers are always on the prowl for any number of things: additional capacity, timeliness of delivery for their customers, and low cost, among others. Processes need to be as productive as they can be. How can this be accomplished?

Principle #8 addresses this with the theory of swift, even flow.

Principle #8: Processes are improved by reductions in throughput time or in undesired variation.

The theory of swift, even flow, as advanced by Schmenner and Swink in 1998 and elaborated by Schmenner in his 2012 book, argues that there are only two ways to increase productivity: reducing throughput time and reducing variation. Any other tactic works only because it either reduces throughput time or reduces variation in quality, quantities, and/or timing. It was noted under Principle #3 that Little's Law ties together increases in the throughput rate, which represents a gain in productivity, with decreases in the waste in a process, waste that keeps the throughput time from declining. Decrease the throughput time for a product or service by, say, removing waste, hold the level of work-in-process inventory constant, and the throughput rate will go up.

A lot of conventional thinking about productivity and cost reduction takes the point of view of the factors of production, as discussed in Chapter 2. The thought is that by improving the way labor works or by automating the process, productivity will soar. Think about the history that was discussed in Chapter 1. Frederick Taylor's scientific management, for example, with time and motion study, specifies how a worker ought to perform every task. Scientific management is all about improving labor as a factor of production. The approach taken by Henry Ford was dramatically different. Ford and his lieutenants sought to automate the job so that the worker would not be needed nearly as much, if at all. Still, that approach focuses on a factor of production too, namely capital (the equipment). Swift, even flow argues that to the extent that these tactics work, they only work because throughput time is reduced or because variation in quality, quantities, or timing has been reduced. Scientific management can miss the fact that the job may not need doing after all, and the Ford approach might introduce an expensive alternative that may cause even more expense to be incurred elsewhere in the process.

Swift, even flow abandons this focus on the factors of production, and instead takes the point of view of the materials or information in the process (i.e. what gets worked on). The concept urges those who seek to improve a process to *become* the materials or the information being processed. It asks two things: (1) are the materials (or information) used in the process subject to variation in quality, quantities, or timing?; and (2) where does the throughput time lengthen? The answers to those two questions can then lead to commonsense solutions that reduce variation and/or throughput time. When the goal for the process is swift, even flow, and when one "becomes" the good or service moving through the process, it is easier to see the variation and the throughput time that could be reduced. Let us look at the sequence and methods of process improvement in a bit more detail.

8.3 The sequence of process improvement

First and foremost, it is important to state that unmanaged processes deteriorate over time. As we discussed in Section 8.1, variety and complexity are likely to creep into a company's processes. This puts pressure on the organization not just to define the standard process, but also to maintain it.

This is an important subprinciple we need to add to Principle #8, as it is often assumed that processes—once set up—will keep running as planned. This is not the case. A stable process is one that requires constant attention. Think of "Murphy's Law": if things can go wrong, they (eventually) will. This also applies to processes.

> **Principle #8:** Processes are improved by reductions in throughput time or in undesired variation.
> a. Unmanaged processes will deteriorate over time.

A stable process is the foundation of any process improvement. So before applying any measure to improve the speed, quality, or costs of a process, it is essential to achieve a stable and predictable process. In short, any improvement of an unstable process is a mirage, as it is unlikely that the improvement can be replicated.

There is in fact a distinct sequence in which process improvement needs to take place in order to yield sustainable improvements—see Figure 8.3. The foundation of any process improvement is a process that is capable, or in other words meets customer specifications. Once this is achieved, the next level is to make this process not just capable, but also dependable (i.e. "in control").

Once the process is capable (of meeting customer expectations in terms of quality) and in control (by delivering this quality consistently, or in Shewhart's

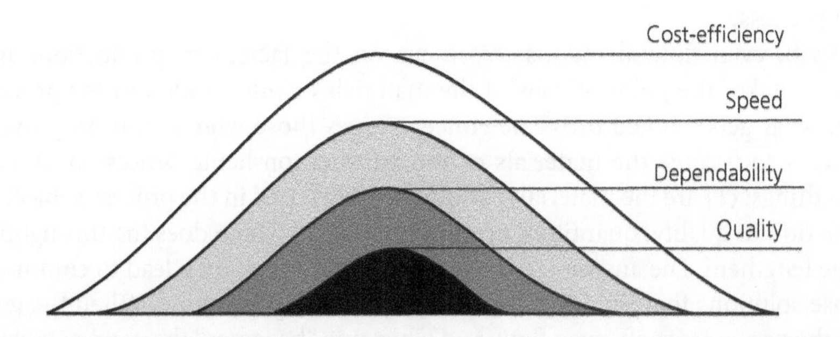

Figure 8.3 The sandcone model of process improvement.

Source: Ferdows and De Meyer (1990).

terminology, by only expressing random variation), then one can think about making the process faster. Here, Lean thinking and other methods come in that look at all activities and cut out the ones that are "muda," that is, those that do not add customer value. In doing so, the process becomes swifter and flows become more even. Swift, even flow is the objective.

A further important and related aspect comes into play with regard to the speed of process improvement. The sooner an operational problem is discovered and its root cause eradicated, the smaller the operational loss related to this problem. Until that point, the operational problem will have to be buffered through excess capacity, inventory, or time, and most likely will lead to internal (scrap, rectification) and external (returns, warranty, lost sales) failure cost. It is for this reason that process improvement is not just a perennial need, but also an urgent need in operations.

We add another subprinciple here that makes this even more specific:

Principle #8: Processes are improved by reductions in throughput time or in undesired variation.

a. Unmanaged processes will deteriorate over time.
b. The total cost associated with an operational problem is inversely proportional to the speed of rectifying its root cause.

Cost-efficiency is of course what most seek to achieve through process improvement, but it is the outcome of process improvement, and not the means by which to improve a process. In other words, it is very simple to cut costs in the short term. Think about a hospital ward, where you can cut back on doctor and nurse staffing levels very easily. Nothing will happen in the short term as the extra work will be absorbed by the remaining staff, through overtime in the best of cases, or through workarounds and shortcuts in the worst case. In the medium term, of course, the overworked staff will make more mistakes, and the patient outcomes will suffer. On paper the operation has become more "cost-efficient," yet of course the outcome has worsened.

The same applies to factories—think of inventory levels. It is very easy to run down inventory levels to improve cost-efficiency. Yet this inventory was generally there for a reason, most likely as a buffer against uncertainty and variation. It is possible to eliminate this inventory in the short term, but without tackling the underlying root causes this is likely to lead to a frenzy of firefighting, as the lack of inventory buffer will mean that many operational problems surface at the same time. The famous "rock–boat" analogy shows this connection (Figure 8.4), whereby operational problems are depicted as "rocks." If you want to achieve a safe passage, you either increase the water level (inventory buffer) or you deal with the underlying root causes (rocks).

If one accepts swift, even flow as explaining productivity, then one inevitably must reject other approaches.

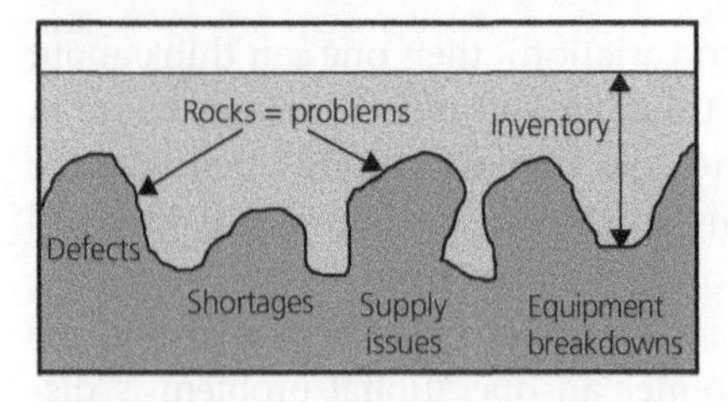

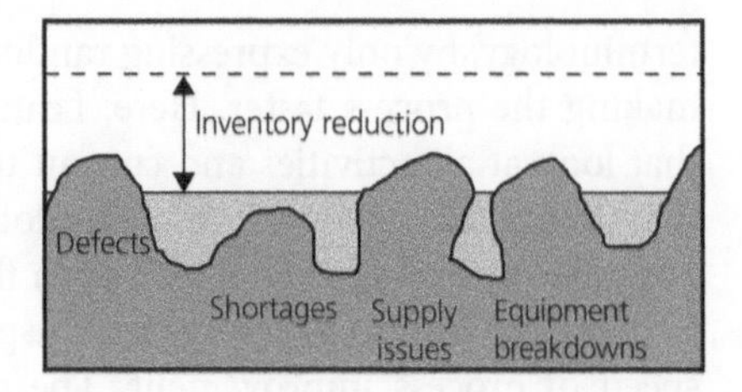

Figure 8.4 The "rock–boat" analogy.

Layoffs and staff reduction: Letting people go is all about labor cost reduction. That cost may be large, but so many other costs could be lowered as well. Moreover, reducing the headcount does nothing to identify waste. It cannot show the way towards a newly designed process.

Automation: Automation, too, is about removing direct labor. It can be oblivious to other sources of waste. It could even lead to "automating" waste, which can be a frightful expense. Automation and its oft-touted flexibility can be as tempting as the Sirens. In the end, however, it can cause managers to stray from the fundamental task of hunting down variation and putting a limit on that variation. It has proved not to be a silver bullet that can effortlessly provide flexibility and low cost. Too many companies have paid too much for automation thinking that it would lead them to greater productivity, and have been disappointed when greater productivity did not appear.

Labor efficiency and machine utilization: These metrics measure specific factors of production—labor and capital equipment—and not the materials (or information) that the process adds value to. What's wrong with that? Labor or machines can be busy, but they may not be adding all of the value that they should. A metric like labor efficiency typically is established as a result of time and motion study. Unfortunately, that study may not be able to uncover all of the non-value-added aspects of any one job, or indeed of any complete process. Much of the time that materials (or information) spend in the process is spent in a queue waiting to be worked on. Labor efficiency and machine utilization ignore this non-productive, wasteful time. Throughput time is thus a more natural and more complete metric that can capture both where value is added and where waste lies.

Scale: Labor efficiency and machine utilization do not affect either throughput times or variation, and, for that matter, neither does scale. Only when scale leads to the design of a different way to make the product is it at all related to increased productivity. Scale only raises productivity when it acts to reduce variation or throughput time. Time after time, speed trumps scale.

Systems: Systems, unfortunately, can conceal waste rather than making it visible. For example, many enterprise resource planning (ERP) systems have lot-sizing routines that use variants of the long-recognized economic order quantity (EOQ) formula. Yet, reorder point systems (i.e. those that use the EOQ) are fraught with problems and are at odds with Lean manufacturing principles. Complacent companies that unwittingly permit their systems to generate lot sizes for production in this way risk doing themselves and their productivity a great disservice.

It is a common problem in practice that process improvement is abused to generate cost savings in the short term. This marks a fundamental misunderstanding: cost savings through efficiency gains are the *outcome* of process improvement, but not the *lever* through which it is achieved. The levers include two basic mechanisms: the reduction of undesired variation, and the elimination of unnecessary activities from the process.

These two levers are strongly linked—when reducing non-value-added steps from the process to cut lead time, often undesired variation is reduced that was caused by these activities in the process. Equally, when reducing undesired variation, often lead time is reduced as unnecessary steps are removed from the process that caused this undesired variation.

8.4 Lean, Six Sigma, Lean Six Sigma, or just "operational excellence"?

A great wealth of approaches to process improvement have been proposed and successfully implemented. Yet seemingly they come in waves, or fads, and then disappear. How can that be? Well, in truth they do not disappear, but get subsumed into the next wave or fad. Virtually all process improvement methods share a common heritage, and thus also will often use (and claim!) the same tools. And this is not a problem, as effectively they all share the same goal: to make the process better. Where it can become a problem is when these improvement approaches become "religions" and do not tolerate competing initiatives. Such competition is unhealthy, and a root cause of backsliding (see Section 8.8).

Where does this competition stem from? Well, while all approaches essentially agree on *what* they want to achieve, they do disagree on *how* to get there. While Lean looks at a process from the point of view of taking out *muda* (waste), *muri* (overburden), and *mura* (unevenness), Six Sigma on the other hand looks for sources of undesired variation. The Theory of Constraints argues that all of the above is futile unless it breaks the constraint and increases throughput at the one and only resource that really matters in the system, the bottleneck. While it is easy to see how these different "lenses" on a process can create a sense of competition or conflict, in reality the actual improvement types are not independent. When you take out unnecessary process steps you generally also reduce undesired variation that these caused, and vice versa. Thus it really makes little sense to see these approaches as competing with each other. They may start in different places, but they are very likely to end up in the same place.

This latter point in particular applies as in effect all process improvement originates from the same set of fundamental ideas that formed the intellectual base of our field. Figure 8.5 traces the intellectual origins of the key ideas that have formed our field.

For companies there is of course a good reason to recite the Toyota, Motorola, and GE narratives. "*It worked for Toyota, it will also work for us*" is a powerful narrative and effectively absolves the company from responsibility, as these methods have been tried and tested by aspirational companies. We, however, as the field of operations management scholars, should stand above the buzzwords and fads, focus on "operations excellence" or "process improvement," and seek to identify the actual mechanisms rather than the buzzwords.

8.5 The elements of process improvement

We have seen a wealth of process improvement approaches over time. While each generally claims supremacy over other approaches, in truth there is a set of routines that underpin any successful process improvement methodology.

Fundamentally, process improvement is a "search" or "meta" routine that seeks to continuously improve the product or service delivery routines in the firm. These routines, or bundles of practices[1] effectively include four elements:

1. **Strategic alignment**: Here the key question is how to link operational process improvement to the wider purpose and objectives of the firm. Common methods include *hoshin kanri* or *policy deployment*, whereby metrics are "cascaded" down in the organization from top-level goals, so that all activities are aligned. The trite and perhaps apocryphal example always given is this. During a visit to the NASA space center in 1962, President John F. Kennedy noticed a janitor carrying a broom. He interrupted his tour, walked over to the man, and said, "Hi, I'm Jack Kennedy. What are you doing?" "Well, Mr President," the janitor responded, "I'm helping put a man on the moon."
2. **Senior management support**: It is now very clear that senior management needs to continuously pay attention to process improvement, in order for it to stick. This includes consistent and frequent communication, detailed

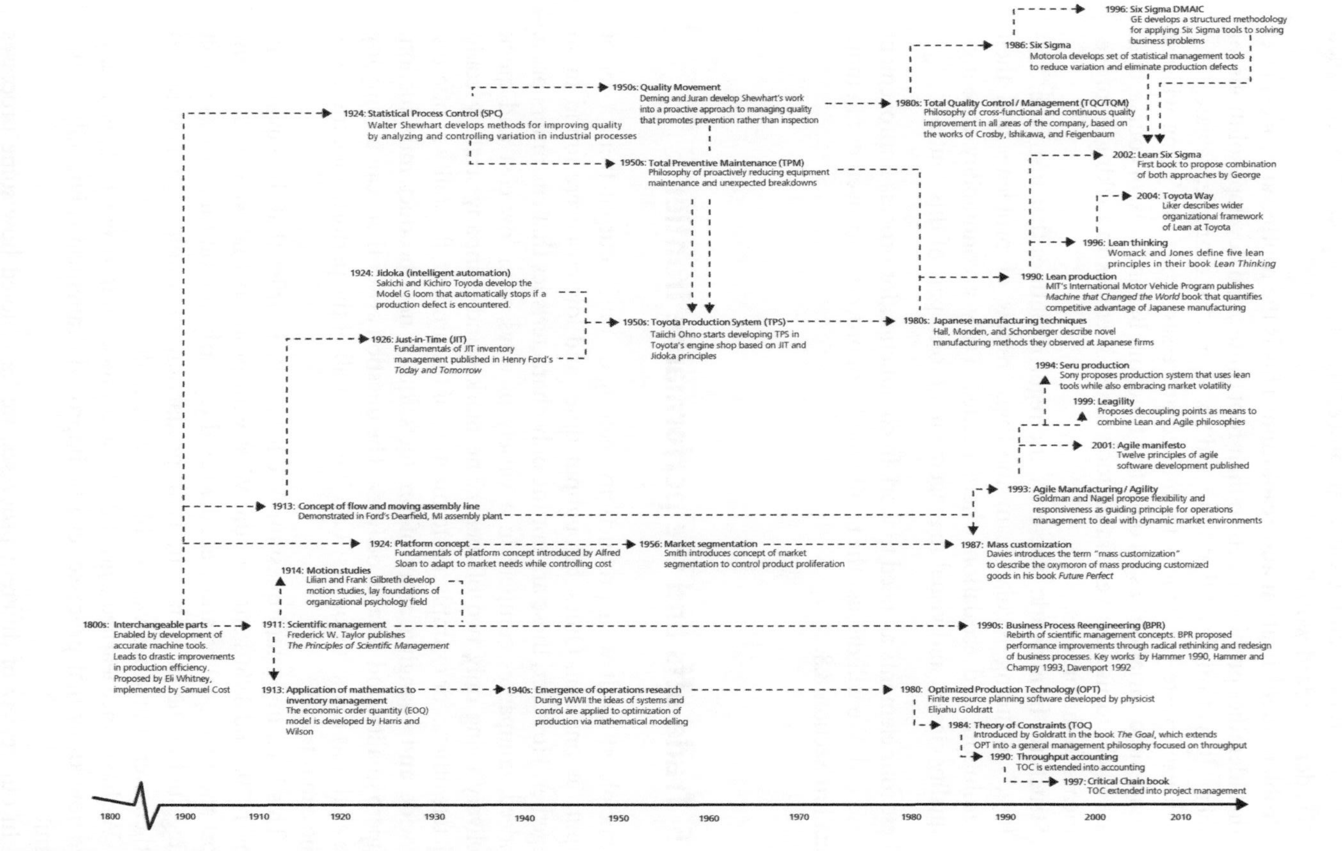

Figure 8.5 Evolution of process improvement concepts.

With special thanks to Dr Lee Schab.

and regular reviews and attention to problems actually being solved, and a rigorous review and escalation procedure. This aspect is often called "Leader standard work."

3. **Problem identification and resolution**: This is the routine at process level that identifies problems, gets to their root causes, and develops solutions for them. It is at this level that Lean and Six Sigma, for example, deviate. Lean will use "waste" as its lens to analyze processes, while Six Sigma will use "undesired variation" as its objective function. Beyond this, of course, both are likely to use the very same tools when it comes to making improvements to the process.
4. **Structural framework**: These are the regular routines that instil the "culture," including regular team meetings, review of problems and their resolution, and escalation where needed. Daily accountability meetings, quality circles, and visual management all form part of this routine.

These four elements all need to work in conjunction for process improvement to succeed. We will discuss the failure modes of process improvement in more detail in Section 8.8.

8.6 Trade-offs and the performance frontier

Principle #8 dealt with productivity, getting as much output from a set of inputs as one can. Quick throughput times and low cost were found to go together. However, these are not the only characteristics that customers prize. Indeed, companies compete in a variety of ways, with low cost and quick delivery being only two of them. The market and company strategy could dictate others: for example, customization of the product, flexibility in offering a wide and changing array of products, quick new product introduction, superb quality, and reliable delivery. The question arises then: can a company be all things to its customers? Can it excel at all of the performance measures one could track?

This is an important question. We have noted earlier that the Japanese in the 1970s and 1980s stunned the West with products that were at once low cost and high quality, and were delivered regularly and on time. It was in fact suggested at the time that the Lean production philosophy that Toyota and others were pursuing was capable of doing it all.

We have since learned a great deal about process improvement. Specifically, we now know that processes can be improved dramatically, but only within limits.

In our review of different processes, we have noted how some processes have strengths that others do not. In a manufacturing context, the job shop is renowned for its flexibility and its ability to customize production to the needs of the consumer. The same is true for the professional service firm in a service context. At the other end of the process matrix diagonal, the continuous flow process is the epitome of productivity and low cost. The same thing could be said for the service factory. For a process to become more productive and thus to lower its costs, Principle #8 asserts that it needs to move down the diagonal in either the manufacturing or service process matrix. That is, swift, even flow calls for the process to reduce its throughput time and/or the variation that it is subject to. We have also seen with Kingman's formula that quick delivery (i.e. a short customer wait) goes along with lower capacity utilization. These truisms suggest that performance along one dimension (e.g. product variety, short customer wait) must be sacrificed for performance along another dimension (e.g. cost, capacity utilization). In other words, trade-offs govern performance measures.

Yet we have also noted that the theory of swift, even flow fits hand in glove with the principles of Lean operations, where quality, cost, delivery, and flexibility can all be enhanced simultaneously. Can these two observations be reconciled? How?

This brings up Principle #9:

Principle #9: The rate of process improvement is subject to diminishing returns.

Stated in another way, improvement along a broad front can be made, but there will come a point where the performances along any two dimensions of a process (think cost or customization or delivery reliability or . . .) cannot both be improved. Then, the performance along one dimension can only improve at the expense of the other. Thus, performance improvement can be made along multiple dimensions but the rate of that improvement will, at some point, slow down and be subject to diminishing returns. And, importantly, there will come a point where improvement in any single dimension will require that performance in another valued dimension will have to decline.

We note as a subprinciple:

Principle #9: The rate of process improvement is subject to diminishing returns.

a. There exists a trade-off between any two aspects of process performance.

This understanding of both improvement and trade-offs is due to what is known as the theory of performance frontiers. The theory of performance frontiers, advanced by Roger Schmenner and Morgan Swink in their 1998 article, argues that improvement and trade-offs can indeed be reconciled. The progression of capabilities that Ferdows and De Meyer proposed with their sandcone model can be reconciled with the notion that one cannot be all things to all people, and that the dimensions of performance have to be traded off

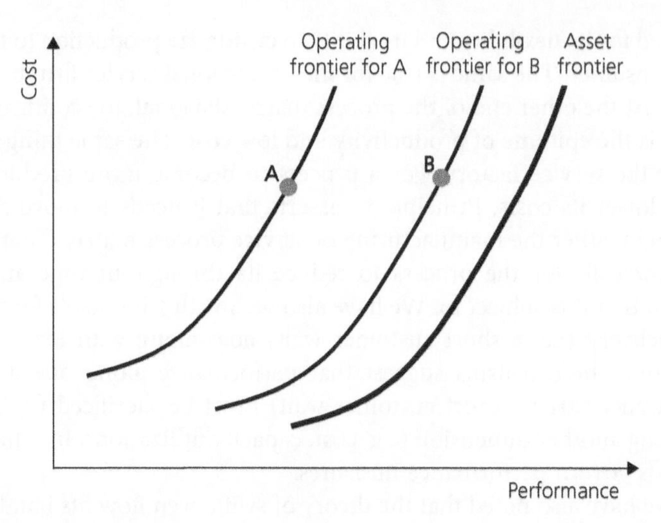

Figure 8.6 Asset frontier with two operating frontiers.

against each other. The theory of performance frontiers identifies two types of frontier, an operating frontier and an asset frontier. The asset frontier depends on investments that would show up on a balance sheet, such as new equipment and technologies. It displays the locus of the best-performing combinations of performance measures of different types that can be had with the investments made. The operating frontier takes the investments of the asset frontier as given. It displays the locus of the best-performing combinations of performance measures available from the management policies that the facility pursues. Figure 8.6 pictures a set of operating and asset frontiers. Cost, on the y-axis, is shown as one dimension of performance. The other dimension of performance, on the x-axis, could be any other one, say customization or delivery or flexibility.

An operating frontier can be repositioned by adopting new policies such as Lean principles or a quality improvement program (e.g. Six Sigma) or factory focus. It can move closer to the asset frontier, a move that is known as "betterment." The asset frontier remains the ultimate boundary for performance, however—see Figure 8.7.

Any movement along the asset frontier represents a trade-off. For example, low cost would be sacrificed in order to attain greater customization. The same is true for movements along the prevailing operating frontier. However, if an operating frontier can be "bettered," as shown in Figure 8.7, one can have both lower cost and more customization. A move from point A1 to point A2 would be one such move. And, if the performance of the operation is located inside any operating frontier (e.g. point A), then performance improvement in multiple dimensions is possible, and, indeed, greatly to be wished.

It is natural to expect that the farther inside an operating frontier one is located, the easier it is to become better along multiple dimensions. And,

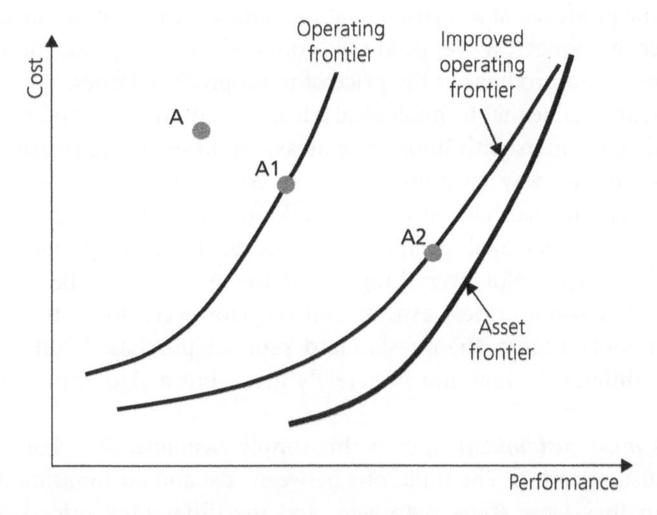

Figure 8.7 Process improvement moves an operating frontier closer to the asset frontier.

conversely, the closer one is to an operating frontier, and especially to an asset frontier, the harder it is to perform better along multiple dimensions. Diminishing marginal returns prevail here.

Any point along the asset frontier is a desirable point at which to be located. And, importantly, no one point on the asset frontier is superior to any other. The points simply represent different combinations of values for the performance measures being considered. This is the point of view that we take with Principle #9. Performance is multidimensional in that it can include cost, customization, flexibility, delivery, and other characteristics that a customer might value, and value highly. But exactly which combination of such performance measures should be chosen is the province of the customer. Indeed, it cannot be known without the involvement of the customer, who determines how much to value low cost vs. customization vs. flexibility vs. any other characteristic.

We conclude with a further subprinciple:

Principle #9: The rate of process improvement is subject to diminishing returns.

a. There exists a trade-off between any two aspects of process performance.
b. Trade-offs can never be broken, but they can be shifted by altering process practice.

FRONTIERS AND MASS CUSTOMIZATION

In the past twenty years, the concept of mass customization has been trumpeted. It asserts that technology and innovative management now permit goods to be produced at low cost and at the same time to be customized for the consumer. No longer, it seems, are we confined to mass production; we can have customized products at the price of mass-produced ones.

It is incontestable that technological advances have made it easier and easier to provide customers with impressive arrays of different models/styles/fits of products. In this way, customization has come to the masses. Moreover, customers can indeed have at least some kinds of products (e.g. Nike shoes, Levi jeans, Dell personal computers) produced to their specifications and delivered to them. Not everything about the product can be individually specified, but some critical aspects can be. However, doing this costs the customer more money than a standard product purchased "off the shelf." The cost differential may not be terribly great, but a significant differential does exist.

Is this *mass customization*, or is this simply *customization*? For us, this is simply customization. The trade-offs between cost and customization are less now than they were some years ago, and the differential price is likely to decline in relative terms, but a trade-off remains and prices are greater for the customized product. How can it be otherwise? There are costs associated with the customer: procuring and processing the customer's information about how they want the product customized and distributing the product directly to them. In addition, the production process itself must take the customization information into account as the product is made. The trade-off of cost versus customization may not be as steep now as it was years ago, but there is still a trade-off.

This implies, of course, that the asset and operating frontiers are frontiers. They can be depicted as continuous curves, and companies can choose which combination of cost and another performance measure (e.g. customization) to target. The lowest cost point is not coincident with the point of greatest customization. Rather, lowest cost and little customization travel together, just as great customization and higher cost do.

THE EVIDENCE FOR FRONTIERS IN WORLD-CLASS COMPANIES

The theory of performance frontiers suggests that companies that are nearer their operating and asset frontiers should be more subject to trade-offs than companies that are farther away from their operating and asset frontiers. Thus, one should expect that the distinction between high-scoring performance measures and low-scoring performance measures ought to be most pronounced in world-class companies.

We do not pretend to offer conclusive proof here, but this expectation is one that rings true to us. Think of companies that have been recognized as world-class for years now, such as Toyota, Zara, McDonald's, or Würth. In each case, the company specifically eschews competition on at least one dimension of performance. Toyota bunches its accessories and options together and does not provide the customer with the ability to "pick and choose" from among them. And the total number of options tends to be lower than those offered by other auto companies. Zara is famed for its fast fashion, where new items can be sent to stores within just a few weeks of their design. Yet Zara stores do not carry large and continuing assortments of their products. Zara does not offer great flexibility in the quantities provided. A fast-selling fashion can come and go quickly, causing at least some customers to shop there regularly so as not to miss out on a potentially attractive purchase. As for McDonald's, there is a reason why "Have It Your Way" is not its slogan. The company offers inexpensive fast food, served quickly, but it does not accommodate customization well. And the German hardware distributor, Würth, is famed for the customization and quick delivery that its salespeople offer, but its prices are considerably higher than its competition.

8.7 Technology and process improvement

When it comes to process improvement, firms often look to technology for salvation. And indeed technology can support process improvement in many ways. It is, however, only a means to an end, not an end in itself. The simple lesson that has been shown over and over is that technology is very powerful in improving a working process, but it is not able to fix a broken process.

For technology to work, it needs to be embedded into a stable process. The basic principle is that the quality of the output of a process is a function of the quality of the inputs into that process (or, in colloquial terms: "garbage in, garbage out"). This lesson was a painful one that plagued many material requirements planning (MRP) and ERP system implementations and continues to do so to this date. Unless the input data, such as inventory accuracy or the stability of production schedules, are given, automated production planning and control (PPC) systems are bound to fail. As a result many firms have found they were unable to generate any positive financial return from their investments in IT systems (the "productivity paradox").

HOW DOES TECHNOLOGY IMPROVE PROCESSES?

Technologies are plentiful, and they support and help improve processes across all sectors in an infinite number of ways. Among many specific mechanisms and applications, there are four general mechanisms by which technology can aid process improvement.

- **Access:** Create information visibility by making information available to others. For example, electronic data interchange (EDI) enables all players in the system to access information throughout the supply chain. ERP systems provide the "data backbone" along which all the data can be transferred and interlinked within the company. So, a purchase order is sent, material is received, and payment to the supplier is initiated—all based on interlinked data handled by the purchasing, logistics, and finance departments.
- **Speed:** Increase speed of communication: by using electronic means it is possible to transmit data much quicker, and at a much reduced transaction cost. This is used to cut lags in supply chain management, for example by transferring orders electronically, and by sharing forecasts and stock levels in real time with supply chain partners.
- **Accuracy:** Ability to calculate accurately and more quickly, thereby improving decision making. For example, MRP systems were a major improvement over manual production planning, where manual explosions of the bill of materials simply became too complex (due to both product complexity and the reuse of components across various products) and therefore were often replaced with estimates based on experience.
- **Connection:** Connect a whole range of stakeholders in the operational process on a global scale. Ecosystems of makers or service suppliers who each performed a small task in the value chain and who coordinated through mutual adjustment have always existed. Jaykumar gave as an example the fifteenth-century textile industry in the Prato region in Italy, and Pisano wrote about industrial commons. The emergence of Internet-based communication and interaction platforms such as the immensely successful retail platform of Taobao and AliPay (Alibaba), which enables them to operate a distribution operation without warehouses or inventories, is an excellent example of this.

In summary, technology used to support and enhance stable processes can be of tremendous benefit. As technology evolves, tools for supporting process efficiency will increase in power and multitude. A recent development here are digital technologies, often referred to as "digitization of manufacturing," the "second machine age," or "Industry 4.0." Let us take a closer look.

THE DIGITIZATION OF OPERATIONS

While there are some services that are exclusively "digital" in nature, any manufacturing process produces an "analogue" or physical product. Therefore what is really meant by the "digitization of operations" is the application of digital technologies to enhance manufacturing and service operations. The key technologies here are shown in Table 8.1, and undoubtedly this list will keep growing as technology advances further.

Table 8.1 Key digital technologies: an overview

Technology	What it is	Where it can be used
Additive manufacturing (AM)	• The layer-by-layer additive construction of products (as distinct from subtractive or tool-based manufacturing) • Production directly from a digital file, therefore it is also called direct digital manufacturing • A common name is "3D printing," although AM includes other additive production methods too	• Initially used in rapid prototyping and architecture • Increasingly used for customized products, such as hearing aids, prosthetics, and high-end products • Many applications in medical sector and aerospace, where geometrical freedom is exploited • Potential applications in spare parts and repair of products in the field
Artificial intelligence (AI)	• Learning algorithms that improve based on past data and tasks	• Decision making of all kinds • Insurance firms use AI to calculate risk premiums, for example
Big data (analytics)	• Machine learning (statistical) tools to identify patterns in large quantities of structured and unstructured data	• Improved decision making due to having access to much larger amounts of data on which decisions are based • Used to create product recommendations, for example, and to generate automatic answers to customer problem queries
Cloud computing	• Virtual computing and storage capacity provided across the Internet	• Distributed applications • Shared file services
Internet of things (IoT)	• Connected devices that communicate with the Internet • Update on location, status, and performance	• Distributed systems of any kind • Real-time sensors, monitoring and ordering devices
Real-time location systems (RTLS)	• Sensors that update a central system on the location of items, e.g. radio frequency identification tags	• Inventory locations, across the entire supply chain

While all of the above will have a great impact on processes across service and manufacturing operations, additive manufacturing (AM) in particular challenges some of the fundamental principles of operations management. Let's revisit the product–process matrix, one of the most fundamental concepts in terms of the design of manufacturing operations.

Standard theory stipulates that as volume increases, the product variety decreases, as increasingly dedicated production assets will be used. Additive manufacturing, however, is effectively agnostic to variety—that is, it can produce variety at (virtually) zero marginal cost.[2] Thus, as AM is being applied across industry sectors, we have seen its application grow from "projects" in product development, to job shop settings in aerospace, to large volume production in hearing aids and running shoes, for example. GE is producing a standard fuel nozzle for their LEAP engine in high volume using AM equipment, as the inherent weight savings and improved fuel flow justify the

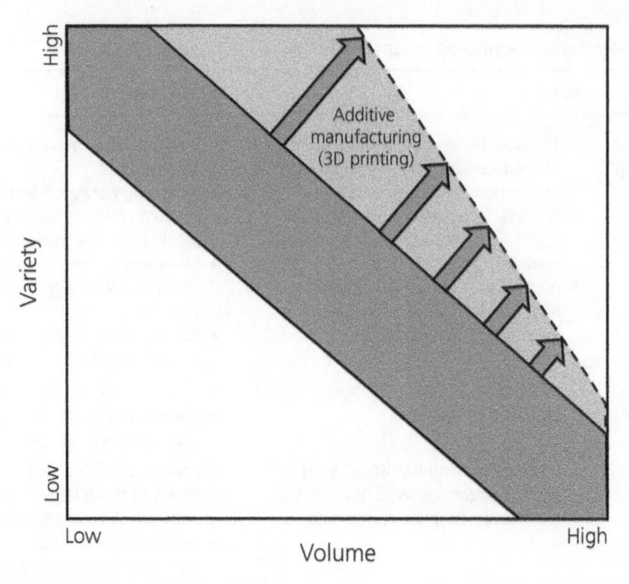

Figure 8.8 How AM expands the feasible space in the product–process matrix.

higher production cost. Hence it is clear that AM challenges the existing notions in the product–process matrix, and increasingly populate the "upper right hand" in Figure 8.8, which traditionally was seen as economically unfeasible territory.

In summary: when applied to a stable process, technology of any kind can produce tremendous improvements in process outcome. And some technologies, like AM, will even challenge us to expand our existing models and concepts. However, by and large, technology's application will not change the principles laid out in this book.

8.8 The hardest act: making improvements stick

Processes take place within sociotechnical systems that comprise machines and people. Hence motivation, incentives, and rewards are as important considerations as capacity, cycle times, and defect rates. Process improvement requires considerable effort in making the changes—in training, and more than anything else, energy in persuading and motivating people to change their entrenched ways. It is not possible to design the perfect process from the start. Constant adjustments are needed to improve. It is for this reason that process improvement methods such as Lean are always described as a *journey* or ongoing effort to improve. The problem here is that many process improvements cannot be sustained, and performance slides back.

Backsliding means that a process improvement slides back towards its original level of performance, so that the initial investment in making that improvement would not be justified. In other words, the firm would have been better off not investing time and resources into improving the process in the first place.

Once the intervention has been made, the question is not just: can the gains be held?, but also: can this process benefit from continuous improvement? In total, there are three possible scenarios (see Figure 8.9). The first and preferred outcome is that the process enters into true continuous improvement, and keeps improving even over the intervention level. Initially it will be easy to make further improvements, but as time goes on these will become harder to make. As we have stated in Principle #9, process improvement is subject to diminishing returns. One would expect to see an S-curve in this case. A second possible outcome, not preferred but at least not backsliding in the strictest sense, is to simply hold the gains. No further improvements are made, but at least the process performance does not regress. The third outcome is the one to avoid if possible—here the performance regresses back from intervention level towards the original performance. One would expect some residual benefits from training, but on balance the combined effort in making the change, training, etc. is effectively wasted.

A particular problem can arise if backsliding occurs over repeated cycles in the "bunny hop," whereby each successive operations manager launches a new process improvement wave, which leads to initial improvements, but

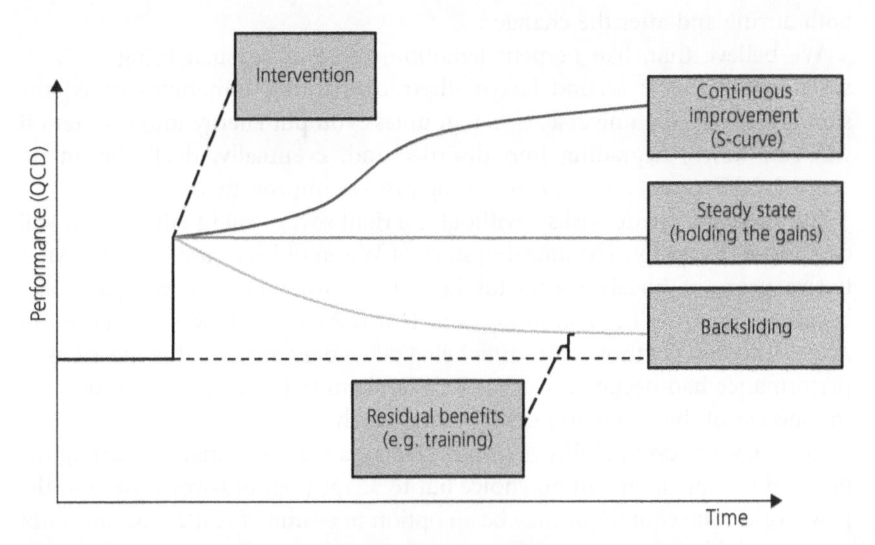

Figure 8.9 Trajectories after process improvement intervention.

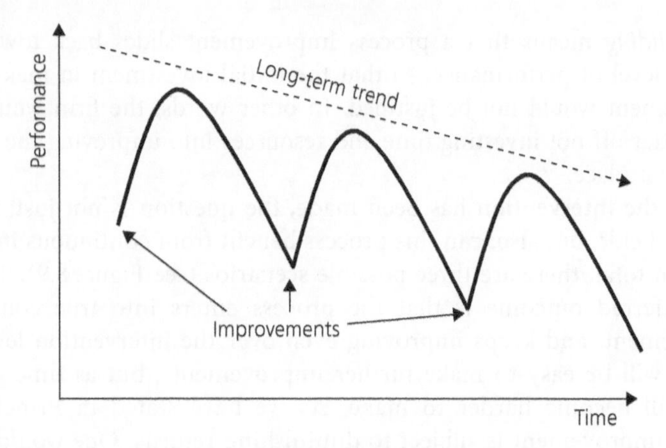

Figure 8.10 The "bunny hop" in process improvement.

then quickly backslides. As team members on the shop floor will become increasingly weary of these recurring initiatives, they will stop contributing and "initiative fatigue" will settle in. On balance, process performance is likely to worsen over time, as shown in Figure 8.10.

ROOT CAUSES FOR BACKSLIDING

There are many root causes for backsliding, but first and foremost, humans are creatures of habit. So there is a strong tendency to revert back to the "old ways." It is for this reason that process improvement needs to be managed, both during and after the change.

We believe that, like perpetual motion, there is no such thing as "self-sustainability." The second law of thermodynamics, sometimes called the supreme law of the universe, says that unless you put energy into a system it will run down, degrading into disorder and, eventually, death (as in no energy). The same applies to sustaining process improvement.

But there are greater risks—without the right sort of energy the system will degrade very rapidly. The amazing story of Wiremold is a case in point. After twelve years of hugely successful Lean transformation, the company had become one of the Lean showpieces in North America. It was written up in *Lean Thinking.* Yet three years after being taken over, many of the measures of performance had declined to what Bob Emiliani (who wrote a case study on the success of the company) describes as "batch and queue."[3]

One view of sustainability is simply "Doing a Cortes"—that is, burning the boats so that his men had no choice but to adapt their old-world ways to the new world. The equivalent may be an option in a time of real crisis, but is not really available to most.

THE FAILURE MODES OF PROCESS IMPROVEMENT IMPLEMENTATIONS

Over the years, we have seen many implementations of Lean—initially in automotive, then in manufacturing in general, and more recently in service and healthcare operations. Many of these initiatives were successful initially, but all too often the benefits were not sustained over a longer period of time. A survey of the leading 1,000 Canadian manufacturing companies in 2007 revealed that "backsliding to old ways of doing things" and "lack of implementation know-how" were by far the greatest obstacles to Lean. In this section, we will outline, from our own personal experience, why these implementations have failed.

1 Senior Management Respect and Support

The first failure mode of Lean implementation relates to senior management support and buy-in. While many would like to believe that Lean can be implemented "bottom-up," by implanting a few tools on the shop floor, then rolling it out to the entire organization, this is a myth. Implementing Lean very soon requires not just changing the layout of the facility or lines, but also changes in the work organization and "culture." Beginning with senior managers themselves, this means having true "respect" for all. If senior managers have this already, then great. If not, several gemba walks and participation in improvement events will often be necessary before Lean properly can begin. Invert the organizational triangle. Also required is a careful review of key performance indicators (KPIs) aligned to purpose. ("Tell me how you will measure me and I'll tell you what I will do"—see Principle #7b.) Behavioral principles will need to be developed and made the norm. Responsibilities, rewards, and incentives, and very often pay, will need review. Changing the role of front-line managers is key. Active participation is essential.

The CEO, of course, is crucial. Not that he or she needs to know the detail of Lean tools, but the CEO should have a belief in Lean so obstacles (including people) can be removed. Perhaps the best way to raise senior manager commitment is to feel the customer experience firsthand. This cannot be delegated to some "mystery shopping"-type team. Follow a selection of actual orders from origin of the demand to use of the product or part in practice. Spend time in the call center actually listening. Talk face to face with users and suppliers.

Finally, it has been said, with some justification, that unless each member of the senior management team possesses their own "well-worn steel-capped safety shoes," process improvement is doomed!

2 Failure to Hit the "Bottom Line"

It has been observed on many occasions that unless progress is reasonably quickly translated into increased sales, freed-up cash, lower unit costs, and/or reduced capital expenditure, interest from top management quickly wanes. This failure can result from one or more of the following:

- Failure to follow through improvements. Waste reduction is futile if not followed through. For instance, set-up reduction must translate into smaller batches and better flow. Movement reduction should be followed by kanban card removal and inventory reduction. Quality improvements must be followed by buffer stock removal... on and on.
- A failure in accounting methods. As we shall see later, inventory reduction can lead to worse results on profit and loss if traditional standard costing is used.
- KPI-driven cost reduction initiatives in the name of Lean that with time lead to increased costs due to defects, safety, morale, and customer loyalty issues.

While the bottom line is important, Lean should not be confused with an initiative solely to improve shareholder value. Lean must have benefits for customers, employees, managers, community, the environment, and shareholders.

3 Initiative Fatigue

In many organizations we have seen multiple improvement programs over time sometimes run in parallel. Such initiative overload leads to confusion ("Is all the good work we have done so far no longer valid?"), to apathy or sitting-it-out ("Why should I take part in Six Sigma: in two months' time we will do something else anyway"), and to open resistance ("These new programs don't change anything: within a few weeks everything will be back to where it was").

So how do you deal with "competing initiatives"? An important point to remember is that most improvement approaches have similar goals: value enhancement, lead time reduction, reduction in defects or variability, and ultimately cost reduction. The problem is not *where you want to go*, but *how to get there.*

When introducing a new initiative, it is hence vital to make people understand how it fits in with the existing strategy or tactics. The name is important, as many perceive "Lean" to be a competitor to "Six Sigma," whereas in fact they can be compatible. It is not by chance that, say, Unipart doesn't call its production system "Lean," but "the Unipart Way."

It is vital to take a long-term view of process improvement, and to send out a consistent message to this effect. If this message is muddled up by conflicting names, team members will immediately question whether the hard work they have put into the current wave will still be valued, and in turn whether it makes any sense to support the "next wave"—as it is unlikely to be around for long before being replaced by the next one.

A WORD OF WARNING ON "CULTURE" AND THE "BOTTOM-UP MYTH"

Lastly, it is important to talk about "culture," or more specifically a "continuous improvement culture." A common goal in many process improvement implementations is to develop a "culture" that supports and carries forward the process improvements. The great danger, however, lies in the implicit assumption that such a culture is self-sustaining. In other words, once it is put in place, it would miraculously continue to exist and grow. Little could be further from the truth: experience, time and time again, has shown that sustaining such an "improvement culture" requires persistent hard work at all levels of the organization. More than anyone else, the CEO or COO (who heads up performance improvement at executive committee level) needs to send the message, support the efforts, and reward the achievements.

Contrary to what we believed in the 1990s, process improvement cannot be sustained through improvements that are made at shop-floor level, and gradually change the entire organization from the bottom up. This "bottom-up myth" has long been expelled by the many cases where great performance improvement work has been done at process level, yet where these improvements hit a "glass ceiling" and often dwindle away. Performance improvement without constant and consistent senior management support and attention cannot work, or at best will lead to some focal gains in efficiency only.

NOTES

1. R. Shah and P.T. Ward, 2003. Lean manufacturing: Context, practice bundles, and performance. *Journal of Operations Management*, 21(2), pp.129–49.
2. M. Baumers, M. Holweg, and J. Rowley, 2016. *The economics of 3D printing: A total cost perspective.* 3DP-RDM, University of Cambridge.
3. B. Emiliani, D.J. Stec, L. Grasso, and J. Stodder, 2003. *Better thinking, better results: Using the power of lean as a total business solution.* Center for Lean Business Management.

FURTHER READING

Bicheno, J. and Holweg, M., 2016. *The Lean Toolbox: The Essential Guide to Lean Transformation.* Picsie Books (Buckingham).

Collins, R.S. and Schmenner, R.W., 2007. Understanding persistently variable performance in plants. *International Journal of Operations and Production Management*, 27(3), pp. 254–81.

Ferdows, K. and De Meyer, A., 1990. Lasting improvements in manufacturing performance: In search of a new theory. *Journal of Operations Management*, 9(2), pp.168–84.

Pisano, G.P. and Shih, W.C., 2009. Restoring American competitiveness. *Harvard Business Review*, July–August, pp.2–12.

Schmenner, R.W., 1988. The merit of making things fast. *Sloan Management Review*, 30(1), pp.11–17.

Schmenner, R.W., 2004. Service businesses and productivity. *Decision Sciences*, 35(3), pp.333–47.

Schmenner, R.W., 2012. *Getting and Staying Productive: Applying Swift, Even Flow to Practice*. Cambridge University Press (Cambridge, UK).

Schmenner, R.W., 2015. The pursuit of productivity. *Production and Operations Management*, 24(2), pp.341–50.

Schmenner, R.W. and Swink, M.L., 1998. On theory in operations management. *Journal of Operations Management*, 17(1), pp.97–113.

9 Coordinating interfaces

9.1 The importance of interfaces

Exciting things happen at boundaries and ideas are often created through outside sources of knowledge. Functions are traditionally managed in silos, therefore it is important to consider how processes operate across the interfaces to operations management—specifically the interfaces with marketing and finance. Beyond avoiding islands of excellence, external knowledge and different perspectives are also important components of innovation. Hence there is great potential for value creation associated with boundary-spanning roles, and the practice of rotating through marketing, finance, and operations.

The aim of operations management is to increase efficiency of production and effectiveness of output, often measured by cost reduction and increased quality. However, a focus on these internal measures of operational performance ignores the wider value created through operational decisions outside of the operations management function. In addition, there may be a delay or indirect impact on the cost of quality performance.

It can be difficult to link operational decisions to financial performance or the marketing strategy of the firm, particularly as these decisions often take place at the lower level of the strategic business unit or plant. However, this should not mean that these operational decisions are not examined in a wider context.

Process improvement has wider implications than just operational efficiency and effectiveness. For example, an improvement in quality of the good or service can be promoted by marketing, or a reduction in the inventory held can reduce assets on the balance sheet. Operational decisions are also noted by investors and shareholders in their valuation of the firm. An increase in operational flexibility provides real options and potential long-term value.

Let us now take turns and consider how operations can enter into some donnybrooks with the other functions of management. We state our final principle:

Principle #10: Processes do not operate in isolation.

9.2 The firm in context

The firm does not exist in a vacuum. Its context is determined by the regulatory framework imposed by the respective national and regional governments.

It is embedded within the firm's network of suppliers and distributors. It most likely serves customers in a wide range of geographical areas. And, of course, it operates in parallel to competing firms that offer similar products and services.

Operations itself cannot operate in a vacuum within the firm. In fact it needs to interface and often integrate with other functions to create value streams in the organization. For example, operations processes need to integrate with development, engineering, and marketing to create a new product development process. Operations needs to integrate with suppliers, procurement, distribution, sales, and service after sales to create an effective supply chain. It needs to integrate with local authorities and other local stakeholders to create an environmentally sustainable operation. And it needs to interface and integrate with human resources, educational institutions, and representatives of the employees to enable a constant flow of talent and its development.

Thus, looking at operations as a self-contained field of research misses the fact that operations has to function in conjunction with the other business units in the company. In line with the notion of a "resolution level" of a process that we introduced in Chapter 2, we can define a process at firm level, at factory level, at line level, at machine level. So, depending on how "detailed" our lens is, we can see the same process as one high-level process, or as a set of connected low-level processes. This largely depends on the question we are interested in. In this case we are interested in the firm-level view, to see how well operations functions in the context of the firm.

The key danger here is that functional optimization does not lead to an overall optimum for the firm. If you optimize each function individually then you can easily create islands of excellence. That means to create functional suboptimization. For example, you could seek to optimize the unit cost in a factory by enforcing a strict level schedule. In case of cyclical demand this results in over-and understocking in distribution, and most likely lost sales—that combined penalty will outweigh the unit cost savings. We introduce a subprinciple:

Principle #10: Processes do not operate in isolation.

a. A set of suboptimal solutions can never produce a global optimum.

The problem of local optimization can be illustrated very nicely when looking at the inventory profile across the automotive industry's supply chain. As one would expect, Lean production has driven down work-in-process inventory at the car assembly plant. However this "lean" production is effectively an island of excellence in a sea of inventory on either side, in distribution and the component supply chain. The distribution inventory effectively decouples the factory from demand volatility, while the inventory in the component supply chain decouples the car factory from an unresponsive raw material end.

Overall, this supply chain clearly works suboptimally—with three-quarters of all capital in this system held in distribution. Here of course we have products made to forecasts, which are unlikely to match actual customer wishes for the most part. As a result we see recurring discounting schemes that seek to push undesired product into the market. We may benefit from lean car factories, but suffer from poor financial returns for the industry as a whole.

What are the root causes of this? Here we come back to Principle 7(b): what you get is what you measure. The key metrics for car assembly plants are unit cost and schedule adherence, while the key metrics in sales and distribution are volume sold and market share. Thus there is no incentive for either the plant or the sales arm to change behavior, and the result is shown in the inventory profile in Figure 9.1.

The former point has an important implication for process improvement, namely that it is not given that a process that is "optimal" in isolation will also lead to a globally optimal solution. In other words we know that the sum of local optima will not lead to a global optimum, hence we need to question any process improvement as to the degree to which it contributes to/works against an overall efficient high-level process. You cannot resolve all operational problems without considering the interactions with the network the process is embedded in.

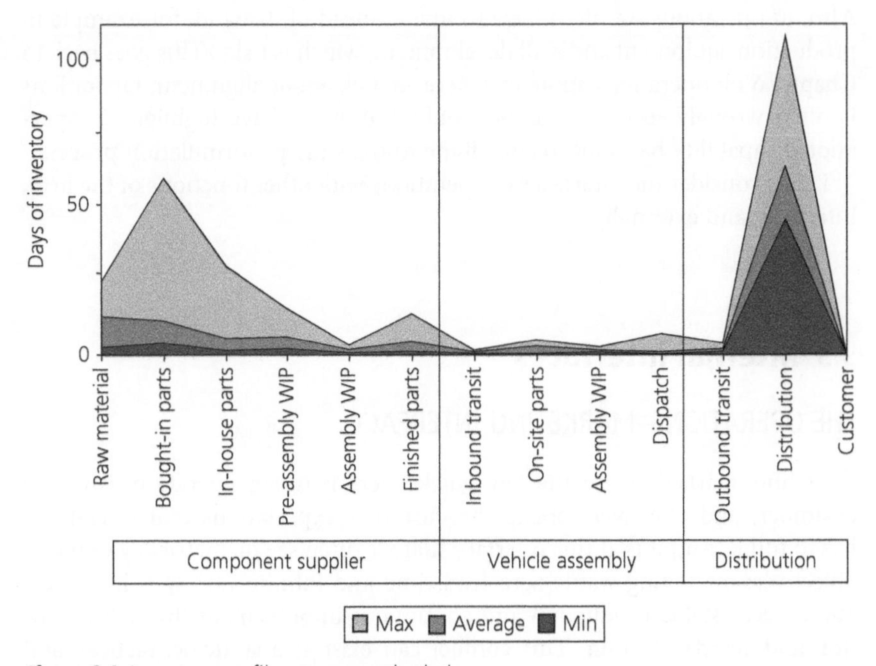

Figure 9.1 Inventory profile across supply chain.

Source: M. Holweg and F.K. Pil, 2004. *The Second Century: Reconnecting Customer and Value Chain through Build-to-Order*. The MIT Press (Cambridge).

Functional objectives will always lead to some strategic tensions. Ultimately it's the CEO who has to reconcile the strategic tensions between operations and its interfaces with marketing/sales, finance, HR, engineering, and strategy. Processes interact with their context, they are integrated into the system they are embedded in. They form value streams together with the other functions. We need to worry both about the process itself and about its interactions with the system it is embedded in. Firms effectively are composed of integrated processes or routines that all contribute to the greater goal of producing a competitive good or service.

So why do these conflicts arise? We have already talked about measurement in Chapter 7. The wrong measures can drive wrong and/or unintended behavior, and behavior that can lead you to optimize local functions over other functions in the business. A second aspect is visibility and communication. It is very easy to restrict your view to your own function, and not consider the implications that your actions have on the other functions in the business. Making these visible, communicating firm-level goals, and aligning performance metrics to achieve these are the key tasks for senior management here.

Operations often is the middleman between marketing and finance, and takes the blame: for instance, if the company grows too fast and operations cannot cope, or in a downturn operations is likely to carry too many staff. Also, in operations we often have to invest ahead of demand, for example in production equipment and skill development, which is risky. This goes back to Chapter 6 on operations strategy, where we talk about alignment. Operations is often wrongly seen as execution only, but as we have highlighted, operational capability has a lot to contribute to the strategy formulation process.

Let us consider the interfaces of operations with other functions of the firm, internally and externally.

9.3 **Internal interfaces**

THE OPERATIONS–MARKETING INTERFACE

Sales and marketing are the key gatekeepers between operations and the customer, and effectively create the customer expectations that operations has to fulfill. And it is at this interface that we often see diametrically opposed objectives: marketing wants zero lead time and infinite variety, while operations seeks stable production and continuous improvement through repetition and standardization. This conflict can exist at a strategic, tactical, and even operational level. Consider, for example, distribution decisions that are made by marketing managers, which will clearly affect operational decisions, including structural and infrastructural ones.

At the firm level what is needed is alignment between operations and channels of distribution, alignment between customer expectations and operational capabilities, as well as alignment between pricing and production capacity.

Marketing and sales interact with operations in a variety of ways, and the battles engaged in can be fierce and continual. Four interactions—or clashes—merit mention:

1. **Production planning**: These are the battles over sales forecasts, where operations often second-guesses what it suspects are overestimates of what will sell during the next several time periods, typically weeks or months. The second-guessing frequently occurs because operations must live with and pay for any excess inventory that is generated. Given this consequence, operations will often disparage the forecasting abilities of marketing and sales, while marketing and sales will distrust anything that operations says it will do. The distrust is particularly strong if operations does not produce all of what marketing and sales forecast and it then turns out that marketing and sales land closer to the mark, forcing operations to play catch-up.
2. **Capacity planning**: This battle is played out on an even larger scale when new capacity must be decided on and the forecast must then extend farther into the future. Here the second-guessing between operations and marketing and sales can involve substantial resources, and thus even more resentment.
3. **Quality**: For the typical operations manager, quality is about conformance to specifications. The operations manager is measured on that conformance. Scrap and rework are costly and are to be avoided. Marketing and sales, on the other hand, are not as concerned with conformance. They are much more concerned about the product's reception in the marketplace and whether it is fit for use. Many of the costs of off-quality—especially inspection and the internal costs of failure—are of less importance to marketing and sales. The conflict between the two functions stems from this difference in approach to quality. Operations will focus on conformance and try to keep costs low in meeting that conformance target. Meanwhile, marketing and sales may want to "upgrade" the product, with obvious implications for cost.
4. **New product development**: The new product development process is one where neither marketing nor operations takes the lead. Typically, engineering (or a similar function) controls the process. Still, there is frequently conflict between marketing and operations. Marketing's input is generally early in the process and operations' input comes later, although both may be part of the combined team charged with introducing the new product. Operations may label marketing as fickle, never knowing what it wants in

the new product, and unwilling to forecast definitively what the sales might be under different options. Marketing, for its part, may tag operations as consumed with cost and unrelentingly pessimistic about the manufacturability of the design.

THE OPERATIONS–ENGINEERING AND DEVELOPMENT INTERFACE

There is potential for conflicts between the new product development function (be it product or process engineering) and operations. There are at least three areas of potential disagreements:

1. **The design for manufacturability**: Can the product or the service actually be produced according to the efficiency requirements imposed by the market? Often designs are too complex to produce and thus unnecessarily increase the complexity and the cost of the operations. A close collaboration between engineering and operations is needed to create a design that can easily be produced.
2. **The pace at which new products and processes are introduced**: New products and processes disrupt the existing operations and often require significant retraining of the operators. This cannot be a never-ending activity. The introduction of new products and processes needs to be carefully planned.
3. **The reserve capacity in operations to run experiments**: Design of new products often requires real-life test runs and experiments using the existing process lines. While this can often be done in off time, it does require set-ups and changes in the processes that disturb the normal operations.

The transfer of new products into the existing processes is often a very delicate process, with operations managers arguing that "these designers have no clue about how the operations processes really work." A first suggestion to help provide a smooth transfer is to have a new product introduction project manager who accompanies the new product or service from the later stages of its development until it reaches full steady state production or service delivery. There has been some debate as to whether this manager should come from upstream (development) or from downstream (operations). In practice it seems to be more effective to have an "ambassador" from operations who goes and receives the product during the last stages of the development process. He or she can bring some process experience to the finalization of the design, and his or her credibility will be higher with colleagues in operations once the product or service comes downstream.

A second piece of advice is to consider the new product introduction as a process in its own right. Over the years, product development management has come up with many processes for introducing products, of which the most common is the stage gate development process. The development process is broken up into a series of stages with clear objectives and performance measures, and at predetermined moments—the so-called gates—the new product development team and senior management will evaluate whether it is justified to continue with development of the product. The introduction of a new product or service into operations is one of these stages, with well-defined goals and objectives, and should be treated as a project to which the principles of process improvement can be applied.

THE OPERATIONS–FINANCE INTERFACE

The other key interface is between operations and finance (or finance and accounting, to be precise). In their seminal critique of management accounting, Johnson and Kaplan described many shortcomings in the way standard management accounting practices lead to a key conflict between management accounting and operations.[1] Particular problems include an overreliance on financial metrics: "If you only manage your company by financial metrics, you are bound to look backwards all the time." It is like driving your car by looking through the rear-view mirror: you know which road you have travelled, but you have no useful insights into what is ahead of you.

Key problems at the operations–finance interface include, first and foremost, a focus on quarterly results—this leads to end-of-period gaming to generate revenue by offering promotions to generate last-minute demand. (This often leads to the "hockey stick" phenomenon, whereby end-of-period gaming leads to sharp and unsustainable increases in sales, or other, which then sharply decline at the beginning of the next period.) More important still, accounting measures are unhelpful to improvement. They require operations managers to explain variances that have little to do with the processes or technologies used. They also fail to provide accurate product costs if they arbitrarily assign overheads to different products.

The fascination with earnings loses sight of the importance of creating value, rather than making money. In operations we focus on creating value through converting inputs into outputs. Our field too often focuses on the intermediate measures of efficiency and effectiveness, and the need to bridge the gap between operations and finance. An example in practice of bridging this divide is the way that private equity firms are now looking beyond reliance on financial engineering and looking into operations principles on how to create value. There is often a time lag between operational decisions and their financial impacts. As Marshall Fisher said in his keynote at the 2006 annual meeting of the Production and Operations Management Society: "a focus on earnings alone misses the values and options created through operational decisions." Plus there may be a lag on earnings.

These shortcomings led to the development of the balanced scorecard and the performance prism, which both promote using a set of metrics that combine leading and lagging, financial and non-financial metrics. The relevant stereotype here is of the accountant or financial manager who fails to understand the firm's operations manager, and vice versa. From a financial standpoint, operations can play a critical role in lowering costs and raising productivity, yet from operations' perspective these same activities can increase the value of the organization and are an investment in the organization's future. It is as if these managers are from "different planets." They value different things entirely. It is instructive to compare these stereotypes.

Let us look a bit more closely into the cost structure and nature of these variances:

- *Accounting and finance perspective*: The breakdown of costs into labor, materials, and overhead is a useful separation and can lead to analysis of the variances in the cost structure over time. Managing the variances is seen as an effective way to reduce costs. It works directly on the factors of production, such as labor and materials.
- *Operations perspective*: The elements of the typical cost structure have little relevance to the operations manager, and managing their variances is of little worth. Labor, materials, and overhead are fixed costs. In the short term, there is nothing that the operations manager can do to contain them. All the operations manager wants to do is produce the volume of good product that is expected.

So, "fully absorbed costs" has a meaning in accounting and finance. Overhead can be attached to the variable costs of a product, and that resulting "fully absorbed" cost can be very useful for determining which product lines are making money, and how much. For operations, however, things are different. Too many operations managers over the years have fallen for this view of profitability so that they love volume at almost any cost. Some managers will accept any production that they can get their hands on, simply to absorb a bit more of the overhead, and they can tie themselves up in knots in the process. For more thoughtful operations managers, fully absorbed costs have no meaning because the operations manager has no control over the volumes demanded.

The same applies to inventory. In accounting and finance, inventory is costly to hold and thus it always needs to be reduced. In this, the operations manager and the accountant/financial manager are in agreement, although for different reasons. The accountant/financial manager worries about the cost of carrying inventory, while the operations manager worries about the inventory itself clogging up the factory. There are instances, however, when having inventory, particularly work-in-process inventory, can be very useful and blanket prohibitions of inventory are misguided.

With regard to equipment utilization, accounting takes the view that equipment is expensive and the company's equipment needs to pay for itself. To do that, the equipment should be operated for a substantial period of each day. For operations, a machine is a sunk cost. It is there to produce when needed. When it is not needed, it is best to leave it idle.

BUILDING THE INTERFACES

Can there be any resolution to this characterization of the interactions of operations with other functions as a frequent zone of conflict? Can some middle ground be struck? We believe it can. And the resolution is best seen by examining the role of operations within the strategy of the company, as was depicted in Chapter 6. This role for operations is both more central and more varied than is frequently acknowledged.

With some understanding, then, of how the operations function fits with strategy, and with our principles of operations management in mind, let us review some of the interactions or clashes that operations may have with other functions.

Marketing and Sales—Production Planning

The best way to avoid conflict is for operations not to be concerned with the marketing and sales forecast. And the most effective way to reduce the significance of the forecast is to shorten its time horizon. Understandably, the longer the lead times for operations, the more important the forecast becomes, and, at the same time, the less accurate the forecast could be expected to be. If the process' throughput time can be reduced, then both the need for a forecast declines and the accuracy of any forecast used improves. This, then, is the best alternative for operations. Reduce throughput time and then one has less need to worry about the forecasting skill of marketing and sales. Operations is thus best served by concentrating on productivity—via swift, even flow—and production planning will automatically improve.

This concentration on productivity should also help to make the process more robust and flexible. As long as the process can accommodate change easily, there should be no need to be concerned about how mercurial marketing and sales are.

Marketing and Sales—Capacity Planning

Here, too, robustness in the operations function is the best way to avoid conflict. If new capacity can be designed with flexibility in mind so that a broad range of capacity targets can be met, then the company will suffer less from the clash between operations and marketing and sales.

Marketing and Sales—Quality

A definition of quality as simple conformance to specifications is too narrow. The importance of the demand curve is simply too great to ignore. As Joseph Juran, one of the quality gurus of the last century, argued, the needs of the consumer must be part of the definition of quality. Quality as "conformance to specifications, as valued by customers," is a better definition. It should also help to relieve some of the conflicts that might break out around quality.

Marketing and Sales/Engineering—New Product Development

A new product can be critical for a company and its position within a—perhaps new—market segment. The product's strategic importance can be substantial. As we have already argued, new product development is a process in its own right, and the company can adopt Lean principles to improve the productivity of the new product development function. Adopting such principles can greatly reduce the battles that revolve around new product development. With faster new product development cycles, the gripes wither about marketing being fickle and unwilling or unable to provide good forecasts for sales of particular product configurations—and operations can be more engaged throughout the entire duration of the project.

Finance and Accounting—Cost Structures and Variances

In our operations management principles, we have argued that cost reduction comes from applying the concept of swift, even flow. That is what can shift a company's position along the industry supply curve. Reducing variation of all kinds and reducing throughput time is the way to reduce cost. Using variances, particularly variances on factors of production such as labor and materials, will not be as insightful or as successful.

Some in the accounting profession have recognized that traditional cost accounting systems have compromised the goals of cost management.[2] In many traditional cost accounting systems, direct labor is used to allocate overhead to products. Yet direct labor is not at all linked to the elements of overhead cost, which are frequently tied to transactions of various kinds (e.g. logistics, materials planning, quality, and product change).[3] Direct labor is a terrible cost driver for overhead expenses. The result of using a poor mechanism like direct labor to allocate overhead expense is to introduce a lot of unexplained variances into the cost system. Such variances, of course, are not unexplained so much as misallocated. Activity-based costing is an improvement on traditional costing as it goes after particular "drivers" for costs and allocates overhead based on those drivers.

Finance and Accounting—Fully Absorbed Costs

When direct labor is used to allocate overhead expenses so that fully absorbed costs can be calculated, and when those overhead expenses are significant multiples of the direct labor cost itself (often 300–800 percent), managers have an incentive to look good by trimming direct labor in any way they can. The more appropriate management action is, of course, to reduce the overhead itself, but that option is too frequently neglected. As total costs rise, the lure of outsourcing the operation becomes stronger and stronger. The result can be a hollowing out of the operational capability of the company, when the opportunity existed for reducing costs of all kinds and actually improving competitiveness.

What is crucial for the company is not how it calculates its fully absorbed costs but rather its relative position on the industry supply curve. That position is enhanced when all kinds of costs—variable and overhead—are reduced. And, as we have noted, that cost reduction comes with application of the tenets of swift, even flow.

Finance and Accounting—Inventory

Cost accounting, as it evolved in the first decades of the twentieth century, became more and more an exercise in valuing inventory for the company's financial statements.[4] In the process, cost accounting lost sight of why inventory should, or should not, exist in the first place. As a consequence, it missed the importance of the just-in-time/Lean manufacturing revolution and could not rethink its mission in such a changed operations world.

We now appreciate that inventories are a means by which the mistakes of the processes can be hidden from view. That is why they can and should be reduced. Carrying inventory costs money—the opportunity cost of capital and the costs of handling, warehousing, obsolescence, shrinkage, transportation, and the like—but, according to our principles, anything that interrupts the swift, even flow of materials in the process costs money. Inventories are but one aspect of this cost, albeit an important one.

Finance and Accounting—Equipment Utilization

When a piece of equipment runs, it does not pay for itself. The only way that things are paid for is by having the factory as a whole ship output to consumers. It is the firm's customers who pay. Traditional cost justifications for capital appropriations requests, which ignore how the equipment fits with the process as a whole, and which are based on such things as reduced direct labor, are deficient. They do not value the process of which the equipment is a part, nor do they fully see how the equipment fits into the scheme of things in positioning the operation on the industry supply curve.

Managing Conflicts

As one can observe, these conflicts can be managed. Our principles and an appreciation for the dynamics of industry supply and demand can promote a rapprochement among operations and its sister functions in the company.

9.4 Primary external interfaces: the supply chain

The term "supply chain management" first appeared in 1982 in a consulting report that stated that firms should manage "total supply chain inventories"—as distinct from each tier managing its own inventory (which meant that in aggregate more inventory was carried in the system than was needed). Supply chain management (SCM) is thus a relatively new discipline: only in the early 1980s did firms realize that their competitiveness was determined not just by what they did, but also by how their upstream suppliers and downstream suppliers were performing. The final product, after all, is a combined effort of all firms in the supply chain. From this insight developed the notion that it is just as important to manage your *supply chain* as it is to manage your own *operation*. Fast cycle times in manufacturing processes can be a powerful competitive weapon, but when firms supply via a slow distributor the customer may never experience the full benefit.

In fact, for most manufacturers, their products are a function of their suppliers' processes as much as of their own processes. Vehicle manufacturers, for example, buy about 60–80 percent of the value of their product ex-factory from suppliers. The actual assembly plant accounts for only about 12 percent of the cost of manufacturing a vehicle, with distribution, retail, and marketing operations costs adding up to another 30 percent of the list or retail price. In this sense suppliers hold much greater leverage over product quality and cost than the original equipment manufacturer (OEM) itself. The final product is thus not the sole achievement of the OEM, but rather the customer experience is co-determined by the entire supply chain in terms of product quality, cost, and delivery. This in turn means that supply chain capabilities are a significant determinant of firm competitiveness. Martin Christopher summarized this succinctly by stating that "value chains compete, not individual firms."

Various conceptualizations of supply chains are evident, such as value chain, value stream, demand chain, and supply network. These can be applied to manufacturing and service supply chains, but also to back office process flows. The term *value chain* refers to how value is added to goods and services by a network of organizations from raw materials through to the end customer. Lean practitioners refer to this as one of the key *value streams* in the firm, enabling an analysis of the current state and designing the future state. The *demand chain* explicitly incorporates the customer where production is triggered in response to actual customer orders. Finally, the *supply network* captures the complexity of multiple suppliers, multiple tiers, and interdependencies that exist between them.

We can also distinguish between forward supply chains and reverse supply chains. Forward (or "open loop") supply chains refer to a system where materials move forward and information feeds backward through the tiers in a linear fashion. Products do not return to the original manufacturer, but are instead recovered by third parties or end up in landfill. By contrast, reverse (or "closed loop") supply chains describe a system where product is returned to the manufacturer for reuse, remanufacture/refurbishment, or recycling. As environmental sustainability has taken on increasing importance, reverse supply chains have become more central to firms' supply chain strategies. Reverse logistics, in particular, is a key building block of the "circular economy," where products are returned, recovered, and remarketed.

The different elements of supply chains are displayed in Figure 9.2 showing forward and reverse, upstream and downstream, inbound and outbound logistics.

SUPPLY CHAIN INTERFACES

Managing supply chains effectively requires the management of multiple types of flows: materials, information, and relationships. Other flows, like technology and money, are also possible.

Integration of Material Flows

At the most basic level, an organization must address a number of decisions about managing inventory across its supply chain. Where to hold inventory? How much? In what form (raw materials, work-in-process, final product)? How to structure call-offs to suppliers? At what point does an order become binding? ERP systems or kanbans (physical and electronic) are used to coordinate material movements from raw materials to end customer.

We have already talked about the importance of aligning the operations of a firm with the requirements of the marketplace—for example, by identifying order winners and making operations choices which are consistent with them. In supply chain design, the need to align supply chain structure to product characteristics has been similarly recognized. Marshall Fisher (1997), for example, in his now seminal paper, highlighted the need to achieve a match

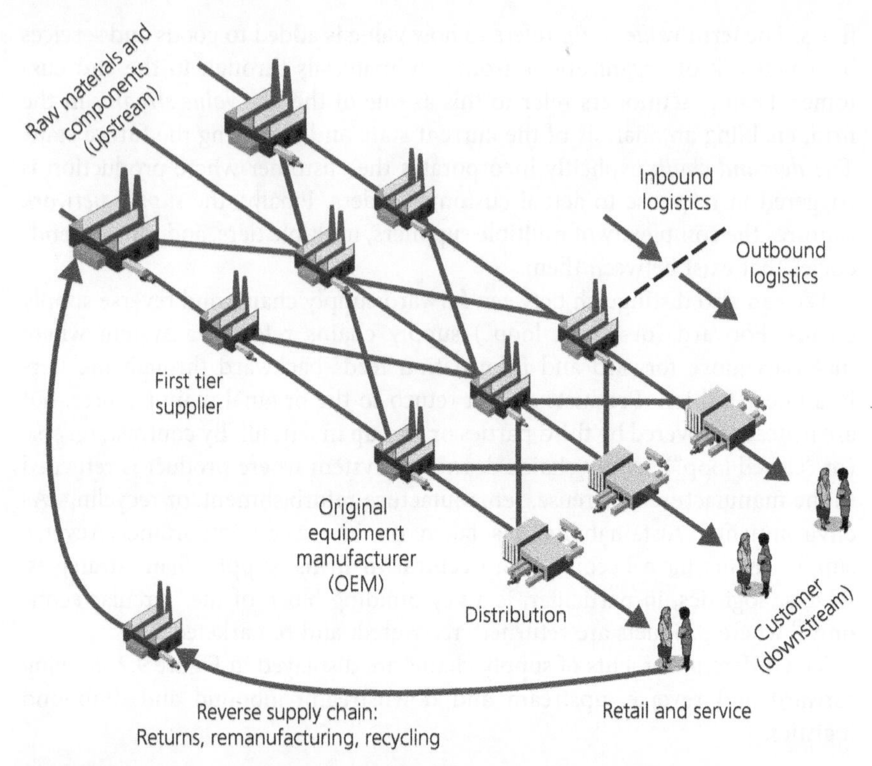

Figure 9.2 The supply chain: forward and reverse.

between supply chain design—either efficient or responsive—and the nature of the end product, either functional or innovative.[5] Functional products exhibit stable and predictable demand, with long life cycles, while innovative products are the opposite, with unstable and unpredictable demand and short life cycles. For functional products, achieving a match between customer demand and supply is quite feasible, and as such firms develop efficient supply chains which minimize distribution and fulfillment costs. On the other hand, to deliver innovative products firms develop responsive supply chains, which, while more expensive to operate, help diminish the supply and demand mismatch. The ideas from Fisher are illustrated in Figure 9.3.

These ideas have been developed further, for instance by incorporating lead time implications into the decisions, by Christopher et al.[6] This discussion creates distinctions around Lean, Agile, and "Leagile" supply chains. Lean supply chains are appropriate in situations of stable demand; by contrast, Agile supply chains are more suited to situations where demand is unpredictable but lead times are short. In this case, being demand-driven is critical to responsiveness. Leagile supply chains are proposed where demand is unpredictable, but lead times are long. Firms may use postponement to achieve a

	Functional products	Innovative products
Efficient supply chain	match	mismatch
Responsive supply chain	mismatch	match

Figure 9.3 Matching supply chain demand to product characteristics.

Source: M. Fisher, 1997. What is the right supply chain for your product? *Harvard Business Review*, 75(2), pp.105–16.

match between demand and supply, as well as base and surge sourcing strategies. The base element of demand is sourced in an efficient, lean manner, with the unpredictable elements moving through an Agile supply chain structure.

Integration of Information Flows

Information is also a critical flow to manage across organizational boundaries. Firms need to coordinate the sharing of operational information related to forecasts, sales trends, and inventory levels in order to reduce cycle times and inventory holdings, and to improve fill rates and customer service. Achieving this level of supply chain integration and information sharing requires systems that support such goals, such as collaborative planning, forecasting and replenishment (CPFR), efficient consumer response (ECR), and sales & operations planning (S&OP).

For supplier management, firms need to communicate supplier performance through monthly reports highlighting supplier behavior on key operational metrics like cost, quality, and problem-solving. Toyota and Honda, for example, use monthly reporting of structured operational information to drive supplier performance. Equally, in today's world of globalized, dispersed supply chains, information flows also enhance transparency and the management of risks. Rapid identification of business disruptions helps improve responsiveness, while transparency of non-financial information related to sustainability risks—environmental or social—has become a legal, if not also an ethical, requirement.

Integration with Suppliers

Managing supplier relationships reflects the processes by which a company manages interfaces with its suppliers. The organization must, for example, segment its supply base in a variety of different ways, such as the relationship stance (arms-length versus collaboration), contract duration (short-term or long-term), sourcing configurations (single, parallel, or multiple sourcing), the desired value from suppliers (productivity only, productivity and innovation, or innovation only), approach to problem-solving (exit or voice), and supplier importance (strategic supplier, preferred supplier, or tactical supplier).

The nature of the supply relationship has a strong bearing on performance: relational or trust-based governance of supplier relations has been found to yield superior performance in terms of quality, cost, and delivery. It is thus the preferred mode for parts that are critical for the final product. Commodities, on the other hand, are best procured through a transactional mode, as here the product characteristics are interchangeable. Table 9.1 sets out the features of the different modes of supplier relationship management: transactional, relational, or a hybrid of the two.

A specific concept about integration with suppliers is that of a sourcing hub. Agrawal et al. have studied the relationships between a main producer, e.g. an automotive manufacturer, and its multiple suppliers and sub-suppliers that use a common material, e.g. aluminum or steel. They propose a fairly simple but effective solution whereby the main manufacturer coordinates all upstream procurement of that common material or component in a sourcing hub for the complete upstream supply chain. Their empirical results indicate a significant cost reduction, quality improvement, and most importantly joint learning through the sourcing hub.[7]

Table 9.1 Modes of supplier relationship management

Transactional coordination	Relational coordination	Hybrid collaborative
Arms-length and transactional	Long-term and relational	Long-term and relational
Open for new suppliers to bid	Set of potential suppliers mostly closed	Open to new suppliers, after a vetting period
Competitive selection by low bid—frequent and speedy exit	Selection based on capabilities—exit rare and slow	Competitive assessment—intermediate frequency and speed of exit
Design simplified by customer to enlarge pool of suppliers	Design controlled by customer, supplier involved via resident engineer	Larger design role for supplier, attention to supplier design capabilities
No equity stake	Often an equity stake	Equity stake depends on criticality of technology
Contracts for governance	Norms/dialogue for governance	Norms and process management routines for governance
Codified procedures	Tacit procedures	Process management routines make procedures explicit

Source: S. Helper, J.P. MacDuffie, and C. Sabel, 2000. Pragmatic collaborations: Advancing knowledge while controlling opportunism. *Industrial and Corporate Change*, 9(3), pp.443–88.

THE KEY CHALLENGE OF SUPPLY CHAIN INTEGRATION: THE BULLWHIP EFFECT

As any process consists of a set of connected subprocesses, we need to also consider the interactions between these subprocesses. For any supply chain, the objectives are simple: get the right products to customers at the right time, right place, right cost, and in the right quantity. However, coordinating the actions (or subprocesses) of the various players in a supply chain process is a significant problem. To meet customer demand, firms in the system must make decisions around forecasts of customer demand, desired inventory levels, and production plans. Each firm has typically an imperfect picture of true customer demand, and their decisions both influence, and are influenced by, the actions of others in the chain. A pattern of inventory overstocking and shortages across the supply chain, with poor forecasting leading to unpredictable production planning, results in an impaired ability to utilize production capacity, and declining customer fill rates impacting on customer satisfaction and revenues.

We refer to these dynamic distortions, where individual firm-level processes interact with the supply chain, as the *bullwhip effect*. The bullwhip effect (or "Law of Industrial Dynamics," as Forrester called it) occurs when small variations in orders from a customer cause amplification in stock levels and orders as they are transmitted along the supply chain. Figure 9.4 illustrates the bullwhip effect in a simple four-tier system, made up of customer, retailer, distributor, and warehouse. Just such a problem occurred many years ago at Volvo with their inventory of green cars. Observing that the company held excess inventory of green cars, the sales department authorized discount offers to dealers, which led to increased demand. The production department, not having been informed about the offer, saw increasing levels of demand and in response increased production of green cars.

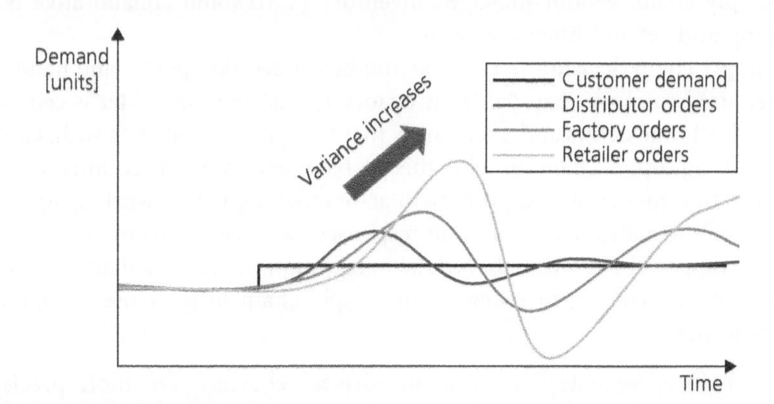

Figure 9.4 The "bullwhip effect."

Such patterns are the inevitable consequence of an unmanaged supply chain system where the following characteristics exist: delays (in the transmission of information and/or materials), uncertainty (of decision making), and decision tiers. We outline the three key drivers of the bullwhip, although note that the literature has generated many others including order batching, price fluctuations, demand forecast updating, and rationing and gaming:[8]

- **Delays**—Delays in manufacturing and procurement exist where information is not transmitted promptly (for example, because forecasts are only updated monthly), or where material does not flow rapidly through the supply chain (due to, for example, long-lead time supply chains). As generations of students have discovered by playing the Beer Game simulation, a common response as downstream customers increase orders and backlogs increase is to continue ordering more and more inventory. Upstream players conflate these backlogged orders with increased demand, and in turn ramp up their own production. As with the theory of swift, even flow—discussed in Chapter 8—reducing or eliminating time delays in a system reduces the severity of the bullwhip effect. These actions reduce inventory holding costs, minimize the forecasting horizon, resulting in more accurate estimates (all else being equal), and improve customer responsiveness.
- **Uncertainties**—Where the players in the system hold imperfect information about customer demand, they must attempt to forecast it. However, any error in the forecast becomes amplified as firms apply different forecasting techniques, policies towards safety stock levels, and ordering behaviors in an attempt to match customer demand with supply. At a systems level, these individual, local efforts result in waves of stock-outs and excess inventory moving up and down the supply chain. Fortunately, concerted efforts by firms over many years have produced systems which generate better information about customer demand and improve forecasting accuracy. These include sharing point-of-sale data across the supply chain, vendor-managed inventory (VMI), and collaborative planning and replenishment systems.
- **Supply chain decision tiers**—The number of decision points and hand-offs required to move material from factory to distribution center accentuates the lead time delays and uncertainty that the system must cope with. Global, far-flung supply chains amplify this problem with multiple countries, transportation modes, and supply chain actors making the network opaque and difficult to coordinate. Common responses have seen firms merging tiers of the supply chain through vertical integration, disintermediating existing players, or seeking to redesign the supply chain to get closer to the end customer.

In summary, we note that "structure drives behavior." Or, more precisely, uncertainty, delay in transmission, and hand-offs will lead to amplification of a signal as it passes from one tier to the next—the "Law of Industrial Dynamics." Thus, we highlight the following subprinciple:

Principle #10: Processes do not operate in isolation.

a. A set of suboptimal solutions can never produce a global optimum.
b. Structure drives behavior.

TAMING THE BULLWHIP

A wide range of concepts and tools have been proposed to manage supply chains and avoid the costly dynamic distortions discussed in the previous section. In this section we discuss the main systems in use: VMI, electronic point of sale (EPOS), collaborative forecasting (CF), and—once put all together—collaborative planning, forecasting, and replenishment (CPFR).

Vendor-managed Inventory (VMI)

VMI (vendor-managed inventory) is one way of reducing supply chain distortions, as it effectively removes one decision point from the system. In a traditional supply chain setting, both retailer and supplier make their own ordering decisions, potentially triggering the bullwhip effect. In a VMI setting the customer passes inventory information to the supplier, instead of orders. The actual inventory at the customer is compared with a pre-agreed reorder point (ROP), set to cover adequate availability. Both parties also agree to an order-up-to point (OUP). When actual inventory is at or below the ROP the supplier delivers the difference up to the OUP. The retailer does not execute any ordering decisions at all, but relies on its ability to control all inventories in the system.

Applying this logic to the water tank model in Figure 9.5, VMI allows the supplier to take over the ordering decision from the retailer. The supplier now has direct visibility of "what is going on" at the retailer in terms of stock levels, and most importantly it also eliminates one decision tier from the supply chain. As we have seen, the bullwhip effect is driven by lead times, uncertainty, and hand-offs or decision points. VMI is a powerful tool in reducing the bullwhip effect: it reduces uncertainty by allowing additional visibility of consumption at the retail tier, it cuts lead times as the supplier does not have to wait for a formal order, and it eliminates a decision point.

Information Sharing (EPOS and CF)

Information sharing can happen in two ways: the retailer or manufacturer can share their actual sales data ("EPOS," or electronic point of sale data, that retailers generally share with their suppliers), or they can share and align their

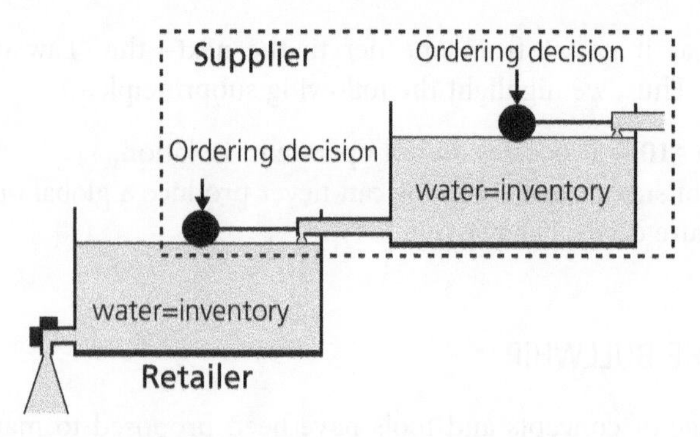

Figure 9.5 The water tank model of vendor-managed inventory (VMI).

Source: M. Holweg, S. Disney, J. Holmström, and J. Småros, 2005. Supply chain collaboration: Making sense of the strategy continuum. *European Management Journal*, 23(2), pp.170–81.

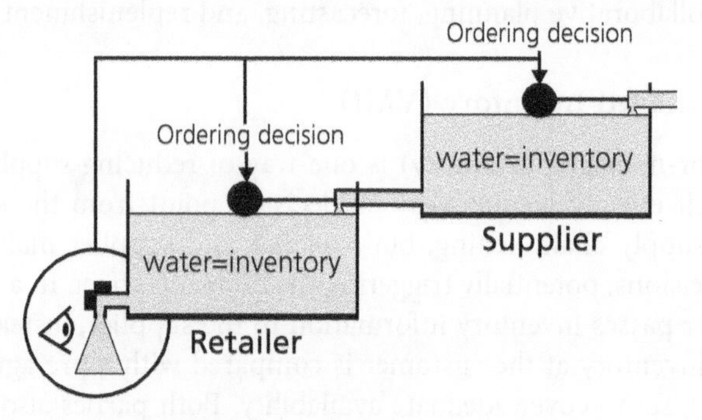

Figure 9.6 Information sharing in the supply chain.

Source: M. Holweg, S. Disney, J. Holmström, and J. Småros, 2005. Supply chain collaboration: Making sense of the strategy continuum. *European Management Journal*, 23(2), pp.170–81.

forecasts with their suppliers (collaborative forecasting, or "CF"). These two types of information sharing serve very different purposes. EPOS data can be very useful for planning short-term execution and driving the replenishment signal (where it works like a kanban: sell one, replenish one). Shared forecasts have no value in the short term, but are essential to align capacities and avoid bottlenecks and overproduction in the future. Also, sales promotions need to be communicated well in advance so that the entire supply chain is aware of the likely short-term increases, and does not overreact when the demand spikes are transmitted through the system. These characteristics are illustrated in Figure 9.6.

Collaborative Planning, Forecasting, and Replenishment (CPFR)

The collaborative planning, forecasting, and replenishment approach (CPFR) was developed by the grocery retail sector (see vics.org), and effectively merges

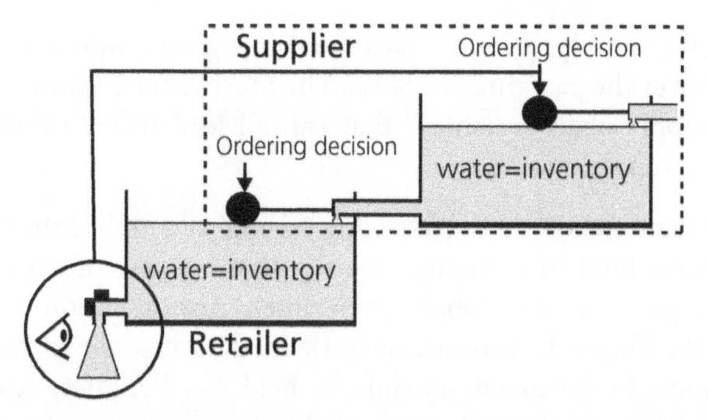

Figure 9.7 The collaborative planning, forecasting, and replenishment approach (CPFR).

Source: M. Holweg, S. Disney, J. Holmström, and J. Småros, 2005. Supply chain collaboration: Making sense of the strategy continuum. *European Management Journal*, 23(2), pp.170–81.

the VMI and collaborative planning elements to form a model of close supply chain collaboration. Shown here in our water tank model, CPFR uses tools to increase the demand visibility (collaborative forecasting), EPOS data to drive the replenishment (continuous replenishment), as well as reduced decision tiers for inventory and order management (VMI). Thus it is a powerful tool for managing high-volume supply chains in the fast-moving consumer goods arena. See Figure 9.7.

SUPPLY CHAIN MANAGEMENT: WHAT ARE WE TRYING TO ACHIEVE?

Managing a supply chain system is different to the management of a factory at local level. Thinking about how to manage multiple interfaces between the organization and its suppliers—in relationships, materials, and information—is critical to managing this interdependency.

It is not given that a process that is "optimal" in isolation will also lead to a globally optimal solution. We know that the sum of local optima will not lead to a global optimum; hence, in evaluating any process improvement we need to question to what degree it contributes to or works against an overall efficient high-level process. In conducting this analysis, Zara realized that they must sacrifice the efficiency of one of their processes in order to optimize the whole: time is central to making their fast fashion model work, and thus they choose to pay more for rapid distribution processes to ensure that lead times from design table to store rack are diminished. Other firms have entrenched their focus on creating local optima—for example, automotive supply chains—subordinating the supply chain system to factory efficiency.

In summary, supply chain management has grown into a very large and diverse field over the past three decades. The most generic framework is that of the "three supply chain enemies" that can all lead to, or worsen, dynamic distortions in supply chains:

1. **Inventory and delays** that worsen any "swing" of amplification. The longer the response time to a change, the worse the swing upstream. This is a particular problem for global supply lines. Also, decision delays require stock, as the longer the forecasting horizon, the worse the forecast becomes, and the more buffer inventory must be held. Finally, safety stock decisions can send false signals, so beware of this trap: inform your supply chain partners if you adjust stock levels.
2. **Unreliability or uncertainty**. Any kind of uncertainty needs to be covered with inventory. Here, unreliable processes cause unreliable delivery, and ultimately uncertainty at the receiving end. The starting point needs to be a reliable and capable process.
3. **Hand-offs or decision points**. Every hand-off or tier in the system bears the danger of distorting the demand signal, as planners tend to have "misperceptions" of the actual demand. So the more people that interfere with the demand flow, the worse the swings generally become. In particular, be aware of "double-guessing" by creating a forecast based on someone else's forecast.

NOTES

1. H.T. Johnson and R.S. Kaplan, 1987. *Relevance Lost: The Rise and Fall of Management Accounting*. Harvard Business School Press.
2. Johnson and Kaplan, *Relevance Lost*.
3. J.G. Miller and T.E. Vollmann, 1985. The hidden factory. *Harvard Business Review*, 63(5), pp.142–50.
4. Johnson and Kaplan, *Relevance Lost*, Chapter 6.
5. M. Fisher, 1997. What is the right supply chain for your product? *Harvard Business Review*, 75(2), pp.105–16.
6. M. Christopher, H. Peck, and D. Towill, 2006. A taxonomy for selecting global supply chain strategies. *The International Journal of Logistics Management*, 17(2), pp.277–87.
7. A. Agrawal, A. De Meyer, and L. Van Wassenhove, 2014. Managing value in a supply chain—Case studies on the sourcing hub concept. *California Management Review*, 56(2), pp.23–54.
8. H.L. Lee, V. Padmanabhan, and S. Whang, 1997. Information distortion in a supply chain: The bullwhip effect. *Management Science*, 43(4), pp.546–58.

FURTHER READING

Agrawal, A., De Meyer, A., and Van Wassenhove, L., 2014. Managing value in a supply chain—Case studies on the sourcing hub concept. *California Management Review*, 56(2), pp.23–54.

Cooper, R. and Maskell, B., 2008. How to manage through worse-before-better. *MIT Sloan Management Review*, 49(4), p.58.

De Meyer, A. and Wittenberg, A., 1992. *Creating Product Value: A Strategic Manufacturing Perspective*. Pitman UK (London).

Forrester, J.W., 1958. Industrial dynamics—a major breakthrough for decision makers. *Harvard Business Review*, 36(4), p.37.

Holweg, M., Disney, S., Holmström, J., and Småros, J., 2005. Supply chain collaboration: Making sense of the strategy continuum. *European Management Journal*, 23(2), pp.170–81.

Lee, H.L., 2004. The triple-A supply chain. *Harvard Business Review*, 82(10), pp.102–12.

Lee, H.L., Padmanabhan, V., and Wang, S., 1997. The bullwhip effect in supply chains. *Sloan Management Review*, 38(3), pp.93–102.

Liker, J.K. and Choi, T.Y., 2004. Building deep supplier relationships. *Harvard Business Review*, 82(12), pp.104–113+149.

Sterman, J.D., 2000. *Business Dynamics: Systems Thinking and Modeling for a Complex World*. McGraw-Hill (Boston, MA).

10 The principles of operations management

10.1 What we stand for

In this book we started from the birthplace of our discipline, have tracked its evolution, outlined the key themes that have emerged over the past century, and have defined the fundamental principles our discipline is based on. As we have made clear, operations management is firmly grounded in the real world. In fact many of the key concepts that underpin the design, measurement, and improvement of processes stem from innovations made in practice.[1]

Operations management is agnostic to epistemology, and thus the methods used to generate valid knowledge. It exists at the nexus of industrial engineering and the social sciences, its two ancestors. The former gives a strong focus on problem-solving, the latter a focus on theory development and testing. Our work is guided and verified by empirical evidence. The essence of our discipline is the design, measurement, and improvement of processes of all kinds, across all sectors of the economy. We see operations as contingent on the context in which it is enacted and, second, that processes in operations are sociotechnical systems. People are complex and varied in their own rights, so merging man and machine in the context of a process—by default—produces a complex system. Therefore we must always abstain from absolute words such as "optimal" or seeking expressions in "closed form," unless for specific and bounded problems, such as focal planning and scheduling.

In the same vein, an operation cannot be "efficient," at least not without qualifying what this efficiency relates to: a standard? Or time? It cannot be "optimal" either, at least not without clearly qualifying under what assumptions this condition of optimality holds true. This is especially the case as the context in which processes are enacted is constantly changing, arguably even more so with the rate digital technologies are entering all aspects of work and life. In this regard it is important to note the role that the context plays in, for example, the definition of "best" practices. What is "best" in one setting may well be "good" at best in another. Contextual validity should never be assumed a priori.

Regardless of changes in technology or other developments, these are the principles that stand the test of time. Irrespective of where the journey will take you, these principles will always apply. Let us review them, and consider how to put them to work.

10.2 A century of operations thinking—distilled into ten principles

The ten process principles distil a century of the essentials of operations management thinking into the fundamental building blocks of our discipline. Each principle in isolation adds value to the management of an operation. Together, they form the essential theoretical basis to understand, run, and improve any operation. The ten principles are set out in Box 10.1.

BOX 10.1 THE TEN PRINCIPLES OF OPERATIONS MANAGEMENT

Foundation principles

- **Principle #1:** All operations are composed of processes.
- **Principle #2:** Variation is inherent in all process inputs, tasks, and outputs.

Design principles

- **Principle #3:** Work-in-process is determined by throughput rate and throughput time.
- **Principle #4:** Complexity in process design amplifies managerial challenges.
- **Principle #5:** Process choice requires fit between the task and the external requirements.

Measurement principles

- **Principle #6:** No single measure can capture the performance of a process.
- **Principle #7:** Process metrics can drive unintended behavior.

Improvement principles

- **Principle #8:** Processes are improved by reductions in throughput time or in undesired variation.
- **Principle #9:** The rate of process improvement is subject to diminishing returns.
- **Principle #10:** Processes do not operate in isolation.

We have derived these principles by drawing upon key elements of prior research and established practices alike. Our foundation principles #1 and #2 build on the early work by Walter Shewhart and W. Edwards Deming, providing us with the importance and universality of the process perspective, and the nature of variation within the process.

We identify three design principles that predict the fundamental behavior of processes in action: Principle #3 uses the work of John D. Little, and his fundamental insights into how throughput and inventory relate. We extend these insights by incorporating the works of Eliyahu Goldratt, Wallace Hopp, and Mark Spearman into the effects of bottlenecks on throughput and capacity utilization. Last but not least, John Kingman's work on expected waiting times provides fundamental insights into the stochastic nature of lead times and inventory build-up.

Principle #4 builds on the work on complexity by Herbert Simon and Warren Weaver, which is of great relevance to any (complex) system that is based on many entities that interact towards a common purpose—including operations.

Principle #5 integrates key notions of Frederick Taylor's work on task separation and Wickham Skinner's notion of strategic operations with the fundamental concept of the product–process matrix by Bob Hayes and Steven Wheelwright on how volume and variety shape processes, and its sociotechnical components (machines and labor).

Measuring performance is the fundamental enabler for managing performance. We draw on a wealth of research on performance measurement, including that of Robert Kaplan, David Norton, Thomas Johnson, and Andy Neely, as well as the work of Arnoud De Meyer with Kasra Ferdows, for Principles #6 and #7.

For Principle #8 we draw on Roger Schmenner and Morgan Swink's theory of swift, even flow and other research by John Bicheno, Kasra Ferdows, Arnoud De Meyer, Matthias Holweg, Frits Pil, and David Upton into how to manage and sustain process improvement across contexts.

The work of Roger Schmenner with Morgan Swink on performance frontiers is a key foundation of Principle #9, along with the general notion of diminishing returns in the economic discourse of production.

Principle #10 builds on the work of the early systems thinkers[2] Ludwig van Bertalanffy and Russel Ackoff who introduced the concepts of open systems and synergy, and the work on the interaction between a system's structure and its dynamic performance by Jay Forrester, John Burbidge, and John Sterman, later extended by Hau Lee, V. Padmanabhan, and Seungjin Whang as the "bullwhip effect."

Our aim in defining these specific principles is to put into one place a coherent, yet parsimonious, perspective of *process theory*. Together they form the bedrock of our discipline. Let's see how to put them to work.

10.3 **Putting *process theory* to work**

As Kurt Lewin so famously remarked, "nothing is as practical as a good theory."[3] So far we have discussed the theoretical foundations of operations management. Operations management is an inherently applied discipline. So what do they mean in practice?

First and foremost, the process model provides the lens for considering any aspect of managing operations: how to *design* a process, how to *measure* its performance, and how to *improve* its effectiveness and efficiency.

In *designing* a process, we consider the process within its system. It is important to set the right boundaries: setting the boundaries too wide yields an unwieldy system; setting the boundaries too narrow will mean missing important interactions with other subsystems. Once the boundaries of the process are defined, one needs to make sure that all tasks identified within that process add value from the customer's point of view. Ideally, we would ensure that the process is designed right first time. In practice there may be several iterations of radical and incremental changes to the processes, which we will refer to later.

It is also vital to achieve fit between these tasks and the environment, as this is a fundamental precondition for an efficient and effective process. As operations grow, the process design is likely to change as well. Where possible, we seek to avoid unnecessary complexity. An exception or workaround may seem useful in the short term, but inevitably will eventually prove detrimental. In the long run simplicity wins!

The set-up of the process largely drives the long-term performance and throughput of the process. As a guiding notion, we seek to achieve swift, even flow of product or tasks flowing through the system.

In *measuring* a process, the fundamental rule applies: you cannot manage what you do not measure. In order to understand performance, we employ absolute metrics that lay out the efficiency and effectiveness of a process. Every process has internal and external stakeholders, and neither can be ignored so they must both be represented in these measures. Underpinning virtually any operations decision is a trade-off. You cannot achieve high performance on all aspects, therefore it is vital to align metrics with the operations strategy of the firm.[4] There is no point in focusing on measures of effectiveness (e.g. customer satisfaction) if your drive is for efficiency (e.g. cost reduction). Never forget that metrics drive behavior, and that setting targets alone does not improve a process. Targets provide a goal, but improvement is derived through change in the process.

There is always room for *improving* a process. We strongly advise observing the actual process in practice—go to gemba (the workplace)! There is no substitute for first-hand observation—either with feet on the ground at the shop floor, or through experiencing the process as a customer. Data can be used to identify where a problem exists, but observations allow you to understand the root causes of the problem. Both observation and data go hand in hand to identify improvements.

Processes are sociotechnical systems, and people co-determine the process' performance. Process improvements are fundamentally change projects, and should be treated as such. The majority of energy will be spent persuading people to take ownership and enact improvements, rather than spending time identifying what needs to be done. Leading change is a core soft skill that complements the knowledge laid out in this book.

Those working within the process generally are best placed to define meaningful improvements. Being part of designing the improvements also increases buy-in to the change. It is very important to celebrate small wins to motivate people to support ongoing improvement, and to show relevance to their daily work. Daily accountability meetings enable quick resolution or escalation and instill a culture of continuous improvement. While we are cautious in using this term, the objective is to create and sustain an "improvement culture" where identifying and delivering improvements becomes a day-to-day routine and an integral part of accepted norms and values. A "culture" develops through continuous attention and review, and quickly wanes if that attention fades.

10.4 **Outlook**

Our aim in this book is not only to equip managers with guidance on how to design, measure, and improve processes, but to demonstrate that there is a coherent set of principles that form the stable core of knowledge in our field. Processes are at the very heart of every organization, yet all too often managing them is not seen as being of strategic importance, and only becomes urgent when things go wrong. Our focus is on the underlying theory on processes, and as such we have deliberately chosen not to focus on real-world cases and examples of the implementation of the principles. Instead we direct the reader to exemplary texts on their application, listed as further reading below, and at the end of each chapter.

Much has been, and is being, written that frames the latest thinking on operations management around another fad or buzzword. Yet, generally what underpins any new fad has its origins in a core body of knowledge, and it is this core knowledge that we present in this book. Our ten process principles have stood the test of time, are empirically proven, and universal. There is no doubt in our minds that—whatever technological advances or organizational changes may be ahead—it will be *process theory* and these principles that we call upon for guidance.

NOTES

1. M.J. Mol, J. Birkinshaw, and J.M. Birkinshaw, 2008. *Giant Steps in Management: Creating Innovations that Change the Way We Work*. Pearson Education.
2. Ludwig van Bertalanffy, an Austrian biologist, was instrumental to the development of a general systems theory in the 1920s, by identifying alternate models of organization as well as the concept of open systems; see L. van Bertalanffy, 1968. *General Systems Theory: Foundations, Developments, Applications*. George Braziller. Russel

Ackoff, a lifelong systems thinker, specifically recognized the interdisciplinary nature of management problems and the need to consider the system as a whole rather than the individual works; see R.L. Ackoff and F.E. Emery, 1972. *On Purposeful Systems: An Interdisciplinary Analysis of Individual and Social Behavior.* Transaction Publishers. John Burbidge was an engineer who applied systems concepts to manufacturing processes, and developed his six laws of manufacturing systems; see for example J. Burbidge, 1983. Five golden rules to avoid bankruptcy. Production Engineer, 62(10), pp. 13–14.
3. K. Lewin, 1951. *Field Theory in Social Science.* HarperCollins.
4. This process of alignment is often called “Hoshin” or “Hoshin Kanri,” or simply “policy deployment.”

FURTHER READING

Bossidy, L., Charan, R., and Burck, C., 2011. *Execution: The Discipline of Getting Things Done.* Random House (London).

Gawande, A., 2010. *The Checklist Manifesto: How to Get Things Right.* Penguin Books India (Delhi).

Schmenner, R.W., 2012. *Getting and Staying Productive: Applying Swift, Even Flow to Practice.* Cambridge University Press (Cambridge, UK).

Womack, J.P. and Jones, D.T., 2010. *Lean Thinking: Banish Waste and Create Wealth in Your Corporation.* Simon & Schuster (New York).

APPENDIX A THE TEN PROCESS PRINCIPLES AND SUBPRINCIPLES

Foundation

Principle #1: All operations are composed of processes.
Principle #2: Variation is inherent in all process inputs, tasks, and outputs.

(a) Variation can occur in quality, quantity, and timing.
(b) Variation in a process can be buffered by a combination of any of the following three means: time, inventory, and capacity.

Design

Principle #3: Work-in-process is determined by throughput rate and throughput time.

(a) The throughput time of a process is stochastic, not deterministic.
(b) Bottlenecks govern the throughput of a system.

Principle #4: Complexity in process design amplifies managerial challenges.

(a) Complexity is a function of the number of static elements (structure) in a process, their heterogeneity, and their dynamic interactions.
(b) A comparable, yet simpler solution will always outperform a more complex one in the long term.

Principle #5: Process choice requires fit between the task and the external requirements.

(a) The higher the volume/lower the variety of the process, the more segregated and specialized tasks will become.
(b) The higher the volume/lower the variety of the process, the more dedicated the assets it uses will be.

Measure

Principle #6: No single measure can capture the performance of a process.

(a) Performance metrics are not necessarily independent of each other.
(b) Absolute measures are preferred to relative ones because of their greater explanatory power.

Principle #7: Process metrics can drive unintended behavior.

(a) You cannot manage what you do not measure.
(b) What you get is what you measure.

Improve

Principle #8: Processes are improved by reductions in throughput time or in undesired variation.

(a) Unmanaged processes will deteriorate over time.
(b) The total cost associated with an operational problem is inversely proportional to the speed of rectifying its root cause.

Principle #9: The rate of process improvement is subject to diminishing returns.

(a) There exists a trade-off between any two aspects of process performance.
(b) Trade-offs can never be broken, but they can be shifted by altering process practice.

Principle #10: Processes do not operate in isolation.

(a) A set of suboptimal solutions can never produce a global optimum.
(b) Structure drives behavior.

APPENDIX B JARGONBUSTER

3C—Concern, Cause, Countermeasure (problem-solving)
3DP—3D printing (a type of additive manufacturing)
3Ms—Muda (waste), Mura (unevenness), and Muri (overburden)
3Ts—Time, Transparency, Trust (efficient supply chains)
5S—Sort, Straighten, Sweep, Standardize, Sustain. Originally: seiri, seiton, seiso, seiketsu, and shitsuke. Also known as CANDO: Clearing up, Arranging, Neatness, Discipline, Ongoing improvement. Sometimes expanded into 6S, with Safety or Security being added.
5 Whys—root cause analysis tool, closely related to fishbone diagrams
6Ms—Man, Machine, Method, Measurement, Materials, Mother Nature (used in root cause analysis/fishbone)
7 Wastes—TIMWOOD(S): Transportation, Inventory, Motion, Waiting, Overproduction (worst waste according to Ohno), Overprocessing, Defects. Often added as 8th waste: Skills or unused human talent.
80–20 rule—Pareto analysis, whereby 80 percent of the impact is caused by 20 percent of the problems
85–15 rule—Deming's rule that 85 percent of faults are caused by poor product and process design, and only 15 percent by the worker
90–10 rule—use 90 percent of machine time for production, 10 percent for set-up and maintenance
A3—a problem-solving tool presenting an issue on an A3 paper template
ABC—activity-based costing
ABC-analysis—inventory categorization technique
AI—artificial intelligence
AM—additive manufacturing
Andon—workers can stop the line (red, yellow, green light system)
APS—advanced planning and scheduling systems
ATO—assemble-to-order (see e.g. Dell model)
BTO—build or make-to-order (syn. MTO)
BTS—build to stock (same as MTF/MTS)
CANDO—another way of naming the 5S: Clearing up, Arranging, Neatness, Discipline, Ongoing improvement
CI—continuous improvement
CNC—computer numerical control
COPIS—Customer, Outputs, Process, Inputs, Suppliers (an alternative version of SIPOC)
C_p/C_{pk}—process capability indices
CPM—critical path method
CRT—current reality tree (root cause analysis)
CTB—critical to business
CTQ—critical to quality

Cycle time—a throughput measure: the time for one production cycle to complete, measured in time per unit of production
DBR—Drum Buffer Rope (TOC)
DFM/DFA—design for manufacture or assembly
DFSS—design for Six Sigma
DMADV—Define, Measure, Analyze, Design, Validate (or Verify); see DFSS
DMAIC—Define, Measure, Analyze, Improve, Control (Six Sigma)
DPMO—defects per million opportunities
DRP—distribution resource planning
EBQ—economic batch quantity (simpler version of EPQ)
EDI—electronic data interchange
EOQ—economic order quantity
EOS—economies of scale
EPOS—electronic point of sale data (e.g. barcode)
EPQ—economic production quantity (EBQ which considers production rate)
ERP—enterprise resource planning (e.g. SAP or BAAN)
ETO—engineer (or design) to order
Fishbone—graphical tool used in root cause analysis (also known as Ishikawa diagram)
FMEA—failure mode and effect analysis
FRP—finite resource planning (ERP system with a TOC module)
FTL—full truck load (logistics)
Gemba—the "actual workplace," i.e. shop floor
Genshi Genbutsu—actual place, actual facts ("go and see for yourself")
Hansei—"relentless reflection"; together with kaizen ("continuous improvement") these are the two pillars of a learning organization
Heijunka—"smooth wave," mixed model and level scheduling
IoT—Internet of things
ISO—International Organization for Standardization (ISO 9001 for Quality Management, ISO 14001 for Environmental Management)
JIC—"just in case"
Jidoka—autonomous machines or "intelligent automation" or "autonomation"
JIS—just in sequence
JIT—just in time
Kaikaku or "kaizen blitz"—focused improvement action
Kaizen—long-term continuous improvement program
Kanban—("sign") signal for pull- or consumption-driven scheduling
KPI—key performance indicator
Lead time—the time from order to delivery, from the customer's point of view
LCL—lower control limit (SPC)
LSL—lower specification limit (capability)
LTL—less than full truck load (deliveries)
MRO—maintenance, repair, and overhaul
MRP—materials requirements planning
MRPII—manufacturing resource planning
MTF/MTS—make-to-forecast/stock

MTO—make-to-order (syn. BTO)
Muda—waste
Mura—unevenness
Muri—overburden
Nemawashi—to reach decisions by consensus (literally: "going around the roots")
NPD—new product development
NPI—new product introduction
OPT—optimized production technology (TOC scheduling software)
OTD—order to delivery (order fulfillment process)
OTIF—on time, in full (delivery)
PDCA—Plan, Do, Check, Act ("Deming Cycle")
PDSA—Plan, Do, Study, Act (alternative version of Deming Cycle)
PERT—project evaluation and review technique
PI—process improvement
Poka-yoke—mistake-proofing or failsafing devices
PPC—production planning and control
QCD—Quality, Cost, Delivery (often added: S for Service, F for Flexibility, M for Morale, S for Safety, E for Environment)
RCCP—rough-cut capacity planning (feedback loop that turns MRP I into MRP II)
RFID—radio frequency identification
RIE—rapid improvement event (another term used for kaikaku or kaizen blitz)
RRS—Runners, Repeaters, Strangers (scheduling)
RTLS—real time location systems
SCRUM—daily accountability meeting (part of Agile product development)
Seru—highly flexible production system
SIPOC—Suppliers, Inputs, Process, Outputs, Customers (Six Sigma)
SKU—stock keeping unit
SMED—"Single minute exchange of dies" (a tool for changeover reduction), single-piece flow
SOP—standard operating procedure
SPC—statistical process control
Throughput time—the time from start to completion of the production process
TOC—theory of constraints
TPM—total preventive maintenance
TPS—Toyota Production System
TQC—total quality control
TQM—total quality management
UCL—upper control limit (SPC)
USL—upper specification limit (capability)
VA/VE—value analysis/value engineering

APPENDIX C THE COST OF INVENTORY

Inventory is the most visible buffer in a manufacturing setting, and thus often the focus of process improvement activities. Before considering the cost of inventory, it is important though to recall that inventory is generally there for a reason. The average inventory level is a function of throughput rate and processing time (Little's Law). Inventory is also an important buffer against any kind of uncertainty, be it demand, supply, or throughput uncertainty (see the "rock-boat" analogy in Section 8.3).

Inventory incurs both direct and hidden costs. Estimates of these costs are often too conservative as they tend to exclude quality, depreciation, and opportunity cost.

The main costs involved are:

- Cost of capital: *product value*i*, with i being the interest rate per unit time
- Opportunity cost: How much would the capital earn otherwise?
- Depreciation of goods
- Stock obsolescence and deterioration
- Quality defects due to handling
- Labor and handling costs
- Warehousing, rent, and energy
- Insurance and overhead to admin labor, space, etc.

Further hidden costs include:

- Longer lead times to fulfill customer orders
- Reduced responsiveness to customer needs
- Underlying problems are hidden rather than being exposed and solved
- Quality problems are not identified immediately
- No incentive for improvement of the process.

As a general rule, it is safe to assume that the *actual* cost of inventory is in the order of $i = 20$–40 percent per annum, which is a multiple of the cost of capital alone.

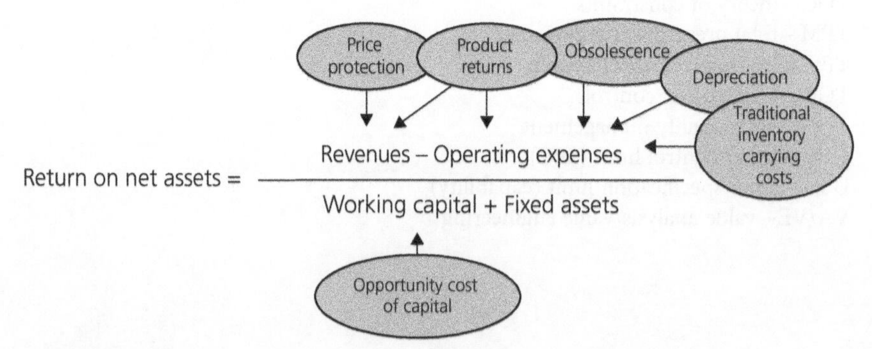

Figure A.1 Linking the cost of inventory to the return on net assets (RONA).

Adapted from Callioni et al. (2005).

Underestimating the cost of inventory tends to lead companies to order larger batches, and in turn hold larger inventories than would be financially optimal.

A good way to represent the cost of inventory was developed by Callioni et al. (2005).[1] Their representation is shown in Figure A.1, linking inventory cost to the RONA formula.

In addition to working capital requirements, product returns impact on both revenues and operating expenses; obsolescence, depreciation, and traditional inventory carrying cost all impact operating expenses.

NOTE

1. G. Callioni, X. de Montgros, R. Slagmulder, L.N. Van Wassenhove, and L. Wright, 2005. Inventory-driven costs. *Harvard Business Review*, 83(3), pp.135–41.

APPENDIX D LITTLE'S LAW

Little's Law[1] states that the minimum work-in-process (WIP) inventory in a process is given by the product of its throughput rate λ and its processing time T. If less than N units of WIP inventory are in the process, parts of the process are starved and the throughput rate will decline. Any inventory in excess of N units of WIP constitutes buffer stock that may be useful to protect against uncertainty, but strictly speaking is not required to keep the process running.

Little's Law states that the minimum WIP inventory in a process N [units] is determined by throughput rate λ [units/time] and the processing time T [time]. Little's Law can be expressed as a simple equation:

$$N = \lambda * T$$

Consider the following example: the FastPC company assembles computers. The assembly process covers ten workstations, which take ten minutes each to complete their tasks. So the total processing time is 100 minutes. FastPC is assembling 240 computers per day, whereby a work day has eight hours, or 480 minutes. So the throughput rate is 0.5 units per minute.

At present FastPC shows a WIP of 110 computers across its ten assembly stations. In this case (shown as scenario A in Figure A.2), excess WIP inventory is carried, as 110 is larger than the minimum WIP $N = 100 \text{ min} * 0.5 \text{ units/min} = 50$ units. In this case (shown as scenario B in Figure A.2), there is just enough WIP inventory to maintain the output rate. If you were to reduce WIP levels below 50 units (as shown in scenario C in Figure A.2), empty slots would develop on the assembly line, starving process steps, and the throughput rate could not be maintained for long and would inevitably decline.

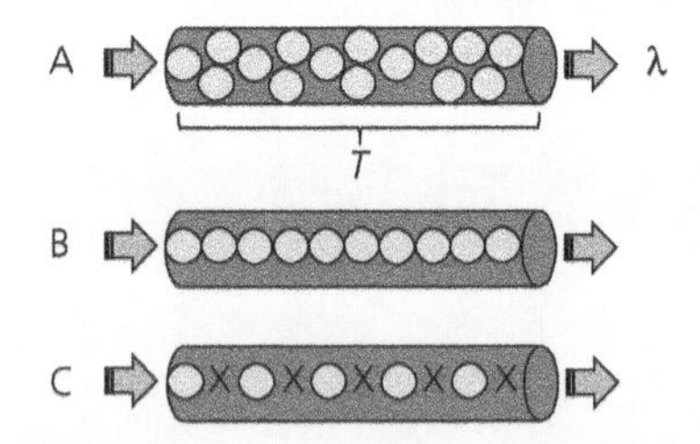

Figure A.2 Little's Law.

NOTE

1. J.D. Little, 1961. A proof for the queuing formula: L = λW. *Operations Research*, 9(3), pp.383–7.

APPENDIX E BASIC TRADE-OFF MODELS

Trade-off models are very common in operations management, as most decisions are based on having to find a balance between two performance metrics. Consider, for example, the problem of sending trucks from a warehouse to customers: the more often you send the truck, the shorter the lead time. Yet at the same time there is a risk that load utilization will drop. Hence a balance has to be struck between shipment frequency and load utilization.

Another classic trade-off model is the balance between ordering frequency and inventory level. The more often a firm reorders its inventory, the smaller the batch sizes and the lower the average inventory level. At the same time, of course, the transaction or ordering costs rise in proportion to the frequency of placing orders. The trade-off model that deals with this problem is called the economic order quantity (EOQ) or Harris-Wilson lot-sizing formula, and dates back to 1913.[1]

The basic idea is as follows: the total cost TC is a function of the batch size Q. It is determined by two factors:

1. The cost of ordering, which is driven by the frequency of ordering: annual demand (D) divided by the batch size Q, times the cost of making one order C_O.
2. The cost of holding inventory, which is the product of the average inventory level $\frac{Q}{2}$ times the annual holding cost for one item, C_H.

The total cost formula thus is given as follows:

$$TC(Q) = \frac{D}{Q}C_O + \frac{Q}{2}C_H$$

The EOQ denotes the batch where total costs are minimal, and is given by this formula:

$$EOQ = \sqrt{2D\frac{C_O}{C_H}}$$

Graphically it can be shown as given in Figure A.3.

The EOQ logic can also be applied to the trade-off between set-up cost and inventory holding cost in manufacturing, where it is called economic batch quality (EBQ), or when considering a rate of production P, the economic production quantity (EPQ), with C_S as the cost of a set-up:

$$EPQ = \sqrt{2D\frac{C_S}{C_H(1-m)}} \quad \text{with} \quad m = \frac{D}{P}$$

The EOQ/EBQ/EPQ models are still used in practice, for several reasons: first, they are quite robust as the result is not very sensitive to errors in estimating any of the parameters, and second, the model is quite simple to implement with MRP/ERP

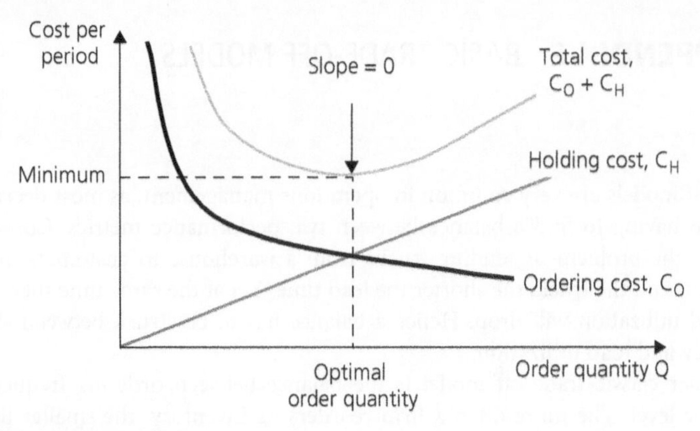

Figure A.3 The EOQ model.

systems, where they are still widely used (check the Inventory Master File where economic and minimum order quantities are stored for each part).

There are, however, many downsides to these models that one needs to be aware of:

- EOQ-based models use some very limiting assumptions, namely that D is known and steady throughout the year, which is rarely the case.
- They assume that the ordering or set-up cost can be correctly quantified (activity-based costing may be a good way).
- They neglect any interactions between different parts as they consider one part at a time.
- These models tend to favor large batch sizes when the cost of inventory is assumed to be the cost of capital (say $i = 5$–10 percent), as opposed to the true cost of inventory ($i = 20$–40 percent). (Consider the cost of inventory, covered in Appendix C.)
- EOQ-based ordering tends to produce lumpy demand, which can trigger the bullwhip effect.

NOTE

1. See F.W. Harris, 1915. *Operations Cost* (Factory Management Series). Shaw, and R.H. Wilson, 1934. A scientific routine for stock control. *Harvard Business Review*, 13(1), pp. 116–28.

APPENDIX F PUSH VERSUS PULL SYSTEMS

The two most basic concepts of how to respond to customer demand are *push* and *pull* scheduling.

In simple terms, pull scheduling is driven by the *replenishment signal* that acts as a trigger in the system: just like in a supermarket, the end customer withdraws a product from the shelf. This empty space then triggers the replenishment from the supplier, which in turn triggers the replenishment of materials.

In push scheduling, production is driven by a *central schedule* (often based on forecast demand) that triggers production, and material is pushed from one stage to the next, according to this central schedule.

So, in *pull* scheduling:

- The final stage of the process sees the customer order first.
- The withdrawal of an item triggers the replenishment from the preceding process.
- The demand signal thus travels from the end customer through each of the preceding process steps.
- Small amounts of inventory are required "to pull from"—pull scheduling does not function without inventory. Using the analogy of a supermarket, these inventory locations often are referred to as "kanban supermarkets."

Pull scheduling is sometimes also referred to as "forward scheduling." Figure A.4 shows a simplified pull scheduling system. Note the small inventory buffers between processes that are needed so that items can be "pulled" and "replenished." These are the "kanban supermarkets," as they function like internal supermarkets within the factory. Also note that there generally is no intervention needed from the central planning and scheduling department. Pull scheduling can work autonomously (within certain bounds of schedule variation).

In contrast, in *push* scheduling:

- A central schedule is calculated that determines exactly what items are needed, and when. These are so-called "time-phased" requirements.
- Based on this calculation of time-phased requirements, schedules for all processes and suppliers are issued as and when material should be processed and shipped. Without this notification material is neither worked on, nor shipped to the next stage, and will remain in WIP inventory.
- The longest lead time item sees the new customer order first. This is similar to the critical path method in project management. Hence this approach is sometimes referred to as "backwards scheduling."

Figure A.5 shows a simplified push system. Note that items only move (or are "pushed") from one stage to the next when an order from the central planning and scheduling department (or IT system) is issued.

While push and pull represent the two opposing strategies, in practice firms will operate both simultaneously at different points. A restaurant, for example, will only

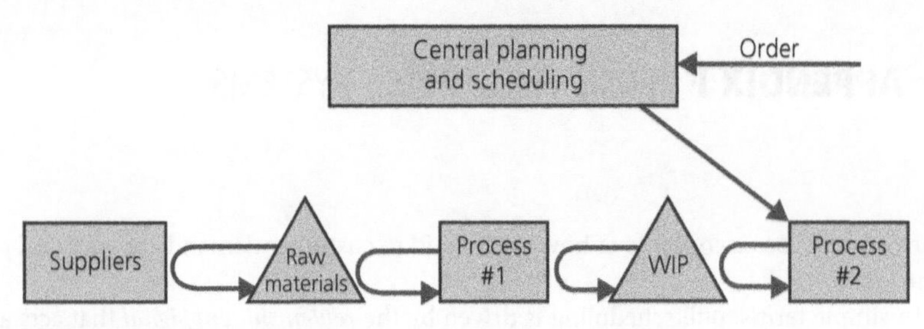

Figure A.4 A pull scheduling system.

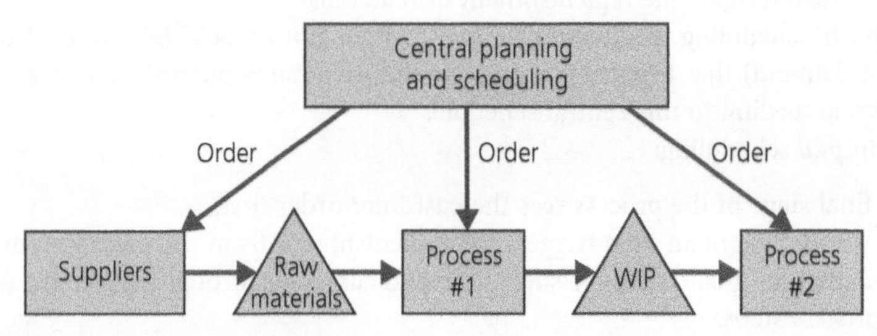

Figure A.5 A push scheduling system.

start preparing your food when you order it (pull). However, it will have to forecast the likely demand for the evening and hold the required ingredients against predicted demand (push). In other words, a restaurant will operate both customer-pull and forecast-push at the same time.

We call this the "push-pull envelope," whereby customer-pull operations are supported by forecast-push systems for those cases where the lead time to provide the goods exceeds the customer's willingness to wait. So at firm level it is important to understand push and pull scheduling as complements, rather than as substitutes.

Another way to think about this is the "order penetration point": how far back does the customer order travel within the operation? In a supermarket, orders are fulfilled from existing inventory on the shelf. This is a typical "make-to-forecast" (MTF) scenario. When you order a Dell computer, on the other hand, your order will travel to the factory, where it will be assembled to order (ATO) using component inventory. When you order a BMW Mini, the components and the vehicle will be made or built to order (MTO/BTO). When you order a Space Shuttle, your order will be sent to the Design department, where it will be engineered to order (ETO).

APPENDIX G THE KINGMAN FORMULA

Sir John Kingman, a Cambridge mathematician, studied the formation of queues in front of a single-server process.[1] He found that queue formation is largely due to load and variation in the system. He approximated the waiting time before a process W_q as follows:

$$E(W_q) \approx \left(\frac{\rho}{1-\rho}\right)\left(\frac{c_a^2 + c_s^2}{2}\right)\tau$$

In this formula, ρ is capacity utilization, τ is the mean service time, c_a is the coefficient of variation for arrivals (the standard deviation of arrival times divided by the mean arrival time), and c_s is the coefficient of variation for service times (standard deviation of service time divided by mean service time, τ). Thus, the waiting time depends on the product of capacity utilization, the variation affecting the process (demand and production itself), and the natural speed of the process (mean service time). The faster the process (i.e. the greater the rate of production, and thus the less the mean service time), the smaller the variability either of the demand striking the process or of the process itself, and the lower the capacity utilization, the shorter is the wait for the customer.

These relationships can be shown graphically, as given in Figure A.6.

Kingman's formula is of relevance to both manufacturing and service operations, particularly in the context of process improvement. Generally service process times, especially in professional services, are much longer than in manufacturing. Furthermore, in service, people (customers) wait in queues rather than products waiting in a buffer, thus we argue that queues are generally more important in service than in

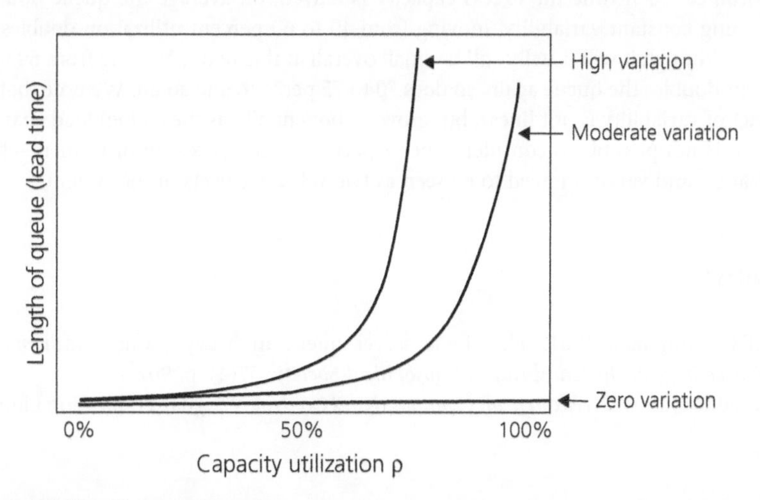

Figure A.6 The Kingman formula.

manufacturing. In other words, while the behavior of a single-server system will be independent of context, the implications of the queue length are not.

Kingman's formula was empirically found to be very accurate for high levels of capacity utilization, which is the most common setting for most operations, especially in manufacturing. Utilization is defined as load divided by capacity, or as demand divided by time available for the work to be done. Or more specifically, as shown in this equation, utilization is directly related to "failure demand" and waste, as follows:

$$utilization = \frac{load}{capacity} = \frac{value\ demand + failure\ demand + rework\ demand}{work + waste}$$

Let us look at this formula more closely: note that there are three types of demand—value demand, failure demand, and rework demand. Value demand is first-time demand. Failure demand is externally generated repeat demand caused by "not doing something or not doing something right."[2] Rework demand is internally generated demand caused by errors that are corrected internally without the external customer knowing about it. We note that the time available for work to be done is reduced by wasteful activity; cutting failure demand and rework reduces the load, sometimes significantly. Reducing waste (or muda) also reduces the load. Waste can cause both rework and excess capacity, thereby affecting both numerator and denominator in the utilization equation.

As a result, reducing failure demand, internal rework, and waste should be a first priority for any service or manufacturer. After reducing these three, there remain value demand and value-added time; each has variation—arrival variation and process variation. Variation, in turn, is of two types—common cause and special cause. Special cause variation is, in general, easier to identify and eliminate, whereas reducing common cause variation may require system redesign.

Utilization is the key factor for process improvement: for low utilization, arrival variation and process variation will have little impact. If utilization, however, is high—above 80 percent as a rule of thumb—arrival and process variation will become of high importance. Each time the excess capacity is halved, on average the queue doubles. Assuming constant variability, moving from 40 to 60 percent utilization doubles the queue, although it will usually still be small overall at this point. Moving from 60 to 70 percent doubles the queue again, so does 70 to 75 percent, and so on. We note that the impact of variability is not linear, but grows exponentially as the system load changes. Thus it is not possible to consider either aspect alone in process improvement—both utilization and variation need to be seen as two related aspects of the system.

NOTES

1. J.F.C. Kingman, 1961. The single server queue in heavy traffic. *Mathematical Proceedings of the Cambridge Philosophical Society*, 57(4), p. 902.
2. J. Seddon, 2003. *Freedom from Command and Control.* Vanguard Education Limited.

APPENDIX H CAPABILITY, CONTROL, AND SIX SIGMA

Background

Process capability and control provide a fundamental basis for managing quality and improving processes. A process is capable if it delivers output that meets the customer requirements. A process is in control if it is performing as expected. A process that is both *capable* and *in control* is able to consistently meet the needs of the customer, which is our definition of quality.

It is important to note that capability and control are two independent outcomes of a process, as shown in Figure A.7. Processes can in fact be capable but out of control, and vice versa.

This reduction of variation is the underlying concept of the *Six Sigma* philosophy. Principally, Six Sigma is about reducing *undesired* variation in a process. Although a relatively recent methodology, the underpinnings of the Six Sigma philosophy are not new. It borrows heavily from the work of Walter Shewhart in the 1920s and Deming's work in the 1950s. Specifically, it argues that everything is a process and all processes have variation, and in order to manage quality, we need to be able to measure the process, understand the variation, and improve it by reducing undesired variation. Most recently, Six Sigma and Lean concepts have often been merged into a generic *Lean Six Sigma* methodology for process improvement (see Section 8.4).

Let us look at these concepts in more detail.

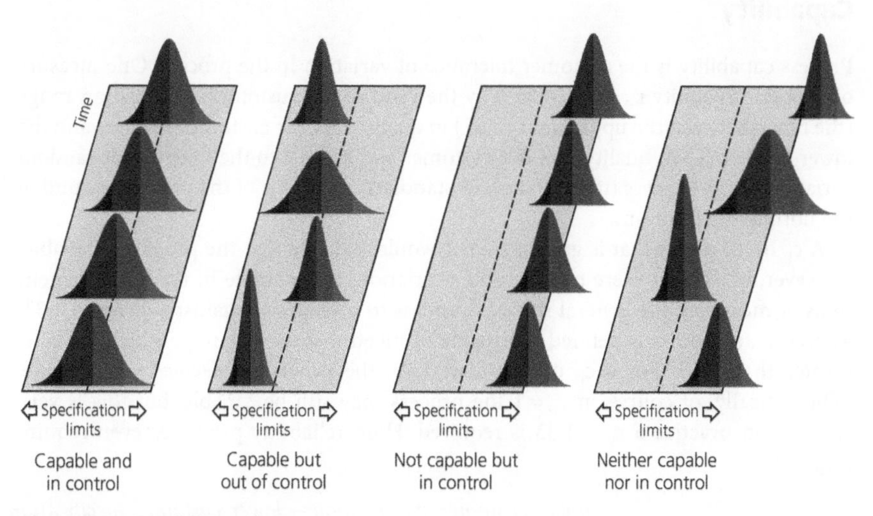

Figure A.7 Capability and control.

Common and special cause variation

Variation is a fact of industrial life, so all processes will exhibit some variation. This is our second principle. Beyond the impact of the changing environment, employees do not perform each task identically, input materials differ, and machines do not produce exactly the same output. Knowing that variation exists throughout the process, it is unsurprising that the quality of the product or service also varies. However, some variation in a process is normal, i.e. it is inherent in the process and displayed randomly. This is known as *common cause* variation. Common cause variation often relates to the effects of ambient temperatures, humidity levels, impurities in input materials, and the like.

What is of interest is the non-random variation, that variation which has an assignable cause. Variation which originates from assignable causes can never be fully eliminated, but importantly it can be reduced. For example, variation may be assignable to untrained employees, damaged input materials, worn parts of a machine, or even the temperature of the environment. Such *special cause* or *assignable cause* variation can be due to lack of knowledge or skills, a failure to adhere to the standard process, a batch of materials unsuited for purpose, as well as wear and tear of machine tools.

Processes are improved by continuously reducing non-random variability through addressing the assignable causes of the variation. In order to address these assignable causes a manager or worker needs a deep knowledge of how the process operates. This means learning about the process at a detailed level and identifying the root cause of the variation. In turn, this provides information on how the process will perform in different situations and therefore a better ability to handle or avoid future variation in the process.

Capability

Process capability is the customer tolerance of variation in the process. One measure of process capability c_p is calculated by the ratio of the customer specification range (the range between the upper limit (USL) in quality that the customer requires and the lower limit (LSL) in quality that the customer will accept) to the inherent or random variation of the process (taken to be $\pm$ 3 standard deviations of the process, assuming the normal distribution).

A c_p of a process that is greater than 1 would indicate that the process is capable. However, given that there may be other variation, for example in the measurement tools or measurer, the general rule of thumb is to measure c_p against a target of 1.33. Therefore, a process is defined as capable of meeting customer requirements if c_p is greater than 1.33. For a c_p of less than 1.33, the process is *deemed* not capable. (Theoretically, of course, at $c_p = 1$ the process may still be capable, but this is very risky, so in practice a $c_p > 1.33$ is required. High-reliability processes even require a $c_p > 2$.)

$$\text{Process capability } (c_p) = \frac{\textit{upper customer specification} - \textit{lower customer specification}}{\textit{6 standard deviations of the process}}$$

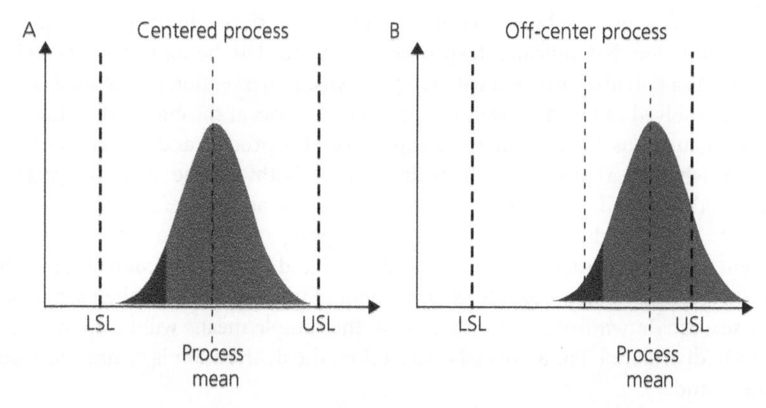

Figure A.8 Centered and off-center processes, in relation to lower and upper specification limits.

However, the c_p ratio does not take into account the position of the mean of the process, or, more specifically, whether the process mean is centered between the customer requirements. Consider the two processes in Figure A.8. Both processes A and B have a $c_p > 1.33$; however, process B is clearly off-center.

To account for whether the process is centered, an alternative to the c_p ratio is c_{pk}. The c_{pk} ratio is calculated by first taking the differences between the upper and lower customer specifications and the mean of the process, and dividing by the 3 standard deviations of the process to obtain the values, Z_{upper} and Z_{lower}.

$$Z_{upper} = \frac{\textit{upper customer specification} - \textit{process mean}}{\textit{3 standard deviations of the process}}$$

$$Z_{lower} = \frac{\textit{process mean} - \textit{lower customer specification}}{\textit{3 standard deviations of the process}}$$

c_{pk} equals the smaller of the two Z values. Process capability $c_{pk} = Z_{min}$.

In the same way as for a centered process to be capable, c_{pk} is required to be greater than 1.33 to be deemed capable. If c_{pk} is less than 1.33, the process is not capable. In the example in Figure A.8, process A has a $c_{pk} = 1.33$; process B has a $c_{pk} = 0.6$ and is not capable, even though the c_p is greater than 1.33.

Control

Once a process is capable, the process is monitored to ensure that it remains in control—i.e. nothing has changed. Statistical process control (SPC) is a quantitative method used to monitor that a process is behaving as expected. SPC collects data on the process during the production of the output (good or service) and compares it to the baseline process performance established by its capability. The data are then evaluated through control charts to determine whether or not the process has changed. Control charts allow managers and workers to monitor real-time variation in the process and discriminate between random, inherent variation in the process and non-random variation that indicates the process has changed. If the control charts highlight that there is a potential problem with the process, an intervention can be made and the problem resolved rather than waiting for quality checks at the end of the process.

The calculations for assessing the capability of a process and the charts used to monitor whether a process remains in control both assume that the process is normally distributed. In reality, a process may follow any one of the many statistical distributions. To address this requirement, sampling and the rule of the central limit theorem are fundamental to measuring capability and monitoring control. The central limit theorem states that, regardless of the underlying distribution, when samples of a given size are drawn from that distribution, the sample means will be approximately normally distributed. For a normal distribution, the distribution is symmetrical about its mean and:

- 68.3 percent of the distribution lies between ±1 standard deviation from the mean
- 95.4 percent of the distribution lies between ±2 standard deviations from the mean
- 99.7 percent of the distribution lies between ±3 standard deviations from the mean.

These properties of the normal distribution are employed to enable a clear understanding of variation in processes.

A control chart is a graphical display of a process characteristic over time. As its basis it displays a center line (CL) that represents the mean value for a capable process. Two other horizontal lines, called the upper control limit (UCL) and the lower control limit (LCL), represent the ±3 standard deviation values of the capable process (see Figure A.9).

As samples are drawn from the process, the sample means are plotted on the control chart against time. As data are accumulated the pattern of the sample means can be visually evaluated to determine whether the data are randomly distributed and therefore whether the process is in control. Any pattern in the data that does not appear random—too little or too much variation—indicates that something in the process may have changed and should be investigated for assignable cause. Evidence that the points are not distributed symmetrically around the center line, sequential points going up or down in a trend, and oscillating points above and below the center line,

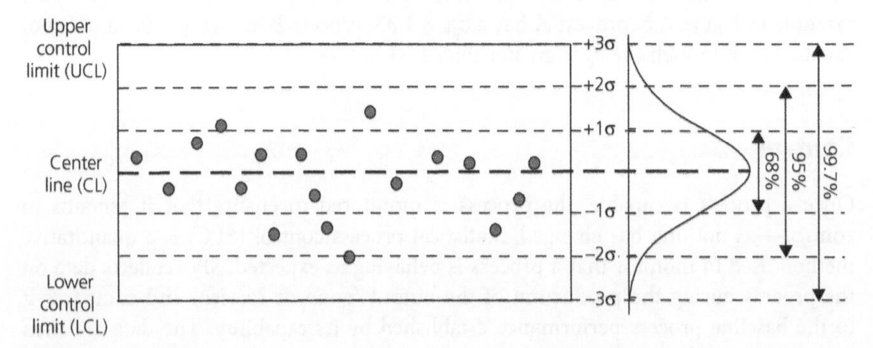

Figure A.9 A basic control chart with lower control limit, center line, and upper control limit.

all indicate that there may be a non-random factor affecting the process. Using the known properties of the normal distribution, for a process displaying random variation, 99.7% of the sample means plotted would lie between the upper and lower control limits. It would be rare for a point to occur outside these control limits, and that would indicate something could have changed and therefore the process should be investigated.

There are three control charts that are routinely used to monitor quality.

p-charts: p-charts are used to monitor the attributes of a process (count data), such as defect rates for example. The baseline percentage of the attribute (p) determined from the process capability delineates the center line. For attribute data the sample size (n) should be large enough to identify defects, i.e. output that does not meet customer requirements. In practice this means that the average sample should capture two attributes (e.g. capture two defects on average). For p-charts, the upper and lower control limits and center line values are calculated using:

$$UCL = \bar{p} + 3\sqrt{\frac{\bar{p}(1-\bar{p})}{n}}$$
$$CL = \bar{p}$$
$$LCL = \bar{p} - 3\sqrt{\frac{\bar{p}(1-\bar{p})}{n}}$$

$\bar{X}$- and R-charts: $\bar{X}$- and R-charts are used for monitoring measures such as time or length (variable data) of the output of a process. Variable data are more specific than attribute data, and as a consequence smaller sample sizes can be used—in general a sample of 4 or 5 is adequate. However, for measured data the process can change in two ways: the mean can shift, or the variation in the process can increase or decrease. Therefore, two charts are used to monitor process control: $\bar{X}$-charts to monitor changes in the process mean and R-charts to monitor changes in the process variation (the range). As for the p-chart, the data from the process capability are used to determine the baseline process mean ($\bar{\bar{X}}$), and define the center line for the $\bar{X}$-chart. For the R-chart: if data on process capability were collected in samples, then the center line is the average range of the samples, $\bar{R}$. Otherwise, the process standard deviation σ is used to calculate $\bar{R} = \sigma d_2$.

For the $\bar{X}$-chart the upper and lower control limits for ongoing sampling using a sample of a particular size (usually four or five samples) are calculated using:

$$UCL = \bar{\bar{X}} + A_2\bar{R}$$
$$CL = \bar{\bar{X}}$$
$$LCL = \bar{\bar{X}} - A_2\bar{R}$$

For the R-chart the upper and lower control limits for ongoing sampling using a sample of a particular size (generally four or five samples) are calculated respectively using:

$$UCL = D_4\bar{R}$$
$$CL = \bar{R}$$
$$LCL = D_3\bar{R}$$

The values of A_2, D_3, D_4, and d_2 are all drawn from the formula in Table A.1.

Table A.1 Coefficients for control chart calculations

	X-bar charts			R-charts	
Sample size = n	A_2	A_3	d_2	D_3	D_4
2	1.880	2.659	1.128	0	3.267
3	1.023	1.954	1.693	0	2.574
4	0.729	1.628	2.059	0	2.282
5	0.577	1.427	2.326	0	2.114
6	0.483	1.287	2.534	0	2.004
7	0.419	1.182	2.704	0.076	1.924
8	0.373	1.099	2.847	0.136	1.864
9	0.337	1.032	2.970	0.184	1.816
10	0.308	0.975	3.078	0.223	1.777
11	0.285	0.927	3.173	0.256	1.744
12	0.266	0.886	3.258	0.283	1.717
13	0.249	0.850	3.336	0.307	1.693
14	0.235	0.817	3.407	0.328	1.672
15	0.223	0.789	3.472	0.347	1.653
16	0.212	0.763	3.532	0.363	1.637
17	0.203	0.739	3.588	0.378	1.622
18	0.194	0.718	3.640	0.391	1.608
19	0.187	0.698	3.689	0.403	1.597
20	0.180	0.680	3.735	0.415	1.585
21	0.173	0.663	3.778	0.425	1.575
22	0.167	0.647	3.819	0.434	1.566
23	0.162	0.633	3.858	0.443	1.557
24	0.157	0.619	3.895	0.451	1.548
25	0.153	0.606	3.931	0.459	1.541

For more detail on SPC see Roy D. Shapiro, 2013. *Managing Quality with Process Control*, HBS 08020-HTM-ENG, or any textbook on quality management.

Six Sigma

Over the last three decades, Six Sigma has become an important and popular quality improvement methodology, but its underlying principles are not new. It was first defined by Motorola, the electronics company, in the 1980s. Early adopters included GE, Honeywell, and Texas Instruments, all of which contributed significantly to the development of the methodology. Today, the Six Sigma methodology is being deployed by manufacturing, service, and public sector organizations around the globe. Yet beneath the Six Sigma branding is a set of tools and principles that are rooted in the work of Shewhart, Deming, and the philosophy of reducing variation in order to improve process performance.

Under the influence of the Total Quality movement popularized in the 1980s, Motorola set out to achieve "total customer satisfaction." Motorola determined that for the operation this equated to products delivered with no defects, no early-life failures, and no excessive post-purchase service. To eliminate these defects and failures, Motorola's operations needed to ensure that product specifications were comfortably within the customer requirements and its processes were capable of consistently meeting these specifications. They would need more stringent quality than the three-sigma quality level (99.97 percent defect-free) originally proposed by Shewhart, as this equated (in their calculations) to 68,000 defects per million parts produced.

Motorola coined the term "Six Sigma" to reflect the required specification of the quality of their products, that is, the product variation ± 6 standard deviations should be within the customer specification. This is twice what was considered natural variation of a process at the time (± 3 standard deviations or 99.97 percent conforming parts) which Shewhart originally identified as a capable process. The Greek letter sigma (σ) is used here to signify the standard deviation of the process. With its goal of six-sigma quality, Motorola aspired for the number of defects per million parts produced to be in single digits, or specifically 3.4 defects per million opportunities (DPMO) for a defective part. (Note: when implementing Six Sigma quality, Motorola experienced 1.5-sigma process walk, so Six Sigma is really 4.5 sigma in the long term.)

Calculating the sigma level for a process

The performance of a process in terms of defects can be easily expressed as DPMO (defects per million opportunities) or as sigma level by using the conversion table in Table A.2. DPMO is calculated as follows:

$$DPMO = \frac{number\ of\ defects\ observed}{number\ of\ opportunities} * 1{,}000{,}000$$

whereby the number of defects equals the total number of defects observed (even though more than one defect may be found on one *defective* product), while the number of opportunities refers to the total number of defects that could have been observed given the sample and measurements taken. To give a simple example: an application form contains fifteen fields of information where a mistake can occur. A sample of 100 forms is drawn, and twenty-six errors are discovered in total:

$$DPMO = \frac{26}{100 * 15} * 1{,}000{,}000 = 17{,}333$$

Using the conversion table in Table A.2 we see that this process operates at a sigma level of 3.6.

Please note that the calculation of the sigma level uses the central limit theorem as justification for applying the normal distribution to all observed processes. Thus, the sigma level can be directly "read" from the probability density function (pdf) of the normal distribution.

Table A.2 Yield to DPMO to Sigma level conversion table

Yield rate %	Defects per million opportunities (DPMO)	Sigma level (Note: 1.5-sigma process walk considered)
99.9997	3.4	6.00
99.9995	5	5.92
99.9992	8	5.81
99.9990	10	5.76
99.9980	20	5.61
99.9970	30	5.51
99.9960	40	5.44
99.9930	70	5.31
99.9900	100	5.22
99.9850	150	5.12
99.9770	230	5.00
99.9670	330	4.91
99.9520	480	4.80
99.9320	680	4.70
99.9040	960	4.60
99.8650	1,350	4.50
99.8140	1,860	4.40
99.7450	2,550	4.30
99.6540	3,460	4.20
99.5340	4,660	4.10
99.3790	6,210	4.00
99.1810	8,190	3.90
98.9300	10,700	3.80
98.6100	13,900	3.70
98.2200	17,800	3.60
97.7300	22,700	3.50
97.1300	28,700	3.40
96.4100	35,900	3.30
95.5400	44,600	3.20
94.5200	54,800	3.10
93.3200	66,800	3.00
91.9200	80,800	2.90
90.3200	96,800	2.80
88.5000	115,000	2.70
86.5000	135,000	2.60
84.2000	158,000	2.50
81.6000	184,000	2.40
78.8000	212,000	2.30
75.8000	242,000	2.20

72.6000	274,000	2.10
69.2000	308,000	2.00
65.6000	344,000	1.90
61.8000	382,000	1.80
58.0000	420,000	1.70
54.0000	460,000	1.60
50.0000	500,000	1.50
46.0000	540,000	1.40
43.0000	570,000	1.32
39.0000	610,000	1.22
35.0000	650,000	1.11
31.0000	690,000	1.00

Table A.3 Necessary adjustments to Sigma level

	Short-term capability	Long-term capability
Short-term data	✓	Subtract 1.5 sigma
Long-term data	Add 1.5 sigma	✓

To illustrate this you can use online tools to calculate the normal pdf by using mean = 0, standard deviation = 1, and x1 = 4.5. In other words, you are asking for the probability of an outcome 4.5 standard deviations away from the mean. You will see that this returns the value of 0.0000033976731, or 3.4 parts per million (ppm).

Thus you can see that the 6-sigma standard really only is a 4.5-sigma standard, as the 1.5-sigma "process walk" has already been applied. Remember that this "shift" or "process walk" to the sigma level is an empirical observation, and thus unfortunately one of the less scientific procedures in Six Sigma, and has led to confusion in the past.

You may find that some organizations talk about "short-term" and "long-term" sigma. This relates to two factors: (1) whether you have short-term or long-term data about the process, and (2) whether you are interested in the short-term or long-term performance ("capability") of the process. Depending on these you would apply the shift shown in Table A.3 to Table A.2. (Note that the most common case is to use short-term data to make long-term predictions, so Table A.2 would show the yield to DPMO to sigma level conversion for this case.)

To be more specific: if short-term data have been collected, then the calculation will be to baseline a process to determine a "short-term sigma." If long-term data are not available but long-term performance needs to be estimated, then 1.5 can be subtracted from the sigma level to estimate long-term performance. The opposite is also true: to estimate short-term performance, add 1.5 sigma to the sigma level.

The value of a 1.5-sigma shift should be used until enough data on the process have been collected to distinguish between short-term and long-term variation. Once enough data have been collected, the exact shift factor for the process can be determined.

For more information see, for example, GoalQPC's *Black Belt Memory Jogger* (2002), and other resources on Six Sigma.

Six Sigma as a management philosophy

Six Sigma has since evolved to be a much broader approach than the pure statistical examination of process variation (although this remains its underpinning element), and now includes an all-encompassing process improvement methodology that aims to define the causes of defects, measure those defects, and analyze them so that the process can be improved and controlled—the DMAIC (Define, Measure, Analyze, Improve, Control) framework.

Six Sigma still predominantly focuses on eliminating defects through reducing variation, yet it is also customer-focused—a Six Sigma defect is defined as anything outside of customer specifications. It is results-based, with an emphasis on data: the performance of the process is measured and monitored. And it uses teams for maximum effectiveness, with an emphasis on structured training and certification (yellow, green, black, and master black belts to designate the level of expertise in Six Sigma tools and techniques). Six Sigma requires significant resources for the management and delivery of process improvements. Overall, in the style of Deming, Six Sigma is management as a system of continuous process improvement that is deployed across the whole organization and is everyone's responsibility.

The DMAIC framework is Six Sigma's structured cycle of process improvement. (In many ways it is a version of Deming's PDCA cycle.) It starts in the *Define* phase by describing the problem, the scope, and the goal of the improvement project—always in terms of customer-focused objectives. The *Measure* phase identifies the current baseline performance with an emphasis on managing by fact and collecting data as evidence of the performance, rather than basing it on subjective opinion. Once the baseline measures have been determined, the *Analyze* phase evaluates the gap between the goal and current performance. Once this gap has been established, it can be analyzed to detect the root causes of the problem. The *Improve* phase develops ideas to address the root causes, redesigns the process, then tests and measures the proposed solutions. After the improved process is implemented, the *Control* phase monitors the process to ensure the improvements are sustained.

Critics of Six Sigma will argue that it offers nothing original, which is true as the basics are not new at all, but they are as relevant as ever. Despite its hierarchical approach to training and formal project-based approach to process improvement, it provides an organizational focus and highlights the commitment required to continuously improve the operation to a high level of quality. Other (valid) points of criticism of Six Sigma relate to its overreliance on statistical tools, and the normal distribution in particular, which requires "large numbers" to be a valid approximation. Also, its formulaic approach is seen to stifle innovation in developing process improvement suggestions.

INDEX OF NAMES

SUBJECT INDEX